D1095258

EX
LIBRIS
J. J.
Douglas

THE CENTENNIAL HISTORY OF MANITOBA

The Centennial

History of Manitoba

James A. Jackson

Published under the auspices of the
Manitoba Historical Society in association
with McClelland and Stewart Limited

1870 MANITOBA CENTENNIAL 1970

The Canadian Publishers
McClelland and Stewart Limited
25 Hollinger Road, Toronto

PRINTED AND BOUND IN CANADA BY STOVEL-ADVOCATE PRESS, WINNIPEG

0–7710 – 4372–4

Contents

List of Maps and Illustrations

Preface

THE MANITOBA HISTORICAL SOCIETY is pleased that it has been able to sponsor a centennial history of the province during this most significant year. The members of the society hold many divergent views on many historical matters. Indeed, this is a healthy condition and fosters spirited altercations within the organization as members attempt to gain a clearer and truer historical picture.

The society is most appreciative that Mr. J. A. Jackson, a scholar of eminence, has undertaken to make available to the public a history written in a popular vein. A latitude given to Mr. Jackson was his entitlement to express his interpretation of history, without any imposition on society policy. Thus, the imprimatur of the society on this publication does not constitute an acknowledgement that the views of the author are official views of the society.

The society acknowledges, with gratitude, the financial support given by the Manitoba Centennial Corporation. Without this support, the project could not have attained fruition.

WINNIPEG, MANITOBA — *W. Steward Martin*

MARCH 24, 1970

Foreword

WHAT IS IT THAT MAKES Manitoba's history so interesting? One thing, as this new story of the province makes very clear, is that it has so much history. That is, Manitoba's history runs so far back. It is quite impossible to understand its history or how people live in Manitoba today, without going back, not a mere one hundred years, but at least 10,000. For everything of that one hundred centuries is still present in Manitoba today: the archaic rocks, the ancient lakes, their more ancient beaches. In Manitoba, one may travel by canoe or by jet plane. The people of its history continue to reside there too: the Indian, the Eskimo, the Métis, the Selkirk settler, the old Canadian and the new. How many communities have preserved all their people, and have added to their history without subtracting from it?

A second thing is the skill and humor with which the author of this history recounts what really happened and how things really were. It is interesting history interestingly told. As Manitobans celebrate the centenary of their province, they can learn with pleasure from this book why and how they came to be what they are—which is to say, most interesting people.

TRENT UNIVERSITY *W. L. Morton*

PETERBOROUGH, ONTARIO

Author's Preface

THE MANITOBA CENTENARY has called forth a commendable number of historical publications concerning the province, its people, the men and events that have shaped its growth. These are valuable additions to the literature of Manitoba's history, which stretches back to the mid-nineteenth century, reinforced by the memoirs and journals of explorers and traders which cast light on events back to the dawn of the seventeenth century. It is hoped that this volume will provide, for the general reader, a background to the main historical themes of Manitoba's past.

The indebtedness of the author is great and cannot be fully acknowledged. Special thanks, however, are due to the Trustees of the School Division of Winnipeg No. 1 and to Carman F. Moir and Gordon T. MacDonell, Superintendent and Superintendent Secondary respectively, for their co-operation in enabling the writer to obtain a necessary and much-appreciated leave of absence from teaching duties.

The work was inspired by the Manitoba Historical Society under the impetus of Dr. Clare Pentland, and its publication was assured by the Manitoba Centennial Commission. Professor W. D. Smith of the Department of History of the University of Manitoba has read the manuscript and has made many useful suggestions, being a constant source of encouragement during the writing. Dr. W. Steward

Martin, Q.C., President of the Manitoba Historical Society, has been a tower of strength, both in the editing of the manuscript and in preparing the way to publication. Raymond C. Wright and Joanne Erickson of the Library of the University of Winnipeg have given assistance far above and beyond the call of duty. Mr. Frank Hall, editor of *Manitoba Pageant,* has made valuable suggestions and criticisms. Barry Hyman of the Public Archives of Manitoba has cheerfully searched out answers to many obscure questions and is largely responsible for the wide choice of illustrations. With the exception of the portrait of Lord Selkirk (which was obtained from the National Archives of Canada), all pictures in the illustrated sections are from the provincial archives. Miss Clementine Combaz, chief reference librarian of the Provincial Library of Manitoba, was always able to come up with requested information.

Many others have cheerfully given assistance and the writer can only regret that much of the valuable first-hand information which was provided him has had to be omitted or at least compressed to satisfy the rigidity of a general account. Any inadequacies, errors, and unconscious distortions are the sole responsibility of the author.

WINNIPEG, MANITOBA *J. A. Jackson*

MARCH 4, 1970

To the memory of
ARTHUR JOHN STARR
Manitoban
mentor, colleague, dear friend
He would have seen that it was better done

Introduction

MANITOBA HAS BEEN a province of Canada for a century. Its story, however, has been a part of that of Canada for longer than this hundred years of direct political affiliation. The chronicles of both are inextricably interwoven in the eras of exploration and the fur trade. Yet Manitoba has a history that is entirely its own. Long before the idea of a transcontinental Canadian state was even a dream, there existed in Manitoba the beginnings of an organized society serving a useful purpose in the North American interior. By 1870, Manitoba society had so developed that it submitted to absorption only after a struggle in which its people demonstrated a consciousness of identity which they forced a reluctant Canadian government to recognize also. The period, 1870 to 1970, certainly marked Manitoba's greatest advance in wealth, population, and other manifestations of civilization. It was preceded, however, by a period of more than two hundred years in which Manitoba's unique identity was firmly fixed. To its first explorers, Manitoba was simply a barrier to the fabled riches of the Far East. As a fur-trading center, the region played a role in the struggle for empire between France and England. Manitoba's history is replete with controversy, both externally applied and of its own manufacture.

The present boundaries are artificial impositions for administrative convenience and were imposed from without. Manitoba's history, even after these boundaries were drawn is the story of the West, in the North American sense of that word. Though the province's historical role has been played over a larger scene, its name arose from a smaller context. Manitoba is graced with three major lakes, among innumerable others. The third in size bears the name that has become applied to the province. The name "Manitoba" is of Indian origin – as, properly, are so many Canadian place names. Lake Manitoba takes its name from a small island just north of its narrows. Here, when the conditions of wind and water allow, the combination produces a rushing whisper of sound. The place was called, according to this account, "the place where the Great Spirit whispers." There are several other interpretations, all of the same basic nature. The name now applies to a very sizeable segment of the north-central part of North America. The most easterly of Canada's three prairie provinces, it stretches northward over a distance of about 750 miles, from the border of the United States to the vast expanse of the Northwest Territories. Unlike its two prairie neighbors, however, Manitoba is not entirely an inland province, since its entire northeastern corner – a distance of approximately 450 miles – opens directly onto Hudson Bay. It is this access to Canada's great "inland sea," along with Manitoba's easterly location, which has made the province the Gateway to the West.

Geologically, the face of Manitoba presents a record both of the titanic upheavals which marked the initial formation of the earth's crust and of the more recent vicissitudes of geological activity. A good two thirds of its land area comprises a part of the Canadian Shield, the most ancient of Canada's geological formations, being in the vicinity of two billion years old. The remaining third runs from very old formations to relatively recent ones. Since the time that these geological foundations were laid down, they have been ground away by recurrent ice sheets, deeply immersed in primeval seas, and sharply gouged by great rivers. About 5,000 years ago, the subsiding of Lake Agassiz, a gigantic glacial lake which at one time stretched as far south as Fargo, North Dakota, and as far east as the fringe of the Whiteshell, resulted in the formation of the three lakes which have figured largely in the development of Manitoba. These are lakes Winnipeg, Winnipegosis, and Manitoba, all of them a part of what is now called the aspen parklands. Connected with numerous other lakes by a vast network of northerly-running rivers, these three great lakes have served as important highways throughout the history of the province.

The face of Manitoba, as it now stands, is a pleasant one. Those portions of the Canadian Shield which are not covered with numerous lakes or vast areas of muskeg are dotted with thick stands of spruce, pine, and birch. Throughout the aspen parklands, the valleys and hillsides are clothed in poplar, oak, elm, and box elder, though all of them, with the exception of the sturdy elm, are kept to a modest degree of growth by the rigors of Manitoba's climate. During the historic past, these trees and their accompanying shrubs penetrated what were once true grasslands, with the result that the province has provided a suitable habitat for a wide variety of animals. The rugged surface of the Canadian Shield was long a haven for numerous species – among them, moose, deer, elk, black bear, fox, muskrat, and beaver. The immense basin of what had once been Lake Agassiz was more the home of elk, deer, black bear, coyote, wolf, and buffalo, while the prairie region, that vast area of grassland west of the Red River and south of the Assiniboine, was host to a range of wildlife similar to that of the Manitoba escarpment. In the grasslands, however, there was a far greater preponderance of buffalo – an animal which, along with the beaver, was to play a fundamental role in the early history of Manitoba.

The first men to come to North America are believed to have made a long and tortuous journey from southeast Asia, northward through what is now China and the Soviet Union, and then across the Bering Strait – or across a land bridge which may have still existed at the time of their arrival. From here, the early nomads moved eastward and southward along the Pacific coast of North America. At one point, or perhaps at several different points, they struck inland across the Cordilleras, and entered upon the great central plains. It is also possible that from their point of arrival in easternmost Alaska they proceeded directly inland and moved through the arctic regions of Canada, rather than along the Pacific shoreline. From the Arctic, they could easily have reached the interior plains by way of the Mackenzie River valley. But whichever route they followed, the first inhabitants of North America did not make their appearance until sometime between 15,000 and 30,000 years ago. In fact, in Manitoba proper, man has not been traced back beyond 10,000 years.

The first human occupants of Manitoba were probably the "moundbuilders." These primitive people made their way into the area of Manitoba, moving along the alluvial ridges of Lake Agassiz as the waters of the lake gradually receded. The moundbuilders, who were primarily hunters, derive their name from the fact that they constructed large mounds in which they buried their dead, usually in a seated position. Remnants uncovered by today's archaeologists include stone tools and weapons, clay pots with decorative rims, flint from North Dakota, ochre from the distant southwest, and chips of obsidian from the Rockies. Thus, it is evident that even at the very dawn of their history, Manitobans were trading far afield – or at least were beneficiaries of trade routes which extended over great distances and in many directions.

No one can say with any certainty what eventually happened to the moundbuilders. It is conceivable that they migrated eastward and became the forefathers of the Forest Indians who later inhabited the region of the St. Lawrence River. Or perhaps they fell victim to, or merged with, the aboriginal invaders who moved into Manitoba during the more recent past, probably from the south and west. In any event, whatever the fate of the moundbuilders, we do know that their society flourished during the period in which Europe was passing through the High Middle Ages – and about the time that Edward I of England summoned his Model Parliament to make a beginning of institutions which would eventually become a part of the life of Manitoba.

The successors of the moundbuilders were the Plains Indians whom the white explorers were to encounter during the 1600's. Among these were the Assiniboine, "the people who cook with hot stones," an offshoot of the Dakota Sioux. By the middle of the seventeenth century, the Assiniboine inhabited the country to the west and south of Lake Winnipeg. At about the same time, the Cree, with links as far east as Labrador and as far west as Lake Athabasca, moved into the area to the south and west of the Churchill River and Hudson Bay. For the most part, the Cree and Assiniboine enjoyed a peaceful coexistence. Both were nomadic peoples – the Assiniboine more so than the Cree – and until they acquired the use of the horse, neither did much to alter the environment in which they lived.

For centuries, the grasslands, the pine forests, the lake-mirrored granite bastions, and the mud flats of Hudson Bay lay quiet and undisturbed but for the sounds of nature. The wind soughed gently through nodding pines, the occasional river crashed stridently to its destiny in the inland sea, and over all hung the pervasive drone of billions of mosquitoes. In the south was added the equally-multiplied chirp of the cricket, stilled at times by the *basso profundo* of the thudding hooves of a stampeding herd of buffalo, disturbed in its grazing by the thunderpeal of a passing summer storm. In this idyllic setting, man played but little part. He crept about the edges of the buffalo herds whose migrations had brought him to the area, cutting off the strays and felling them with his primitive weapons. The Indian was a nomad, and for all practical purposes the buffalo was his entire sustenance. Buffalo robes provided warmth in the sudden cool of summer nights and in the paralyzing cold of winter. Buffalo hides served as material for clothing and for tepees; pieces of buffalo bone were used as needles and buffalo sinews served as thread. The larger bones of the buffalo became tools and weapons, its dried manure was the universal fuel in a land largely devoid of wood, and, above all else, its flesh was a major source of food. Dependent in this way on a buffalo-centered economy, the Indians moved northward in early summer, trailing the herds into the reaches of western Manitoba; then moved southward in winter, retreating, like their prey, beyond the reach of northern blizzards. What is now the home of more than three quarters of Manitoba's population was then an uncultivated grassland, the permanent home of no man. Manitoba's aboriginal inhabitants knew no agriculture and had not advanced in animal husbandry beyond the breeding of dogs, which they used as work animals as well as a source of food. Here, no rich and romantic kingdom was to be found, no empire like that of the Incas, far to the south. Here was only a primitive people, living peaceably in close relation to their natural environment.

This primitive existence was soon to change. The coming of the horse and, shortly after, of the white man brought an entirely new way of life to the Indian. The horse, descended from those lost in the sixteenth century by the Spanish *conquistidores* far to the south, made the Indian the master of the buffalo. With the horse, the Indian was able to follow the wandering buffalo at will and could easily outpace a stampeding herd. The coming of the white man began a period of culture contact which was far-reaching in its consequences. At turns both friendly and hostile, rewarding and damaging, the relationship of Indians to whites was to constitute a significant theme in the province's history.

1

Exploration and Fur Trade

MANITOBA WAS TO WAIT well over a century after Columbus' discovery of the New World before the first explorations of the white man disturbed its primeval wilderness. By this time, Europe was aware that the northern part of North America was not simply a rich treasure waiting to be plundered, as had been the civilizations of Mexico and Peru. Here, rather, was a formidable barrier to the riches of the Far East, a barrier which evidently could not be sailed *through* and which must therefore be got *around*. The Elizabethan navigators, Davis and Frobisher, had taken time off from the task of singeing the beard of the King of Spain in order to probe the northern reaches of this New World, only to be driven back by the unrelenting ice. In the opening decade of the seventeenth century, the intrepid Henry Hudson had ventured into the strait and bay which now bear his name, to fall victim to a tragic death which gave rise to new hopes that this might be the way to India. These hopes, however, were firmly denied when Button, Munck, James, Foxe, and others ascertained that the bay was but an inland sea which provided no easy outlet to the west.

Thomas Button, an intrepid Welshman in the English service, was the first white man to winter in Manitoba. He spent the winter of 1612-13 with his two ships at the mouth of a river that he named the Nelson in honor of his navigator, who had died of scurvy. The country he called New Wales, a designation which many of his countrymen might have considered a libel. With his crews decimated by scurvy, Button abandoned one of his ships in the spring and sailed home. For this exploit, he was raised to the rank of admiral.

For another generation, Manitoba was left to its lonely grandeur. But even before the short and tragic sojourn of Button, events to the east were acting to bring Manitoba permanently into the affairs of European man. In 1608, Samuel Champlain finally gave up his long and futile effort to penetrate the Appalachian barrier. He now moved to Quebec and the St. Lawrence River, which gave him relatively easy access to the interior of North America, though it did not give him so much as a glimpse of his goal of the "western sea." By the time of Champlain's death in 1635, the French were familiar with three of the Great Lakes (Ontario, Erie, and Huron) and were aware of greater "fresh-water seas" beyond. Goaded by a triple spur, the French pressed westward: to the west were souls to be converted; riches in fur to be collected; and, above all else, the western sea which would lead to the incalculable wealth of the Far East.

In 1641, the year before the founding of Montreal, the Jesuit fathers Jogues and Raymbault built a mission at Sault Ste. Marie. Although the Iroquois scourge of 1648-49 destroyed Huronia, the lure of furs and of the far horizon was not to be denied. From a purely economic point of view, what really mattered in the destruction of Huronia was that the Iroquois had prevented all but the slightest trickle of furs from reaching New France. To persuade the western Indians to brave the hazardous journey to Quebec, Médard Chouart des Groseilliers was sent by the French authorities to the west of Lake Michigan. Here he encountered the Illinois, the Sioux, and the Cree. From the latter tribe he purchased furs of a hitherto unknown thickness and richness which had been trapped near a "sea of the north." On his return to Quebec in 1656, Groseilliers brought with him a considerable fortune in some thirty canoe-loads of pelts, as well as a determination to exploit for himself this Golconda of fur.

In 1659, together with his brother-in-law, Pierre Esprit Radisson, Groseilliers again travelled west of Lake Michigan to the forests of what is now Wisconsin. In the spring of 1660, the two adventurers slipped away from the missionaries who had accompanied them and made their way to the north shore of Lake Superior, where they joined forces with the Cree. From this point on, their trail is somewhat obscure. The two men claim to have gone overland to Hudson Bay, though this seems highly unlikely, since they returned to Montreal by the late summer of the same year. Where they actually travelled, however, is purely a matter of academic interest. The important thing is that they arrived in New France with many furs and with a valuable fund of information. Most of their furs they lost to the authorities for violations of trading regulations, but their information they carried to the English at Boston, partly out of resentment at their loss and partly in the belief that the English would place greater value on their knowledge.

Putting two and two together, Radisson and Groseilliers had concluded that the Cree "sea of the north" and the inland sea which Hudson and others had discovered were one and the same. Thus, there was no need to undertake an arduous, expensive, and time-consuming journey from the headwaters of the St. Lawrence to the inland paradise of fur; it could be reached with relative ease in large sea-going vessels, and the cargoes of fur could be picked up where they were trapped and transported directly to the European market. These advantages were equally obvious to the English, who had much valuable knowledge and experience of northern navigation. Here, then, was a portentous meeting of minds.

Through the good offices of Colonel George Cartwright, a friend to James, Duke of York and brother of King Charles, the two Frenchmen journeyed to England. Once there, they gained the attention of the English king, a man with a penchant for adventurers and a ready ear for tales of any wealth that might help to satisfy the endless demands made on his purse. A pilot expedition was soon outfitted through the aid of several sponsors: among them, Sir George Carteret; the king's cousin, Prince Rupert of the Rhine; and Rupert's secretary, James Hayes. The expedition was delayed by the misfortunes of the Dutch War, by difficulties in financing, by faulty vessels and by the perversity of the elements. Finally, however, Groseilliers set sail in the *Nonsuch* and reached the mouth of the Rupert River in James Bay late in the summer of 1668. Here he engaged in a brisk trade with the Cree and returned to London in 1669 with a rich haul of furs. The experiment, therefore, was a success and there remained but to convert the operation to one of a more permanent nature.

Though the desire for profit in the fur trade was undoubtedly paramount in the minds of its promoters, there were also deeper concerns affecting the establishment of the new venture. The prospect of an easy route to the "western sea" helped the framers of the new company to gain the necessary backing of Charles II and his ministers. Although the discovery of a northwest passage was intended to be a prime aim of the company, it was one which they tended to neglect. In fact, it was not until the early nineteenth century that interest in this goal was revived. Even then, the renewed concern was due more to a need to defend the company's trade monopoly than a desire to master the arctic seas.

Under the guiding hand of James Hayes, whose interest lay more in immediate gains than in abstract concepts of empire, the founding group was held together and the necessary paper work put in order. On May 2, 1670, the Great Seal of England was affixed to a "Royal Charter of the Governor and Company of Adventurers of England Trading into Hudson's Bay." The first great landmark in the history of Manitoba had been set in place. Charles did not stint in giving away what was not his any more than had his grandfathers, James I of England and Henry IV of France. When stripped of its almost Shakespearean language and translated into terms of modern geography, the charter can be seen to give to the Hudson's Bay Company absolute power over all of the north-central portion of North America. More specifically, the company's writ was to run westward from Labrador to the Rockies and northward from the source of the Red River to Chesterfield Inlet. What is even more impressive is the fact that the whole of this area was secured for an annual rental of two elks and two black beaver, payable when the king, his heirs, or successors should visit the company's territories! Clearly, Prince Rupert, the first governor of the Hudson's Bay Company, and his fellow shareholders had struck an excellent bargain.

The French, however, did not willingly allow the English to reap this wealth in fur. In due course, the newly-claimed Rupert's Land was to figure in conflicts of empire. The French on the St. Lawrence were early aware of the new threat to their trade in fur. Already engaged in stiff competition with the English trading out of New England and New York, they quite naturally resented this northern intrusion. Perhaps the perceptive and resourceful Jean Talon, the Intendant of New France, foresaw that this initial squeeze on his colony would later be transformed into a vise-like grip. Be that as it may, his reaction was swift.

In 1671, Talon dispatched Father Albanel, the Sieur de Saint-Simon, Sebastien Provencher, and a party of eight Indians to James Bay via Lake St. John. While wintering on the lake, they heard of the English presence on James Bay and on reaching the mouth of the Rupert River in June, 1672, they found the HBC post, Fort Charles, deserted. They made haste to claim the lands in the name of Louis XIV and to bestow gifts on the local Indians in the hope of persuading them to carry their furs to Montreal. The French, however, were soon forced to build trading posts in the region themselves and to engage in direct competition with the HBC on James Bay. The result of this competition was to direct the company's efforts to the west and the north. Posts (or "factories," as they were called) were established at the mouths of several rivers: the Moose, the Albany, the Severn, the Nelson, and the Churchill. In this way, Manitoba acquired its first permanent white occupants and the details of the western shores of Hudson Bay were soon more clearly defined.

In spite of the continued interference of the French, it was already evident that the HBC would be content to remain on Hudson Bay, letting the Indians come to the bay with their furs and making no major effort to investigate the interior which appeared no less barren and inhospitable than did the coast. Before a peaceful and profitable denouement could be reached, Manitoba's shores were to be shaken for the first time by the roar of cannon fired in anger.

In 1670, and for some time thereafter, the English and French had been at peace with one another. Indeed, they were allies against the Dutch under the Treaty of Dover. These considerations, however, did nothing to halt their mutual hostility in the Hudson Bay area. In 1686, with England and France still at peace and the measure of the new king, James II, yet to be taken by his people, Pierre Le Moyne, Sieur D'Iberville, at the head of a party of one hundred French, arrived at James Bay after travelling overland from the St. Lawrence. This foremost scion of the most noteworthy family of New France was now to create part of the great reputation which still enshrines his name in places as far apart as Manitoba and Louisiana. With vessels that were built on the spot, he quickly captured the HBC posts on James Bay.

In 1688, James II, having shown a tolerance of Roman Catholicism which was as yet unacceptable to the English, was thrust into exile. In 1689, James's son-in-law, William of Orange, now King William III, declared war on the French. The redoubtable D'Iberville soon ousted the English from all but one of their remaining footholds on Hudson Bay. For the next decade, the fortunes of war played back and forth over the once placid waters of the bay. Fort Nelson was the last post held by the English and this they lost in 1691, although the fort was to change hands four times over the next six years.

The French, however, could not stand long against English sea power. To their fatal lack of maritime strength was added the major drawback of a lack of French ambition with regard to Hudson Bay. The cause of this was to be found in the colonial policy of France with regard to Canada in general. When New France became a royal province in 1663, Colbert had stipulated that settlement be confined to the area of the St. Lawrence River and that the fur trade be limited to encouraging the Indians to come there with their catch. In 1696, Louis XIV spelled it out very clearly to Governor Frontenac:

> They must, pursuant to his Majesty's invariable orders, observe as their main rule in all departments of the Government of that Colony, to concentrate it, and to make it derive its support from the employment of the settlers within its confines and from their trade with the Kingdom and with the Indians who will necessarily bring peltries into the Colony in order to procure there those goods of the Kingdom which they require.

This emphasis on a restricted colony persisted to the last days of French power in America. Indeed, it was precisely this policy which served to give England and her chosen instrument, the Hudson's Bay Company, a free hand to exploit the fur resources of Rupert's Land.

By the Treaty of Utrecht of 1713, a treaty which ended at once the War of the Spanish Succession and Louis XIV's efforts to dominate Europe, France bowed to English naval invincibility and, adhering to her narrow Canadian colonial policy, renounced all claim to Hudson Bay. Henceforth, French interest in the bay was nonexistent and in the rest of Rupert's Land was for many years quite limited. Within the limits imposed by the dictates of Paris, however, the French continued to maintain contact with the West. Their only practical approach was by way of the route which linked Pigeon River, Rainy Lake, Rainy River, and Lake of the Woods, a route which was hotly contested by the Sioux and the less warlike Cree and Assiniboine. As a result, French efforts were continually thwarted by Indian conflicts and by their inability to resolve them.

The French remained in contact with the fringes of the West through the *coureurs de bois*, who worked out of Kaministikwia at the western end of Lake Superior. The ability of these men to live among the Indians paid high dividends. Many prime beaver pelts destined, according to the HBC, to find their way northward to the bay were diverted instead to Montreal. This drain on furs was not great, but it was the subject, from time to time, of comment by HBC traders. These men began to manifest real concern only when, in 1732, the number of pelts delivered to York Factory declined from a previous 52,000 to 37,000. There was now something very much amiss, from the viewpoint of the HBC, in the area southwest of the Laurentian Shield. The explanation for this sudden depletion of the English fur trade lay in a new French stratagem. In 1732, the governor of New France appointed Pierre Gaultier de Varennes, Sieur de La Vérendrye, to the command of the northern posts. To this day, the name of La Vérendrye is inextricably bound up with the history of Manitoba. He, together with his sons and his nephew, was the first to see the territory of Manitoba as the link connecting the routes to the south, the west, and the north of the continent. A native Canadian, born at Trois-Rivières, he had grown up with a knowledge of the forests, the Indians, and the fur trade. He had also fought in the wars of Louis XIV and had been wounded at Malplaquet, one of the great victories of John Churchill, Duke of Marlborough, who had at one time been governor of the Hudson's Bay Company. Without ever having it as his conscious aim, La Vérendrye was later to make that company pay dearly for his wounds.

While the main French effort in America had been diverted to the area of the Mississippi and to the containment of the English on the east coast, La Vérendrye looked westward for the elusive "western sea" which had lured his predecessors as far back as Champlain. In his attempts to reach that sea, he had as little success as they; but because of his extensive explorations, he is generally regarded as the discoverer of the Canadian West. He was also a thorn in the side of the HBC, forcing it for the first time to look to its trading laurels beyond the shores of Hudson Bay.

In spite of its charter commitment to pursue diligently the search for a northwest passage, the HBC was particularly remiss in exploring the Canadian hinterland. In fact, in the first eighty-four years of its existence, the company sent only one man into the interior – and he was not sent as an explorer so much as a "public relations" man. His primary aim was to encourage the Indians to bring their furs to Hudson Bay and to urge them to end the fratricidal quarrels which impeded the smooth trade in beaver pelts. In this, he was but an early forerunner in what was to be one of the HBC's principal activities, that of peacemaker among the Indians. The man sent out on this assignment was a natural choice for the task. He was Henry Kelsey, a natural *coureur de bois* who had entered the service of the HBC at the age of fourteen. As early as 1686, with only one companion, Kelsey undertook a 200-mile journey along the coast of Hudson Bay north of the Churchill River in search of the "northern

Indians," that is, the Eskimos. He found no Eskimos, but he did encounter two musk-oxen, one of which he shot. He called these animals "buffillo" and described them as "misshapen" beasts. Kelsey was later to correct this zoological error on his most famous venture west and south of the bay. Travelling as peacemaker and fur-trade drummer somewhere south of The Pas, possibly in the neighborhood of Swan River, he saw the true buffalo, and was the first white man to do so in the Canadian West. He noted in his journal the great numbers of the animal and the ease with which the Indians stalked and shot it. But he did not, at least in writing, speculate on its future role as the mainstay of the northern fur trade; nor, more is the pity, did he comment on its edibility.

Kelsey's travels are noteworthy for more than his being the first white man to sight buffalo on Manitoba's soil. The very uniqueness of his journey on behalf of the HBC – the only one in almost a century – demonstrates the company's dominance of the fur trade. The HBC now knew that it need not set itself up in the barren and dangerous interior. The Indian, out of need, was obliged to go to the company on the bay. His only alternatives, until the arrival of La Vérendrye, were either the hope of encountering an itinerant French trader or the hazardous journey through lands dominated by Sioux to the more-or-less permanent French *postes du nord* at the Lakehead. The trip to the bay was much to be preferred, since generally it was shorter and certainly it was safer. Above all, it was becoming more and more necessary to the Indian. He was by now accustomed to the white man's weapons, utensils, cloth, tobacco, and, possibly, his alcohol.

Convenience and safety were by no means the only factors which the Indian took into account when choosing to do his trading with the English on the bay. English trade goods were generally of higher quality than those of the French and had been from the very outset. As early as Queen Anne's War (the War of the Spanish Succession in Europe), Governor Vaudreuil of New France was complaining angrily to Paris about the preference shown by the Indians for English goods. Indeed, his anger was directed largely at his own compatriots because of their most unpatriotic preference for things English, with the one redeeming exception of gun powder. Thus, even in the frontier areas of North America, the first stirrings of England's industrial revolution were already discernible, giving her an advantage which was to become greater with the passing of time. The trade goods of the English were better and cheaper: their hatchets held an edge longer, their copper copper pots did not easily melt or show flaws, their guns were not likely to explode on being fired (no matter how enthusiastically overloaded), and their blankets were of higher quality and were much more colorful than those of the French. On top of this, the greater economy of the direct route from the Atlantic Ocean into Hudson Bay, a route which had been pointed out by Radisson and Groseilliers, meant that English prices were much lower than those which the French were obliged to charge because of their higher overhead. With all of these factors working to their advantage, it is small wonder that the English felt that they need not overly concern themselves with a search for customers.

It fell to La Vérendrye to spoil the fur-trade monopoly enjoyed by the HBC. Neither he nor his fellow traders were long or fully to enjoy the spoilage, but he did quite literally blaze the trail which was to bring the company to its knees in the following century. La Vérendrye's motives were several, though his main concern was always the will-o'-the-wisp "western sea." Just as the French posts along the Ohio and the Mississippi were designed, no matter how ineffectively, to restrict the English to the east coast of America, La Vérendrye's strategy was to outflank them in their northern fastness on Hudson Bay. To do this, he would make his way across the Canadian Shield to the west of Lake Superior and strike northward along its western edge, thus intercepting their trade.

This was a crucial move, since a command of the fur trade was essential to La Vérendrye if he was to obtain sufficient backing to continue his explorations. In this respect, La Vérendrye was caught in a dilemma which was typical of the early North American explorers. In short, he had to make a profit in furs in order to satisfy his backers' often excessive demands for monetary gains. This took up much of the time and resources which he might better have spent on exploration. At the same time, the French authorities, both in Paris and in Quebec, suspected that he was neglecting his explorations purely in the interest of gaining profit from the fur trade.

La Vérendrye made it plain from the time of his taking command of the *postes du nord* that he would establish a regular series of posts westwards from Kaministikwia and would attempt to maintain them on a basis of permanent occupation. This he set out to do. In 1731, he built Fort St. Pierre on Rainy Lake at the mouth of the Rainy River, and in 1732, he built Fort St. Charles at the northwest angle of Lake of the Woods. He had now reached the very threshold of the West. He sent his son further westward to build Fort Maurepas

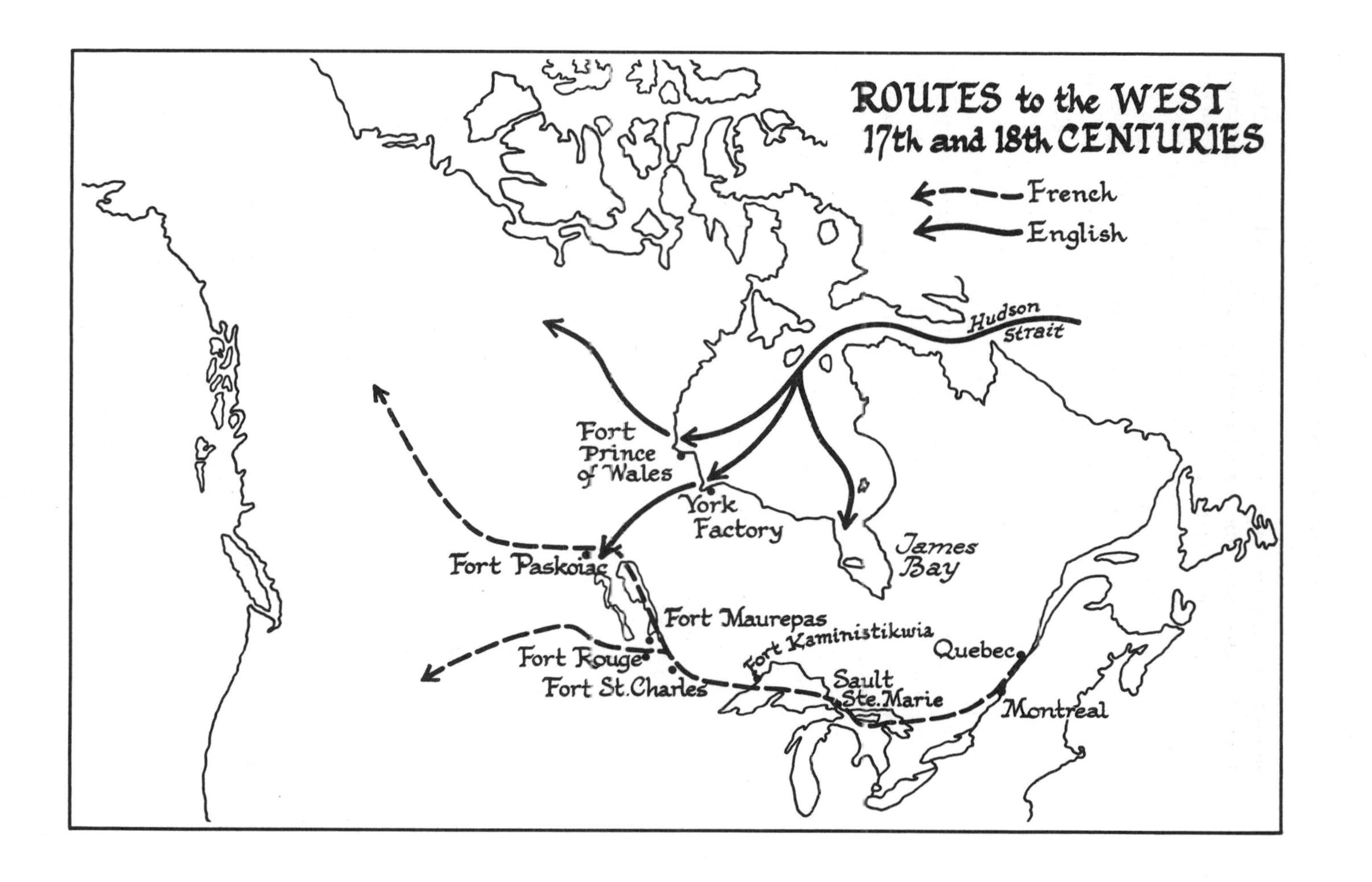
ROUTES to the WEST
17th and 18th CENTURIES
French
English
Hudson Strait
Fort Prince of Wales
York Factory
James Bay
Fort Paskoiac
Fort Maurepas
Fort Kaministikwia
Quebec
Fort Rouge
Fort St. Charles
Sault Ste. Marie
Montreal

on the lower Red River in 1734. This post, named in honor of the French minister of marine, was moved to the lower Winnipeg River in 1735. In 1736, La Vérendrye suffered the buffetings of a cruel fate. La Jemeraye, his nephew and faithful second-in-command, died near what is now Letellier while en route to meet his uncle at Fort St. Charles. Early in June, La Vérendrye sent his eldest son, Jean Baptiste, together with the Jesuit Father Aulneau and twenty-one armed men from Fort St. Charles to Kaministikwia to pick up and convoy much-needed supplies and trade goods. Less than a day out from the fort, they were slaughtered by the Sioux while camping on an island in Lake of the Woods. The suspected location of this occurrence is now identified as "Massacre Island." La Vérendrye paid a bitter price for the French alliance with the Cree and Assiniboine.

La Vérendrye steeled himself to carry on. The winter of 1736-37 he spent at Fort Maurepas on the Winnipeg (near the present Fort Alexander) familiarizing himself with the land and seeking data on what might lie to the north and west of Lake Winnipeg. He sent one of his two surviving sons to live with the Cree at the north end of the lake as a source of information and as a gesture of alliance. The need for men and money drove him back to Montreal in 1737; but in 1738 he returned and built a post at the juncture of the Red and the Assiniboine rivers, as he had promised his Assiniboine allies he would do. This was the short-lived Fort Rouge, located probably on the north bank of the Assiniboine near its junction with the Red, the genesis of the city of Winnipeg. Some authorities place Fort Rouge on the south bank of the Assiniboine. If it was so, then the post was obviously only of a temporary nature since the land of the south bank is low and was flooded in high water. In the same year, he ascended the Assiniboine and established Fort La Reine near Portage la Prairie. Then he struck overland, southwestward to the upper Missouri, seeing first-hand the hills and valleys of southwestern Manitoba and following the age-old tracks of the migrating buffalo. He sought and found the Mandan villages, fanciful tales of which had been told to him by his Assiniboine guides. Far from being white and dwelling in houses, these Indians tended to be clay-colored from contact with the mud huts in which they lived. They did, however, grow corn and their women were fairer both of hair and of skin than were other Indians. His great disappointment was the discovery that the river of the Mandans, the Missouri, flowed south and, as he had rightly suspected, into the Mississippi. Once again, the "western sea" receded before his eager grasp.

Henceforth, La Vérendrye devoted his activities to the area north and west of Lake Winnipeg and more to the practical problem of tapping the fur trade of the HBC, meanwhile strengthening the hold of the French through the construction of posts. In 1739 came Fort Dauphin near Lake Winnipegosis, and in 1741 Fort Bourbon on Cedar Lake, whence the Saskatchewan River finds its way to Lake Winnipeg. The Saskatchewan was on the main route of trading parties to the bay and an establishment there should have given the French a decided advantage. Impatient with La Vérendrye's lack of concrete results and aghast at the cost of his ventures, the authorities at Quebec removed him from command of the northern posts in 1744. In 1749, La Vérendrye was once again appointed to the command of the *postes du nord*. He was then in his sixties, very old for a man of the mid-eighteenth century and even older for a man about to brave the rigors of the western frontier. La Vérendrye, however, was never again to face that test. While preparing to go once more into the west, he died at Montreal in December, 1749. Thus, less than a decade before the outbreak of the French and Indian War, which as the Seven Years' War was to spell the end of French empire in America, Pierre de La Vérendrye passed from the Canadian scene.

Little time or opportunity was now left to the French to exploit the trade route which he had marked out. In fact, it remained for the Scots and the Americans who took over the Montreal-based trade in 1760 to reap the benefits in fur. La Vérendrye had moved the HBC to stir restlessly in its long sleep by the bay and to begin a somewhat leisurely course of inland operations. It was only, however, when the Scots and the Yankees made full use of the avenues which he had opened up that the HBC became feverishly active. La Vérendrye bequeathed to the land of Manitoba a clear definition of its purpose as the North American crossroads between north and south, and between east and west. Perhaps even more significantly, in his oft-repeated admonition to those who manned his posts, that they should live off the land by growing their own crops to supplement a meagre diet based on locally-killed game, he pointed the way to the future.

2

Crossroads and Larder of the West

WHATEVER LA VÉRENDRYE'S dreams may have been, their realization still lay far in the future. The story of Manitoba was to continue to be the story of the fur trade for more than a century after his death; but the activity of the French in western Canada, which he had initiated, did not live up to its early promise. A general apathy descended on French operations in the west; their trade languished, and soon the final struggle for empire in North America summoned back their small legions to the St. Lawrence and the Plains of Abraham. In the interim, only the last flickers of French activity were to be seen, with the result that the HBC relaxed its tentative inland approaches, being content with a few exploratory efforts designed to encourage the Indians to bring their furs to the bay.

The story of these activities is a brief one. In 1743, the first inland post of the HBC was established as Henley House, one hundred and twenty miles up the Albany River from James Bay. In 1755, every member of its small staff was murdered and the post was looted by local Indians, with the help of others who were friendly to the French. The company had not yet mastered the art of living among the Indians and this disaster did not encourage the founding of further inland establishments. Henley House was not set up again until 1766, after the French had gone from North America.

To the west, things went somewhat better. In 1754, Anthony Henday moved inland from York Factory to Paskoyac and thence southwest to winter among the Blackfoot between the North Saskatchewan and Red Deer rivers. Here, Henday encountered buffalo in large numbers, "grazing like English cattle," and remarked on the skill of mounted Indian hunters. Returning to York Factory in June, 1755, he brought with him many rich furs and many Indians, but no Blackfoot. The Blackfoot refused to make the journey because of the long distance, their unfamiliarity with the canoe, their dislike of substituting a diet of fish for their accustomed fare of meat, and the disinclination of the Cree and Assiniboine to let them pass peaceably. The latter tribes had already assumed the role of middleman and did not wish to have their profits cut off by a direct association between Blackfoot and whites.

Others were also active in the interior of what was then known as Rupert's Land. In 1753, the year before Henday's journey, the Chevalier de la Corne, successor to La Vérendrye as commander of the *postes du nord,* set up Fort à la Corne at the forks of the Saskatchewan River, a last far-flung gesture of French power. The next year, in a deed of far greater significance, he planted the first wheat in the prairie West. (There remains no record of the yield, if any.) In 1757, Joseph Smith and Joseph Waggoner, again from York Factory, carried the message of the HBC via lakes Winnipeg, Winnipegosis, and Manitoba to the Assiniboine, bringing back fifty-seven canoe-loads of fur and accounts of the slaughter of buffalo by the Assiniboine Indians. Thus, by the time of the outbreak of the French and Indian War, the English from Hudson Bay were in active competition with the French, both on the prairies and on the western part of the Canadian Shield. In 1759, Alexander Henday and Joseph Smith made another great sweep from Hudson Bay to the Assiniboine, bringing back, in June of the following year, sixty-one canoes of furs. Just three months later, on September 8, 1760, Pierre de Rigaud, Marquis de Vaudreuil-Cavagnal, last Governor of New France, surrendered all of his vast viceroyalty to the English at Montreal. Before pursuing the far-reaching consequences of this monentous event, it is necessary that we pause to glance backward in time, and northward in direction, to the events that had meanwhile transpired on Hudson Bay itself.

The HBC had never shown any real concern about the challenge to its position made by the French penetration of Rupert's Land. Its actions, though invested with potential for the future expansion of the fur trade, in no way suggested that the company regarded itself as being in danger. On the bay itself, however, the story was much different. Here, defence against French incursion was a paramount consideration. With bitter memories of the French success in the bay during King William's and Queen Anne's wars, the English began, during King George's War, to prepare defences against the possible return of a French fleet. Even before this, a good beginning had been made at the mouth of the Churchill River. The first permanent establishment had been built there for the HBC in 1717 by James Knight, whose vivid description of the area was often to be echoed: "I never see such a misserable place in all my life."

In 1732, with the encouragement of the British Admiralty, the HBC began the thirty-year task of building Fort Prince of Wales, "the Louisbourg of the North." Indeed, in terms of both cost of construction and military ineffectiveness, it closely resembled the French bastion on Cape Breton. Fort Prince of Wales, today largely reconstructed as a national historic site, had four bastions, each ten feet high and linked by parapets pierced with gun ports. Forty-two cannon were emplaced; a magazine, with walls five feet thick, was constructed of stone; and sturdy wooden buildings were erected within the walls. By the time that Fort Prince of Wales was ready, the French and Indian War was already under way. York Fort was further armed, and Moose and Albany were put into a state of defensive readiness. These warlike preparations, however, were never put to the test, since the French and Indian War was resolved without disturbing the peace of Hudson Bay. It was not until 1782, during the American Revolution, that Fort Prince of Wales was finally attacked by the French. At this time, the redoubtable La Pérousse achieved a bloodless victory over thirty-nine Englishmen under the command of Samuel Hearne. With commendable good sense, Hearne capitulated in the face of heavy odds.

By now, new events were beginning to trouble the even tenor of the company's trade. These were less immediately devastating than the depredations of La Pérousse at Fort Prince of Wales, but in the long run they proved more important to the HBC and figured more significantly in the history of Manitoba. The whole of Hudson Bay remained permanently and tranquilly British after the Treaty of Paris ended the American War of Independence in 1783. Similarly, the territory of Rupert's Land remained British, although far from tranquil with regard to matters of the fur trade. With hardly a dropped paddle-stroke, the French fur trade of Montreal quickly became the British fur trade of Montreal and, in a short time, a far more formidable competitor to the HBC than the French had ever been. The great majority of those who came into this trade were either Scots or Americans, cousins of the men of the HBC, and Yankees from New England and New York. As early as 1761, with the ink not yet dry on the Articles of Capitulation that were signed by Vaudreuil at Montreal, Alexander Henry the elder was at Michilimackinac with a French partner, where he found that others had preceded him.

The number of independent traders soon increased and their fur-garnering ventures carried them further into the west and north along the route pioneered by La Vérendrye. Attempts on the part of the imperial government to restrict trade in the interest of establishing peaceful relations with the Indians of the Great Lakes region proved all but useless. The urge for quick profit could not be denied by the decrees of a remote authority. Traders became so numerous and their activities so ruinously competitive that the situation soon corrected itself through the elimination of the inefficient by bankruptcy. The survivors grouped themselves into partnerships, which gradually became larger and finally merged in 1784 to form the North West Company. Henceforth, until its union with the Hudson's Bay Company in 1821, the NWC dominated the Montreal fur trade to the virtual exclusion of all others. Its monopoly was never as complete as had been that of the HBC in northern Rupert's Land, nor did it go unchallenged. For a time, between 1799 and 1804, the New North West Company provided some formidable competition, until its partners, most of whom were dissatisfied Nor'Westers, were reabsorbed into the parent organization. The New North West Company was familiarly known as the XY Company, because its bales were so labelled in order to distinguish them from those of the NWC. The Montreal traders, or "pedlars" as they were at first contemptuously known to the HBC, soon made their presence felt. Here began a new era in the history of the fur trade and of Manitoba.

The North West Company soon pushed its operations far beyond those of the French. They moved west along the North Saskatchewan, and north from there to the Beaver River and to Lake Ile à la Crosse. In 1778, Peter Pond, the Connecticut Yankee, made his way across the Methye portage to Clearwater River and then to the Athabasca, which flows into the lake of the same name. At the western end of Lake Athabasca, he founded Fort Chipewyan, named for the Indians of the district. He did well to name the post in their honor. Not only did he receive from them furs of a hitherto undreamed-of richness, but he was also the first white man recorded to become familiar with pemmican, a foodstuff which the Indians had devised to sustain themselves in a country where game was only chancily come by. Without pemmican the northern fur trade could not have been carried on. It was as the source of pemmican that the forks of the Red and the Assiniboine first became a factor in western Canadian development. Pond also set up the base from which Alexander Mackenzie was to find his way in turn to both the Arctic and the Pacific oceans.

Both before and after Pond, the "pedlars from Montreal" were to furnish many names of undying fame. Simon McTavish, Joseph Frobisher, James and John McGill, Simon Fraser, William McGillivray, Nicholas Garry, David Thompson, and many others were to have their share of grief and glory in the process of achieving lasting fame. Between them, during the last quarter of the eighteenth century and the first quarter of the nineteenth, they devised, developed, and extended a system of trade which was entirely different from any that had ever before been seen in North America, though it did have a parallel in the contemporary American trade out of St. Louis.

To make a return journey from Montreal to the fur country in the course of a single year had always been both arduous and hazardous for those encumbered with furs or trade goods. The custom of spending the winter in the northern fastness had been routine since the days of Radisson and Groseilliers. When it began to trade extensively in the far north and west, the NWC had to come to terms with extremes of terrain and climate. There evolved an apparently elaborate, but essentially simple, two-part operation. This operation pivoted on a central base that was shifted early on from that of the French at Michilimackinac to one at the western end of Lake Superior. This latter base was Grand Portage, at the mouth of the Pigeon River. Later, it was moved north along the lake to Fort William (the Kaministikwia of the French) at the mouth of the Kaministikwia River. The shift was made to avoid the possibility of clashes with the United States when the international boundary was set from Lake Superior to Lake of the Woods by Jay's Treaty in 1794.

Early each summer, the partners of the North West Company and their *voyageurs* would begin to stir over the length and breadth of their trading empire. From the far north and west, fur-laden canoes were paddled down to central points such as Fort Chipewyan on Lake Athabasca, Ile à la Crosse, Nipawin at the forks of the Saskatchewan, and Fort Gilbraltar at the junction of the Red and the Assiniboine. They would then be combined into brigades and proceed to the head of Lake Superior. The men who assembled and organized these brigades were the "wintering partners," known colloquially as "the northmen" or "the men of *le pays d'en haut*." At the same time, the "Montreal partners" or "*mangeurs du lard*" (pork eaters) would load similar brigades of great freight canoes at Lachine with a vast array of trade goods for the coming year plus the account books which covered the details of the trade of the previous year. In addition to its cargo, each canoe carried enough food for ten men (chiefly salt pork and corn meal) plus forty pounds of personal baggage for each man. The canoes, which measured thirty-six feet long by six feet wide, could each carry a load of up to 6,000 pounds. From Lachine, the Montreal partners retraced the route of Champlain: up the Ottawa, the Mattawa, across Lake Nipissing, and down the French River to Georgian Bay, traversing thirty-six portages along the way. They then proceeded via the North Channel and Sault Ste. Marie to Lake Superior and thence to the Lakehead. Here, they met in the early summer with the northmen and transacted all necessary business.

First, however, they held a great and sustained celebration, a necessary relief for both groups from the hardships of their respective journeys. The festivities were conducted in the best French-Scots manner, with innumerable toasts, much feasting, and *feux de joie,* culminating in a grand ball to which all, especially the Chippewa girls, were welcome. During the course of the celebration, the winterers were brought up to date on the news of the outside world and both winterers and Montrealers exchanged gossip about the state of the fur market. Their interest covered every facet of the operation, from the Arctic Ocean to the fashion salons of Europe. Business was usually settled quickly and amicably; the previous year's accounts were scrutinized and the profits were divided equitably among the partners. The current fur crop was tabulated and sorted for the eastern journey, and trade goods were stowed in the canoes which were to return to the *pays d'en haut*. New winterers transferred to the outgoing brigades, and veterans who were coming out took their places in the brigades bound for Montreal. Comparative peace would then reign at the Lakehead until the following summer.

This was the major contact, though not the only one, between the garnerers and marketers of fur for the NWC. General news and trade information were continually being carried east and northwest by courier. There was, however, no general exodus from the centers of fur gathering. The posts had to be manned and trading carried on at all times, so that any one individual might spend up to three years in the wilderness before coming out for a much-deserved holiday. This he would likely spend in Montreal, in Britain, in the United States, or wherever his home might happen to be. After a few stints in the wilds, he might gravitate into the ranks of the "Montreal partners" and their exclusive Beaver Club, or he might even retire on the strength of his share of the profits. As time went on, and especially after the 1821 union of the NWC and the HBC, a growing number of those who retired did so in the country which they had learned to love. Many had taken Indian wives and were therefore inclined to remain in Rupert's Land for the benefit of their families. Before the union of 1821, this aspect of the fur trade was as yet undeveloped, but from it Manitoba was to gain her first native sons. In settling down in the country which had sustained them, the men of the HBC would eventually follow the example set by the men of the NWC. In the meanwhile, they had to meet the now real and present danger of direct competition.

Where the French had been, at worst, a mere irritant to the HBC, the Montreal traders had become, almost overnight, a ravenous wolf in their fold. Demands were soon being made by the officers in charge at York Factory and at Fort Prince of Wales for the establishment of interior posts, particularly on the Saskatchewan River. It was intended that these posts be located in advance of those of the "pedlars" so as to intercept the Indians. Not only were the interlopers dealing with the Indians in or near the trading grounds, but they were doing so with similar goods at competitive prices. With the elimination of inefficient traders through bankruptcy and with the strengthening of efficient traders through the partnership of the NWC (with its resultant economies in operating costs), the threat of the Montreal traders soon assumed frightening proportions. A close study was made on the ground in the late 1760's and early 1770's by a number of HBC men such as William Pink, William Tomison, Matthew Cocking, and the already-famous Samuel Hearne. All noted the established presence of the Montreal traders and the persuasiveness of their methods. They also noted that the effectiveness of the Montrealers was not due entirely to their prices or to their liberal dispensation of rum. The new breed of trader had with him many *Canadiens,* whose relations with the Indians were, as always, closer and often better than those of the English. In this regard, Cocking reported: "It surprises to perceive what a warm side the Natives hath to the French Canadians."

In June of 1774, Cumberland House was established by the HBC just upriver from The Pas. In quick succession, other posts were built in an effort to secure the Saskatchewan fur country: Oxford House, Edmonton House, Carlton House, Buckingham House, and Gordon House. The appearance of these posts, however, did little to stem the advance of the newcomers. In fact, all during the years of the French Revolution and the Napoleonic domination of Europe, the Montrealers remained in contention for the fur trade. The brashness, inventiveness, and general spirit of derring-do of the Nor'Westers was matched by the longer experience, greater financial resources, and toughness of fiber of the "men of the Bay."

The struggle was for a long time merely a matter of trade rivalry and involved little or no personal animosity on either side. After all, there were furs enough for everyone. In fact, in many locations, the posts of the HBC and the NWC were within hailing distance of one another, and they were on a "hail fellow, well met" relationship. It is reported that for some years the Nor'Westers were hosts at a Christmas wassail for the HBC men at The Pas and were feasted, in turn, by the HBC men at Cumberland House with a proper Scottish New Year's hogmanay. It must be remembered that at the dawn of the nineteenth century, the company of fellow whites, or indeed the company of any man, was hard come by in the vast emptiness of Rupert's Land. Moreover, the harsh and demanding conditions of existence made a helping hand a natural and even a necessary gesture. As competition increased, however, tempers did wear thin. Friendships cooled and co-operation diminished, except in times of mutual misfortune. Until the nineteenth century was well under way, the situation was characterized by nothing more serious than ill will. It was not until after the Battle of Trafalgar had ensured England of security from French invasion and Napoleon had begun to feel the chill of a Russian winter that rivalry turned to active hatred and to acts of war.

When the trouble finally did come, it came in Manitoba, although it did not stem directly from the trade in fur, but from the buffalo hunt which made the fur trade possible. As the trading antagonists built their opposing empires, they increased their dependence on the pemmican that was provided by the buffalo. Since the richest source of buffalo was the extensive grazing grounds south of the Manitoba lakes and west of the Red River, it was here that the fate of the fur trade would be decided. Thus, the main current of Manitoba's history now began to turn inward on the province and to give it a life of its own.

Almost without exception, every traveller who moved through west-central North America in the first six decades of the last century, for whatever reason, wrote an account of his experiences and observations. Some, like Milton and Cheadle and the Earl of Southesk, did so as adventurous dilettantes. Others, such as Henry Youle Hind and John Palliser, did so with considerable scientific pomposity. Without exception, they all made special note of the buffalo and the buffalo hunt. All agree that the buffalo roamed in immense numbers and that the Indians were most adept in their pursuit and slaughter of the animal, as well as being wasteful in the numbers they killed. Yet none of these writers seems to agree on even the approximate number of buffalo at any given time or place and they are equally at variance in their accounts of the migration of the herds. One American army officer, observing from Fort Dodge in Kansas, reported that herds migrated northward early each summer, complete with cows and calves, but never returned to the south. Perhaps he subscribed to a widely-held Indian belief that the buffalo, placed in eternal supply by the Great Spirit, came forth from certain lakes or streams. In truth, however, though buffalo herds ranged over the entire center of the continent, individual herds apparently moved through only a relatively narrow range. For example, those herds sought by the Red River hunt ranged south from roughly the Manitoba lakes to the upper Missouri, and west from the Red River to the Cypress Hills.

The buffalo was a "sometime thing." Neither its movements nor its wintering or summering grounds could be determined with any accuracy. Alexander Ross, the first historian of the Red River and of Manitoba, wrote that finding the herds was like a "leap in the dark." Alexander Henry would report buffalo without number in one locale in one summer and would then note that there were none at that spot in the summer of the following year. In 1812, there were herds grazing within gunshot of the junction of the Red and the Assiniboine in July and August; while in 1817, hunters had to go as far afield as the Pembina Hills to find them. Spring floods, late frosts, the endemic prairie fire, or simple contrariness seemed to govern the movements of the herds more than any dictate of the seasons or any response to instinct. Their movements, in fact, were as unreliable as those of the geese were reliable.

Red River became the center of the buffalo hunt for both of the great trading companies at the beginning of the nineteenth century and remained the focus for the united companies until after the creation of Manitoba as a province of Canada in 1870. As a result of the union of the NWC and the HBC in 1821, Red River was provided with the nucleus of a permanent settlement, one which was reasonably populous for that time. It was also strategically situated, since it lay on the principal east-west route of the NWC and bordered a waterway which was much used by the HBC. Moreover, while the Red River carried hunters into the buffalo country of Dakota, the Assiniboine,

Souris, and Qu'Appelle rivers led to the buffalo grounds of the west and southwest.

Red River, however, was by no means the sole source of buffalo-hunting parties, nor was it the permanently-occupied site closest to the largest herds. In 1793, John McDonald of Garth reported that the main supply center for pemmican for use in the Athabasca trade was to be found between the two branches of the Saskatchewan, the same locality in which Peter Pond had first come upon it in 1778. Moreover, many buffalo continued to be taken far to the west and south of Red River, and these, in due course, found their way (in the form of pemmican) into the northern reaches of Rupert's Land.

The Red River buffalo hunts were undertaken on an organized basis early in the nineteenth century. As soon as there was anything like a permanent settlement, its inhabitants, primarily Métis with some English and Scottish halfbreeds, came to regard the twice-a-year buffalo hunt as their principal source of income and far and away their chief avocation. Taken as a whole, the Métis and the halfbreeds of the Red River were, at best, indifferent farmers and they looked on the hunt as a welcome diversion from the drudgery of their small and unproductive farms. They embarked on the twice-yearly hunts with what clearly amounted to an excess of zeal. The earlier hunts, prior to the setting-up of the Selkirk settlement, were sponsored by the rival fur companies. Their aim, outdoor sports aside, was to provide the pemmican which was not only essential to the northern trade but which was also a winter food supply for the few permanent residents. By 1820, with the fur-trade war in a state of permanent armistice and the union of the companies already on the horizon, the hunt became a highly organized affair which was generally held in mid-June and again in October. Following 1846, there were at times two hunting parties in each season originating in the Red River colony or, as it was then known, the District of Assiniboia. The Red River hunt travelled south to Pembina and sought the buffalo in what is now North Dakota. The second party, known as the White Horse Plain hunt, went west on the Assiniboine into the valley of the Qu'Appelle. The organization of the two hunts was similar, since both of them were modelled on the example of the Indian forebears of the hunters, with some refinements being developed as a result of the greater number of hunters and the use of the ubiquitous Red River cart.

The size of a hunt could be estimated by the number of carts involved, while the yield of buffalo products could be deduced by the number of laden carts which returned to the settlement. In 1820, 540 carts participated; in 1830, 820 carts; and in 1840, 1,210. The latter hunt, described in detail by Alexander Ross in 1852, yielded 1,089,-000 pounds in all. The price paid by the HBC at that time was 2 pence per pound, probably 10 to 15 cents per pound at today's values. In 1840, the company paid out £1,200 for buffalo tallow, dried meat, and pemmican. This sum, Ross notes, was greater than the cash value of the farm crops of the area. The yield per animal was not great: one buffalo cow would furnish, at best, one half-bag of pemmican (at 100 to 110 pounds per bag); three quarters of a bundle of dried meat (at 60 to 70 pounds per bundle); one quarter of a bladder of marrow (at 12 pounds per bladder); and one fifth of a sack of tallow (at 200 pounds per sack). The above figures, derived from Ross, are mere approximations and there are as many variations of yield as there are estimates. The yield of tallow, for example, is usually listed as being much higher, up to 75 pounds per cow. The bull was not greatly sought after in times of plenty. Of the bull, only the hump and tongue were considered edible, though its hide was prized as much as that of the cow. There was much wastage, resulting from a number of different factors: wanton slaughter; careless butchering; spoilage due to heat and water; and the depredations of dogs and wolves.

The following description of the organization and conduct of the hunt, taken from Ross' 1852 account, can be regarded as being typical of that of Red River in full vigor. In 1840, the total number of those who participated, including men, women, and children, was 1,630, a good half of the population of the settlement, if not more. Their first concern was to choose the officers of the hunt and of the camp. Thus, the adult males gathered together and chose ten captains. Of these ten, one became "captain of the hunt," or "great war chief," and head of the camp. He was presiding officer of the camp and of the hunt on all matters of a general nature; he also served as its resident magistrate. Each of the ten captains had ten soldiers under his command; and apart from the ten captains, ten guides were also chosen. These guides were entrusted with directing the progress of the hunt on the trail according to a daily roster.

The camp flag was entrusted to the guide of the day and the camp moved at the dictates of the flag. The raising of the flag in the morning signalled the departure of the camp and one half-hour was allowed for moving preparations. Any reasonable cause for delay, if communicated to the guide, would cause the departure to be postponed. The flag, however, would remain flying, since it was lowered only to signal a buffalo run or encampment for the night. While the flag flew, whether the camp was moving or not, the guide remained in full command. All the captains, soldiers, and other guides, as well as the rest of the personnel, took their orders from him. When the flag was lowered, the guide's office was fulfilled and the ordering of the camp became the responsibility of the captains and soldiers. These men would direct all carts into a circle, shafts outward, thus forming a stockade for defence against possible Indian raiders. Throughout the history of the Red River buffalo hunt, this was a necessary precaution, since the predatory Sioux were always likely to cause trouble in their efforts to steal horses or to inflict more serious damage. If such an assault were expected, the horses and oxen were kept within the circle; if not, they were tethered outside. The participants in the hunt lived in tents or tepees that were set up in lines within the circle of carts at the dictate of the captains and soldiers. The business of setting up camp was usually accomplished within a half-hour, since the participants, particularly the officers, usually had considerable experience in these matters.

On the first evening in camp, the captain of the hunt, in the company of his lesser captains, their soldiers and the guides, gathered together with other respected hunters to hold council and to lay down the rules of the hunt. These rules varied only slightly from year to year and variations were tolerated only when conditions so dictated. The general rules were as follows:

1. No buffalo to be run on the Sabbath.
2. No one to run buffalo before the general order to do so.
3. No party to diverge from the route chosen, go ahead, or fall behind without permission of the guide.
4. Each captain, in daily turn, with his ten soldiers to keep watch and patrol the camp.
5. Failure to live up to these rules to be punished by the offender's having his bridle and saddle cut up for the first offence, to have his coat removed and cut up for the second offence, and to be flogged for the third offence.
6. Any thief captured to be paraded through the camp and his crime broadcast before him. (Ross noted that theft was a rare offence among the hunters, and among the inhabitants of Red River generally.)

The hunt moved off between 6:00 and 7:00 A.M. and stretched about five or six miles along the plains when on the move. A short rest was taken at about 2:00 P.M. for the benefit of the animals, and the whole company camped for the night at 5:00 or 6:00 P.M., having covered up to twenty miles during the day. On this particular hunt, horses were used to draw the carts; with oxen, progress would have been much slower. When camp had been made, the captains and soldiers issued sure orders which were generally obeyed without question, carts and tents being placed according to their dictates and often with their assistance. When the camp had been settled, the usual evening council would be held to discuss the day's events and the prospects for the morrow. Those who were not occupied with the council prepared an evening meal of bannock and whatever game had been taken on the march: pheasant or prairie chicken, rabbit, squirrel, or even crow, but often nothing. Ross went on at some length about the near or even complete privation of most of the party before the buffalo had been run. "Feast or famine" was their way and their nature.

The 1840 hunt did not sight buffalo until their twentieth day out of Red River, by which time they had reached the Sheyenne River southwest of present-day Fargo, North Dakota. On the morning of July 4, an appropriate day considering their location, some four hundred mounted hunters were ranged in line. At the signal of the captain of the hunt, they advanced – first at a trot, then at a gallop, and finally at a dead run – toward the grazing buffalo a mile and a half away. They were within four hundred to five hundred yards before the buffalo showed signs of alarm. As the buffalo began to stampede, the hunters were among them, firing repeatedly, apparently at random but in fact with deadly aim and effect. The fattest cows were the first targets and the plain was soon littered with carcasses. The first run, or "race," took about two hours and accounted for 1,375 buffalo, as indicated by the number of tongues that were brought into the camp that night.

Not all hunters were equally skilled. Much depended on the excellence of their horses, and these animals formed rather a motley herd. Of the four hundred mounted hunters, only about fifty had a chance at the prime cows. The best hunters accounted for ten to twelve head apiece, while the poorer hunters took only two or three. There were many accidents due to the rough ground, to goring or trampling by the frenzied herd, or to guns that burst as a result of overloading. A well-trained horse would run to within three or four yards of a buffalo and then spring out of its way as the stricken animal fell. The poorer and shyer mounts would remain ten or fifteen yards away, thus reducing the effectiveness of their rider's aim in the general disorder of milling movement, dust, smoke, noise, and confusion. A good shot, however, could kill repeatedly from a distance of twenty to thirty yards. Surprisingly, there were few disputes as to who had killed which beast. In spite of the chaotic nature of the event and the great distance covered, each hunter could retrace his steps and unfailingly pick out those buffalo which he himself had slain. This spectacle was repeated each hunting day, with greater or lesser numbers of buffalo being killed. In the evening, the hunters would give a shot-by-shot account of their prowess, as do their modern golfing counterparts over sometimes the same ground.

Ross noted that there was little which was fair about the actual run of the buffalo. The best-mounted hunters always had first choice, and the poorer ones were left with whatever they could get. Not even smaller herds or detached groups of buffalo were left to the weaker participants. Fortunately, however, the proverbial generosity of the Métis and halfbreeds produced an equitable distribution of the spoils. As a result, no one went hungry or returned empty-handed to the settlement.

Following behind the hunters were the carts with the old men, women, and children. The first beasts slain were the first butchered. Their hides or robes were taken, as were their tongues and humps, both of the latter being considered great delicacies. An impromptu feast was then held while the rest of the carcass was dismembered, the fat removed, the meat cut in strips, and the bones cracked for their marrow. If their luck held, the hunters would make several runs each day over a period of two or three days. At the end of this time, a day's halt was called for the drying and singeing of the meat and for the preparation of pemmican. For this purpose, the buffalo meat was dried on low racks in the sun, or over low fires if the weather so dictated. A better end-product was achieved if, as Ross wrote, "the meat were made a little crispy with the heat of the fire."

Most pemmican was made on the spot. The dried and crisped meat was pounded into a powder which was known as "beat meat" and which was also used as a trade commodity. Beat meat was poured into 100-pound sacks of buffalo hide, with the fur outside, and mixed with an equal amount of either boiled tallow or buffalo fat. When cooled and sewn shut, this mixture provided a highly concentrated and nutritious food, without which the fur trade of the far north could not have been carried on. If circumstances permitted, the mixture, when hot, would have added to it berries or whatever other edible plant products were available. In the case of the Red River hunt, Saskatoon berries were the usual additive. This addition produced a more valuable variety of pemmican, one which was often reserved for the officers of the trading companies. Even more highly prized was pemmican to which had been added blueberries, nuts, or wild rice. This "gourmet variety" was rare in Red River, since most pemmican was made before these condiments had ripened and in areas in which they were not easy to come by. Whatever its precise nature, pemmican, due to the conditions of its manufacture, no doubt contained a greater or lesser admixture of small stones, leaves, twigs, and buffalo hair, plus a soupçon of dirt.

Pemmican was practically unaffected either by time or by the elements. There are recorded instances of sacks of pemmican which were stored, or even buried in the earth, for periods in excess of fifty years and which, when a stone-like outer crust had been removed, were still palatable. This palatibility, which added much to its acceptability to the fur traders, is attested to in many contemporary accounts. These accounts are supported by individuals who have partaken of pemmican that is of more recent manufacture, though admittedly with the advantage of a sanitary twig and hair-free process. Pemmican could be sliced and eaten in its natural state, heated over a fire while supported on sticks, or fried. It could also be stewed with vegetables if occasion offered.

Pemmican's nutritive value is as much testified to as is its palatability. This high degree of nutrition may be gauged from the fact that a *voyageur's* daily ration, according to the explorer David Thompson, consisted of either eight pounds of fresh meat or one and a half pounds of pemmican. At Fort Qu'Appelle in the winter of 1867-68, the daily ration per man was twelve pounds of fresh buffalo meat, six pounds of dried meat, or three pounds of pemmican. Sources other than the buffalo, such as deer, elk, moose, or caribou, made acceptable pemmican. With the exception of the latter, however, these animals were simply not available in the numbers needed to satisfy the demands of the northern trade. The long-sustained abundance of the buffalo, plus the relative ease with which it was killed, made it by far the major source of pemmican.

The Red River buffalo hunt constituted Manitoba's first processing industry and, as such, was almost the sole *raison d'être* of the Red River settlement. To supplement this industry and to provide greater variety to the fur-trade diet, was the principal reason for the establishment, after 1811, of an agricultural settlement at Red River. However, it was this same settlement which, when viewed by the NWC as a future threat to the buffalo hunt, led eventually to the flaring-up of a long-smouldering conflict between settlers and traders.

3

Lord Selkirk's Settlement

THOMAS DOUGLAS, fifth Earl of Selkirk, is one of the few completely selfless men to appear in the history of Canada and is perhaps the only one, hitherto, to appear in the history of Manitoba. He did not seek wealth, since he possessed more than enough for his own needs – and, in fact, risked much of his personal fortune in his ventures as a colonizer. Selkirk enjoyed a modicum of fame and an honored place in society simply by virtue of his birth. Had he actually sought power, this ambition would surely have shown through in his long and bitter struggle with the North West Company. As it was, Selkirk was unwilling to exercise the power that he could have claimed as overlord of Red River. He was, quite simply, a humanitarian. In fact, Selkirk's concern for his fellow man involved him in great outlays of money, endless expenditures of energy, and great personal harassment, including arrest and the threat of imprisonment. Finally, depleted in purse and broken in health, he died at the age of fifty, his hope and his faith as yet undimmed. The path chosen by this truly great colonizer led him to Manitoba as surely as the desire for profit attracted his fellow Scots of the Hudson's Bay and North West companies. Selkirk's aims, however, were as remote from theirs as they could possibly have been.

Selkirk was a Lowland nobleman, a member of the Douglas family, which has provided Scotland with many notable sons. He lived well, in the manner of the more conservative gentry of the late eighteenth and early nineteenth centuries. As a seventh son, he had unexpectedly fallen heir to his father, the fourth Earl, Dunbar Douglas, after the various hazards of imperial service had struck down all of his older brothers. As a child of eight, Selkirk had seen his mother terrorized, though without losing her aristocratic calm, by John Paul Jones, hero of the American Revolution. Jones raided the family home at St. Mary's Isle, Kirkcudbrightshire, during the absence of Selkirk's father and elder brothers, making off with the family silver in what was largely a gesture of defiance toward the "laird" of his childhood home. He later returned the silver, along with his apologies, to the Countess of Selkirk. Because of this childhood trauma, Selkirk has often been set down as a man who suffered a pathological dislike of the United States and whose chief motives as a colonizer were simply to keep the Scots and Irish away from the States and thus to preserve the interests of Britain in North America.

Whether or not there is any substance to this view, Selkirk was certainly a good Britisher. At the time of the War of 1812, for example, he instructed his governor in Assiniboia, Miles Macdonell, to be ready to contend with the Americans in a guerilla war in the event that the Americans ventured that far north. There is little evidence that Selkirk actually disliked the United States, although he did go on record as being somewhat upset by its extremes of democracy. Selkirk travelled to the States from time to time and during the period of the gradual breakdown of Anglo-American relations which led to war in 1812, he was asked to become Minister to the United States. He welcomed this opportunity, and although the appointment did not materialize, it is unlikely that it would even have been offered to him had he been known to be anti-American.

Selkirk was primarily a humanitarian, deeply concerned with the poverty and degradation which descended upon his people with the coming of the Industrial Revolution. He was a progressive and paternal "laird" and the suffering of his crofters was for him a great source of unhappiness. What were known as the "Highland clearances" became the order of the day at the time of the Napoleonic Wars. Enclosure had been a growing threat to pastoral England since even before Henry VII and the dawn of modern England. Toward the end of the eighteenth century, it spread like a cancer throughout the islands of Great Britain and Ireland. The mills demanded wool and its price rose. There was much profit with little overhead cost in the raising of sheep. Thus, the hapless tenant farmer, be he yeoman or crofter, was dumped unceremoniously from his small holding, which was then cleared and enclosed for the raising of sheep. The dispossessed farmer might be absorbed into the burgeoning industries of the new cities such as Manchester or Birmingham, or, closer to home, Glasgow. There, the erstwhile crofter and his family might rot in the utter bleakness of the industrial slums. The only alternative to soul-searing adaptation was starvation.

The government made no effort to improve conditions nor would it even recognize that conditions were in need of improvement. The victims of the new order had no voice in that government, nor was the conscience of the state to be aroused in their behalf for another generation. The consciences of those who profited by the new conditions were not to be alerted at all. Such relief as was provided was of a private nature and necessarily small in relation to the great need. The churches did what they could to alleviate both the immediate and long-range results of enclosure. They were the pioneers in fostering migration as a possible remedy. They could, however, do very little to alter the situation. Selkirk, for his part, did all that he could to help and tried to persuade his wealthy and influential friends and kinsmen to do likewise. In terms of absolute numbers, his colonizing was the proverbial "drop in the ocean." He was well aware of this and persevered out of purely humane considerations and in the hope that his example might encourage others to take up a similar role. He was a pioneer – a trail-blazer, as La Vérendrye had been – moving somewhat ahead of the wave of history. Like La Vérendrye, he is worthy of all honor for having pointed the way for his successors.

In a manner typical of the Scot, Selkirk approached the problem of emigration carefully. Apparently, he never gave serious consideration to areas outside of British North America, and for many years he confined himself to studying the question from all angles, considering costs, land grants, possible government assistance, crops, and markets. Early on, he had thought of a settlement in the vicinity of Sault Ste. Marie. He was discouraged in this by the English government of Lord Addington, which feared possible infringement on the charter of the HBC, since the company had, in the recent past, received the additional sanction of Parliament. There was, however, another and perhaps more pertinent reason for the government's reluctance to assist schemes of emigration. The wars of the French Revolution were now becoming the war against Napoleon, and people in authority realized that the Peace of Amiens of 1802 was but a truce. Scotland, in particular the Highlands, was a rich source of recruits and each man who emigrated was a man lost to the war.

Despite the government's failure to support Selkirk's aims, he did secure a land grant in 1803 in Prince Edward Island, where he put his long-laid plans into effect with some measure of success. He spent the summer of 1803 with his colonists, working among them, always "the careful laird." In the fall of that year, he went to Canada and made arrangements for a settlement in Dover and Chatham townships on Lake St. Clair. This settlement was named "Baldoon," in honor of a family holding which, ironically, had later to be sold in order to help support the colony. In the course of this journey, Selkirk spent several days in Montreal, where he enjoyed the hospitality of the Beaver Club and heard tales of the *pays d'en haut*. His interest in the far west, an interest that he had acquired earlier, was now further intensified.

In November, 1807, Selkirk married Jean Wedderburn. Through her, he developed a lasting friendship with both her brother, Andrew Wedderburn-Colvile, and her cousin, John Halkett. Together, these two agreed with Selkirk on the usefulness and feasibility of an agricultural colony located in Rupert's Land. Colvile and Halkett had considerable experience both in the administration of colonies and in trade, and they were impressed with the idea that such a colony might supply the HBC and thereby reduce its operating costs. Both men were shareholders in the HBC and were active in its general court, or annual shareholders' meetings, and both were attracted by any plan which might produce savings and, perhaps incidentally, impede the progress of the NWC. By this time, the rivalry and animosity between the two fur companies was no longer insignificant. An indication of this is to be seen in the fact that the annual dividends of the HBC dropped from eight percent in 1794 to four percent in 1807.

The idea of a settlement was always the paramount one with Selkirk. He saw, in the valleys of the Red and the Assiniboine, the perfect location in which to realize his dreams. Here was a land which could easily sustain a large population; and here was a ready market for the agricultural surplus which he was sure could be produced and which would give his settlers a cash income to improve their living standard. An additional attraction lay in the fact that here he need not conform to the dictates of a colonial bureaucracy. His colony would, indeed, be "Lord Selkirk's settlement."

Selkirk began to accumulate HBC shares with a view to exercising influence on, if not control over, the London Committee of the company. Shares were not cheap, nor were they easy to come by in the market. More important, many of the members of the London Committee were unreceptive to the idea of an agricultural settlement anywhere in Rupert's Land. They were well aware that fur trade and settlement could not prosper side by side, and that in the end one must give way to the other, with the odds favoring the agricultural settlement. Thus, they feared the likely effects of Selkirk's project on their already diminished profits, not to mention the reaction of the company's officers in the field. Selkirk persisted, however, recruiting the financial resources of his family and even the help of a most unlikely ally. This was the great explorer, Sir Alexander Mackenzie, who saw that in the control of the HBC lay an easy means of ending its conflict with his own North West Company. The alliance, however, did not last long. Mackenzie's ambition was for a fur-trade empire, and he therefore shrank from the idea of encouraging settlement.

Eventually, the troubles of the HBC began to favor Lord Selkirk's ambitions. In 1809, the company failed to pay a dividend for the first time in twenty-five years, although it was by no means in financial straits. To the crippling competition of the NWC had been added the closing of the European fur market as a result of Napoleon's Berlin and Milan decrees. Moreover, the effects of heavy war taxes were also being felt. The company was therefore faced with the necessity of either increasing revenues or lowering costs. It could have increased its revenues through diversification into other fields, such as lumbering or the white-whale fishery of Fort Prince of Wales, but these operations were dependent on the war – and wars are notoriously unreliable, both as to scope and as to length. On the other hand, a prosperous agricultural community on the Red River might serve to lower costs substantially. With many misgivings, and under heavy pressure from Andrew Wedderburn-Colvile, now a director of the HBC, the company undertook to grant Selkirk's wishes. Selkirk himself, with his dreams unexpectedly coming to life, began to summon associates to help put his great venture in hand.

Even before the Red River grant had been made, Selkirk recalled Miles Macdonell from Baldoon in Upper Canada. Macdonell had served well in Canada; he was an ex-soldier and had the capacity to command and to gain the support of the Highlanders. Thus, he seemed a logical choice to command the first party of emigrants, who would prepare the ground for the oncoming crofters. From his experiences in both Prince Edward Island and Upper Canada, Selkirk had come to appreciate the value of such preparatory work. There was also Colin Robertson, a former Nor'Wester who had been forced out of that company when it was reorganized in 1804. Robertson was ready to put his experience at Selkirk's command, and he was also

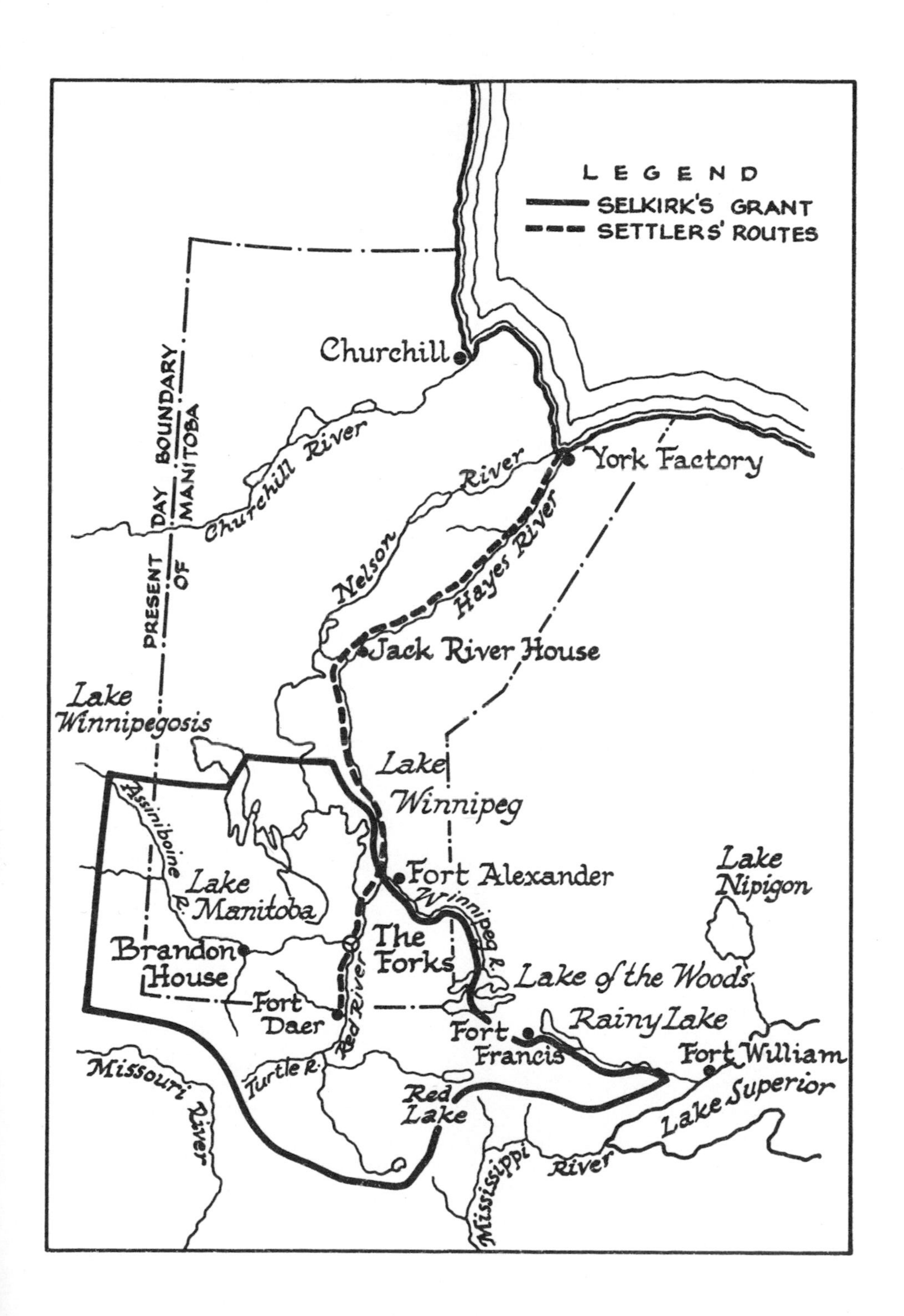
LEGEND
SELKIRK'S GRANT
SETTLERS' ROUTES
PRESENT DAY BOUNDARY OF MANITOBA
Churchill
Churchill River
York Factory
Nelson River
Hayes River
Jack River House
Lake Winnipegosis
Lake Winnipeg
Fort Alexander
Lake Nipigon
Assiniboine R.
Lake Manitoba
Winnipeg R.
The Forks
Brandon House
Lake of the Woods
Fort Daer
Red River
Rainy Lake
Fort Francis
Fort William
Missouri River
Turtle R.
Red Lake
Lake Superior
Mississippi River

ready to meet the aggressive tactics of the NWC with strong measures, if need be. It was Robertson who suggested to the HBC the practicality of arming its trading parties. In this, at least, he had the support of William Auld, superintendent of the Northern Department of Rupert's Land, an area which included Red River. In fact, while Auld was in London in the winter of 1809-10, he approached the HBC officers with recommendations for a more aggressive policy toward the NWC.

Auld returned to Rupert's Land in the summer of 1810, carrying with him the company's orders to prepare for the possibility of a settlement at Red River. He was, as a good fur trader, opposed to the settlement and by mere inaction did much to impede its ultimate success. However, he did inform his colleagues of the dreaded prospect, and word of the proposed move was soon common gossip in the dining halls of the posts of both companies, as well as being communicated to partners of the NWC in London. The partners at Montreal were alerted to prepare for a "year of trial," and the projected settlement was regarded as the greatest threat which the NWC had yet faced. The natural dangers of the wilderness the Nor'Westers could cope with; but they were now faced with the possibility that the very heart of the buffalo grounds, the crossroads of their trade, would pass into the hands of a "Bible peer" whose ignorance of the country itself was exceeded only by his ignorance of the fur trade. Thus, in the eyes of the Nor'Westers, the gauntlet had been thrown down by the HBC – and it was at once picked up by the NWC. It was not to be a fair fight.

On June 2, 1811, the London Committee of the Hudson's Bay Company granted to Selkirk and his heirs outright, for the nominal sum of ten shillings, the consideration required to make the agreement binding, an area that is nearly as large as the whole of the United Kingdom. This area covered all of what is now the populated part of Manitoba and stretched westward into Saskatchewan, southward into North Dakota and Minnesota, and eastward almost to Lake Superior. In size, it was truly a "kingdom," as Selkirk's wife was often to tease him. For his part, Selkirk aimed to use his kingdom in an enlightened manner. There would be room for all of the dispossessed Highlanders, and for the Irish as well.

The greater Selkirk's ambition to populate the colony, the greater the fear that was engendered in the partners of both the NWC and the HBC. In fact, the HBC, after having reluctantly taken the first step, now withdrew all active support. The whole project was to be executed by Selkirk himself and the HBC would have as little to do with it as possible. This change in policy pleased the company's agents, and during the whole of its short and turbulent history, the Selkirk settlement was forced to endure not only the active opposition of the Nor'Westers, but also the apathy and poorly-concealed antagonism of most of the men of the HBC.

On July 26, 1811, Selkirk's advance party left Stornoway for York Factory, on the first leg of their journey. Selkirk had moved quickly once his grant had been made official. Much preliminary planning had already been completed, and Macdonell was given detailed instructions as to how to proceed. He was better equipped with instructions than he was with either men or materials. Of the 105 emigrants bound for Hudson Bay, only thirty-five were heading for Red River. The Highlanders might have been greater in number and better equipped had it not been for the propaganda of the North West Company. Recruits were discouraged by doleful accounts of the fate which awaited them at the hands of ravaging savages, or as the result of the even fiercer weather. These tales were passed by word of mouth and some were published as letters, signed "Highlander," in the *Inverness Journal*. The "Highlander" was Simon McGillivray, brother of William McGillivray; both men were nephews to Simon McTavish, and all three ranked high in the councils of the North West Company. Indeed, Simon McGillivray spoke the simple truth when he described the prospect of wintering at York Factory, where "it is my firm belief that many will perish before the Spring from excessive cold and want of food." The Nor'Westers contrived difficulties with the customs officers for the men of the HBC. Even the maritime safety regulations were invoked against them, making it necessary for them to leave behind valuable supplies. In short, the NWC spared little effort or expense in its attempts to kill the Selkirk settlement even before it was born.

After a stormy passage of sixty-one days, the Highlanders reached York Factory on September 24, to a reception cooler than that provided by the already fast-waning sun. Because it was much too late in the season to attempt the long inland journey, Macdonell was required to take his men twenty-three miles up the Nelson River to the nearest wood supply and there to place them in temporary winter quarters. The winter passed slowly, but not without incident, and the dire predictions of "Highlander" very nearly came to pass. Ill-housed and ill-nourished, Macdonell's party was racked with dissension and disease. Orkneymen and Irishmen fell easily to quarrelling, and both groups mutinied against the harsh regime imposed by Macdonell. Auld, the superintendent at York Factory, gave whatever assistance was required of him, though only grudgingly, and contrived even to help set the men to fighting among themselves. Only one man died from scurvy, but several were sent home by the first ship next summer for the part which they had played in the mutiny.

The spring of 1812 was long and cold, and the river ice, which usually broke up in May, held solid through June. As a result, it was the first week in July before Macdonell and his men, now reduced to twenty-two in number, could put out into the Hayes River. They were encumbered by a small cannon, but were without the supplies and farm implements which they had been obliged to leave at Stornoway in the far-off Hebrides. When the immigrants reached Oxford House, they numbered only nineteen, since three men had deserted en route. The journey had been a nightmare of drudgery, and desertions would surely have been more numerous but for the fact that there was no easy avenue of escape. At Oxford House, Macdonell gained the services of four men, including an Indian guide. He also acquired the colony's first livestock, in the form of a bull and a cow, who were promptly named Adam and Eve. From Oxford House, the party made its way to Lake Winnipeg and coasted three hundred miles along its eastern shore without incident. After traversing the great swamp which forms the delta of the Red River, the men began to work their way upstream against the placid and slow-moving current. At this point, the low banks of the river permitted them glimpses of a pleasant country, a rolling plain covered with endless buffalo grass and occasional clumps of brush. The shores of the river itself were clothed with trees and bushes, wildflowers grew in profusion, and golden rod was in bloom. Along the verges of the stream, bullrushes ripened and myriads of waterfowl wheeled and churned overhead. It appeared a fitting Eden to which to bring themselves, as well as their bovine Adam and Eve. Finally, on August 30, 1812, the party reached the junction of the Red and the Assiniboine.

After resting for a day or two, during which time he took a preliminary look at the center of his new domain, Miles Macdonell was entertained at dinner by his cousin and brother-in-law, Alexander Macdonell. A member of the North West Company, Alexander Macdonell was in charge of Fort Gibraltar, the NWC post at Red River. In return, Miles invited his cousin and his guests (winterers John Wills and Benjamin Frobisher, who were en route to Athabasca) to attend the formal "ceremony and seizin' of the land." This ceremony took place on September 4, on the east bank of the Red River opposite the mouth of the Assiniboine. A color guard was provided by the

HBC, and the cannon which had been hauled with such difficulty from York Factory was fired. The deed which transferred the land from the Hudson's Bay Company to Lord Selkirk was read both in French and in English, thus marking Manitoba's first official bilingual occasion. Miles Macdonell formally took over from William Hillier of the HBC and was proclaimed Governor of Assiniboia. Present, aside from the officers already named, were a number of Indians and Métis who were in the employ of the HBC. Alexander Macdonell had forbidden the servants of the NWC to attend what he must have regarded as being, at best, a subversive performance. Toasts were drunk by the gentlemen present and a keg of spirits was broached for the "people" to conclude the small and dignified ceremony.

The season was too far advanced for there to be any hope of a crop that year, but in anticipation of the next year, Macdonell arranged for the planting of winter wheat. He planted this wheat near his projected post, some two miles north of Fort Gibraltar at the base of a great bend of the Red River. Both this point and the post itself were to bear the name Douglas, in honor of the family of the Earl of Selkirk. Later that fall, most of the men moved south to the junction of the Red and Pembina rivers, on the fringe of the wintering grounds of the buffalo.

In June of that year, a second party of eighty settlers, under the command of the Irishman Owen Keveny, had left Sligo. Keveny's command was increased by one through the birth of a girl just two days out of York Factory. This event, however, did not delay the group and it arrived at Pembina, on October 27, 1812, having been directed through by those who were still at Fort Douglas. Here, they suffered through the winter in a collection of makeshift huts which was named Fort Daer. Roughly one hundred in number, the group subsisted on such buffalo as could be obtained from the Métis who lived around Fort Pembina. Pembina had been unoccupied for a time, but the NWC reactivated the post solely for the purpose of denying supplies to the settlers by standing ready to purchase anything which the Indians might offer for sale. Despite this expression of opposition on the part of the NWC, friendly relations existed between the people of both camps. After all, they were alone in a vast wilderness and had ties of a common blood and homeland. Many of the settlers must have sorely missed that homeland, in spite of all its miseries, as they fought the cutting wind, the vise-like cold, and constant pangs of hunger.

On June 28, 1813, a third party, made up largely of young Highlanders, sailed from Stromness. On this occasion, Lord Selkirk himself was present to bid them *bon voyage.* Unfortunately, the Earl's best wishes did little to protect the emigrants. Their vessel was plagued with typhus, the dreaded "ship fever" of the day, and five people died en route. Conditions were only aggravated when the nervous captain debarked his fifty passengers at Fort Prince of Wales, instead of carrying them to York Factory as he had contracted to do. Here, two more perished, while the remainder endured a miserable winter in crude huts at the mouth of the Churchill River. In April, 1814, the survivors set out for York on snowshoes, accompanied by a party of HBC servants. The men dragged their meagre goods on sleds, breaking trail for the women who followed. They reached York Factory in three weeks and when the ice broke in the Hayes River (this time in the middle of May), they pressed on, reaching Red River in June. Here, they discovered a situation in which the colony's efforts to survive involved not only its struggle with the forces of nature, but also its conflict with the men of the North West Company.

In the spring of 1813, the settlers at Fort Daer had returned to Fort Douglas to find that their winter wheat had not sprouted. The length and severity of the winter had killed the seed, as in fact it would that of similar plantings in the future. To complicate matters, Keveny's party had been forced to carry reduced supplies in order to accommodate the expensive Merino sheep which Selkirk had insisted on sending to the Red River colony. The sheep, however, were a doubtful asset. Most of them succumbed to the climate, to other ills, or to the ravages of the dogs, who found them much less formidable than the buffalo and perhaps even tastier. Implements were therefore still in short supply. Nevertheless, crops of wheat, peas, and English barley were planted. All failed to ripen, probably because of early frost, a phenomenon which long harassed farmers who had gained their experience in a more temperate climate. Having failed to raise a crop in the summer of 1813, the settlers once again took up winter quarters at Fort Daer. This time they were left alone, since neither of the companies manned its post at Pembina River. This second winter was easier than the first, though only comparatively. Since they now had some experience and encountered only a relatively light snowfall, the colonists were at least able to keep themselves supplied with buffalo meat.

Their spirits revived, and with them the confidence of their governor, Miles Macdonell. Though he had been cautioned by Selkirk to move with great care, Macdonell now decided to challenge the North West Company. Thus, on January 8, 1814, he issued a proclamation which placed a one-year embargo on the taking of pemmican from the Selkirk grant. This hand-lettered proclamation, which was posted throughout the district in the vicinity of the various posts, prohibited both companies from exporting any "flesh, grain, or vegetables" (except under licence from Macdonell) and provided compensation for any food which was confiscated. The proclamation was obviously directed at the North West Company, and it is fair to note that the company was taken somewhat by surprise. They did not expect such a move, at least not so soon, and especially from a colony that was in winter exile at Pembina. Macdonell had boasted that he possessed the power to withstand any assault which the Nor'Westers might make against him and it is true that at the time they were not in a position to challenge him.

Some of the Nor'Westers felt that the position taken by Selkirk's lieutenant was legal and these men wished to adopt a "wait and see" policy. Others, such as Alexander Macdonell and John McDonald, *le borgne* (the one-eyed), preferred to ignore the embargo and to crush the upstart. Selkirk had long before counselled Macdonell to make no move which might cause the Nor'Westers to go to the courts. Imperial legislation of 1803 had provided that the courts of Upper Canada would judge cases which arose in "Rupert's Land and the Indian territories," and in Canada, the NWC was not without influence. Selkirk hoped to have his own British-appointed courts set up in Red River, or at least to gain provision that trials would take place in England.

Macdonell, however, had the bit in his teeth. He sent John Spencer, the Sheriff of Red River, to seize NWC pemmican on the Turtle River. Pemmican that was being brought down the Assiniboine was also taken, in spite of the Nor'Westers' efforts to hide it. With the help of an HBC officer named Howse, Spencer took possession of pemmican at Fort la Souris. Macdonell's cannon, set up in front of Fort Douglas, blockaded the Red River. A Nor'Wester party at la Souris was divested of its arms but was permitted to proceed to Fort Gibraltar. There, the assembled *bourgeois,* in anger and chagrin, damned the colonists and their meddlesome governor and some partners again counselled violent retaliation. Such action might well have taken place had not John McDonald of Garth, now in his sixties, arrived at the Forks from the Pacific en route to retirement in Montreal. At one time a heavy-handed and ruthless participant in the struggles between the old and new North West companies, McDonald had since mellowed and become more judicious. He advised moderation, and fortunately for the colonists, his advice prevailed.

Miles Macdonell was now prepared to be reasonable, having, as he thought, made his point. He agreed to return the confiscated pemmican to the NWC in return for a promise that 175 bags of pemmican would be delivered to Fort Douglas that fall and that the NWC would pay for the transportation of oatmeal from York Factory to Red River. These terms of agreement were accepted, albeit unhappily, by the Nor'Westers at Fort William. They decided to bide their time, but were by no means reconciled to the presence of the colonists. Indeed, the pemmican embargo and the cannon of Fort Douglas served to underline the danger in which the settlement had placed their lifeline of food and fur. It was at this juncture that the third party of settlers, that which had departed Stromness in June, 1813, arrived from York Factory. In all, some eighty-three new settlers joined the colony in the summer and fall of 1814.

The arrival of the newcomers stiffened Miles Macdonell in his resolve to eliminate the NWC, who, in the meantime, were busily at work arousing the Métis and halfbreeds with tales of how the farmers from Scotland would destroy their time-honored life of the hunt. Macdonell ordered the confiscation of two hundred bags of pemmican which were en route to Fort Gibraltar. Then, in October, 1814, he sent notices to the *bourgeois* at Fort Gibraltar, Bas de la Rivière Winipic (La Vérendrye's Maurepas), and Fort Dauphin advising them that they were trespassers on Lord Selkirk's lands and that they should leave the country within six months. This warning, it was later stated, was only intended as a general notice of ownership and not as an immediate attempt on the part of Macdonell to gain possession of the posts. Such legal niceties meant little to the Nor'Westers, even had they taken note of them. The Nor'Westers were by now fully aroused and they, in turn, further inflamed the Métis.

The winter of 1814-15 was an eventful one at the Forks. While Napoleon was plotting the "hundred days" from his exile in Elba, the Nor'Westers schemed at an overturning that was equally important in terms of their own survival. During the winter, the Selkirk settlers remained at Fort Douglas, even though they had salvaged only enough of their crop for seed for the next year's planting. Pemmican, however, was plentiful, thanks to the unwilling generosity of the NWC. That company was also generous in other ways, and for other reasons. Alexander Macdonell had been to Fort William and had returned with unwritten orders to eliminate the settlement by whatever means might prove necessary. Thus, he frequently entertained the crofters at Fort Gibraltar with many a dram against the chill of winter. On such occasions, the settlers were reminded of the dangers which they had to face at the hands of savage men and an even more savage nature. At the same time, they were offered safe passage to Canada, where land and its appurtenances awaited them. Miles Macdonell was depicted as a deranged individual who would lead them into dangerous courses of action; he should therefore be deprived of arms and ammunition. For the North West Company, it was a winter well spent in acts of subversion.

Meanwhile, Miles Macdonell had gone from Fort Douglas to York Factory in July, 1814, possibly to see to the speeding of future parties of settlers from Hudson Bay, or possibly with thoughts of giving it all up and returning to England. He had been in indifferent health and had written to Lord Selkirk asking to be relieved as governor. In any event, at York he suffered a physical and perhaps mental breakdown. His HBC hosts felt obliged to remove any weapons from him lest he do himself harm. By the time that Macdonell finally returned to the settlement in the early summer of 1815, much damage had already been done. Sherriff Spencer had been arrested on a Canadian warrant which was brought from Fort William by Duncan Cameron and which charged him with illegal seizure of NWC pemmican. The redoubtable cannon had, with the help of defectors, been stealthily removed and the Métis and halfbreeds were now well aroused against the settlers.

In June, 1815, Macdonell was persuaded to surrender to Duncan Cameron on the promise that no harm would come to the colony if he did so. Otherwise, the colonists might well be charged with shielding a fugitive. In the same month, he was taken east under guard of Duncan Cameron for trial in Canada. With them, went one hundred and forty of the erstwhile settlers, again exiles, after having accepted the Nor'Westers promise of free land and safe passage to the east. Unfortunately, the self-sacrifice of Miles Macdonell availed the colony nothing. No sooner had the party sailed than NWC servants rode down the standing crops and put the torch to barns and stables. Only the lush greenness of the crops prevented them from burning. Alexander Macdonell, once again in charge at Fort Gibraltar, ordered the remaining settlers out of their homes. Clutching their infant children and as many of their small possessions as they could carry, the sixty-odd settlers hurriedly took to their boats and headed north on

Lake Winnipeg to a precarious refuge at Jack River House on Playgreen Lake. With their departure, the fort and the remaining buildings were burned by the excited Métis with the full knowledge and consent of their NWC masters. Only a small blacksmith shop to the east of the Red River escaped, by virtue of the spirited defence put up by John McLeod and two companions. Fort Douglas, a grist mill, and a total of thirty buildings were destroyed and the crops were left as though flattened by hail. The North West Company had, apparently, achieved a complete victory.

Colin Robertson, the former Nor'Wester who had appeared at the outset of Selkirk's work with the HBC, was again active in his cause. He had persuaded Selkirk and the HBC to compete with the NWC in its own country by using its own route. Accordingly, he had outfitted one hundred *voyageurs* in Montreal and was en route to Red River and the Athabasca when his party passed that of Duncan Cameron somewhere west of Fort William. This encounter caused Robertson to hurry on to the Forks, where he found that with the help of nature and the buffalo hunt, John McLeod and his two companions had worked wonders. Nature had caused the flattened crops to rise and flourish as no crop at Red River had ever done before; and the buffalo hunt had removed, at least for the time being, the menace of the NWC employees.

Robertson moved quickly. He journeyed to Jack River House and persuaded the refugees to return, so that Fort Douglas was at least partially restored. At the same time, he did not neglect his main mission. He sent his aide, John Clarke, to the northwest with the *voyageurs*. On Lake Athabasca, they established Fort Wedderburn, named after Selkirk's wife and brother-in-law. This fort, however, proved a tragic failure. Pressed for time, Clarke had entered the barrens without adequate food supplies. The winter was long and bitter, and no further provisions could be found, with the result that sixteen of the party died of starvation. This tragedy served to emphasize the value of pemmican and the importance of controlling its source of supply.

At Red River during the summer of 1815, the settlement showed more life than ever before. Grain and vegetable crops succeeded beyond expectation. With the remission of NWC harassment and under the inspired leadership of Colin Robertson, the colonists gained new hope and confidence that they would yet prevail. When a new party of eighty settlers under Robert Semple arrived in November 1815, their faith in their ability to survive and to progress was greatly increased. These Sutherlandshire recruits were all farmers and they were soon settled in for a relatively comfortable winter. Robert Semple was to be the new governor, in place of Miles Macdonell, who was still in eastern Canada. Semple was commissioned not only by Selkirk as Governor of Assiniboia, but also by the HBC as Governor-in-Chief of Rupert's Land. Semple's combined office, however, was more indicative of Selkirk's power in the HBC than of the company's increased interest in the reinforcement or extension of the colony. Both Selkirk and Semple hoped that the prestigious titles and inferred powers of the new governor-in-chief would be sufficient guarantee of the future good behavior of the Nor'Westers. Unfortunately, their hopes were in vain.

As an indication of the importance that was attached to his dual office, Semple was to receive the munificent salary of £1,500 per year. He was a man of great energy and resolution, and apparently a man of good judgment and balance. In the appointment of Semple, however, Selkirk once again proved that he was not always a good judge of men. Semple was a Loyalist, born in Boston in 1777 of a family which later returned to England. He had wide experience both in travel and in business and though he was, beyond any doubt, a man of substance and standing, he had no knowledge of the west, nor of the fur trade. To make matters worse, the new governor did not have much time in which to learn or to properly judge how to apply what little he may have learned in Assiniboia. The apparent prosperity of the Red River colony, the quiet of the Métis and the halfbreeds, and the complete absence throughout the winter of threatening gestures on the part of the NWC – these factors lulled him into a sense of security and well-being. In spite of the many and timely warnings given him by Colin Robertson and in spite of his own knowledge of the intent of the Nor'Westers, Semple remained undisturbed. Robertson had intercepted the letters of the Nor'Westers and he therefore knew of the threatening mood of opposition among the partners of the NWC. Semple, however, chose to ignore the warnings and to rely on external appearances, trusting to the weight of established order and good government, which he felt were a sure defence for the colony.

Colin Robertson had no such illusions and he openly sought to ensure the safety of the colony by every available means. He openly courted the Indians, both with gifts and with lower prices than those which it had formerly been the custom of the HBC to charge. He was not so successful at courting the halfbreeds or Métis, though he cannot be faulted for having failed to try. In October, 1815, before the arrival of Semple, he tried to arrest Duncan Cameron in retaliation for the arrest of Miles Macdonell, but was overawed by Cameron's companions and his threats of the penalties for false arrest. In mid-March, 1816, an opportunity presented itself. With the aid of the colonists, Robertson raided Fort Gibraltar and seized both the incoming and outgoing mails, the contents of which proved, beyond any doubt, that ill times lay ahead. John McDonald, "the one-eyed," had written: "The day of retribution is drawing nigh." He was not composing a sermon! Duncan Cameron had penned an invitation to James Grant at Fond du Lac (now the city of Duluth, Minnesota) inviting him to send men to Red River on the enticement that they "might make very good booty if they went cunningly to work, not that I would wish them to Butcher anyone *God Forbid*." From Fort Brandon, Alexander Macdonell had written to Duncan Cameron: "We will see some sport in Red River before the month of June is over." Even more prophetic, in terms of the distant future, was the conclusion of Duncan Cameron's letter: "The new nation under their leaders are coming forward to clear their native soil of intruders and assassins."

On the occasion of the pillage of the mails, Duncan Cameron was placed under arrest by Robertson. Fort Gibraltar was seized and the stolen cannon returned to Fort Douglas. While Robertson busied himself by reading the Nor'Westers' incriminating mail, Semple was not idle. He took a party of men and occupied the NWC posts at Pembina and Brandon House. When he returned to Fort Douglas, however, he and Robertson were involved in an inevitable clash of wills. Always enthusiastic, brash, and as ruthless as his former partners of the NWC, Robertson was all for destroying Fort Gibraltar and putting Fort Douglas in a state of readiness to withstand a siege. Semple demurred; to him, the proposal seemed rash. He could see no reason for pursuing such action purely on the basis of the fevered scribblings of the *bourgeois* of the NWC. All was outwardly calm; and surely these men realized that were they to attack Fort Douglas, they would be trifling with the might and majesty of the state. Because of Semple's adamant position, Robertson determined to return to England, taking Cameron with him to stand trial there on charges of treason and conspiracy to murder. He demonstrated his brashness and joy in the seeming victory by flying a pemmican sack from the mast of his York boat. As the boat pulled out into the Red River,

Robertson shouted a piece of advice to Semple: "Destroy Fort Gibraltar, lest it again become the center of danger."

This advice, at least, Semple took. Beginning the following day, as much of the ramparts as could be dismantled were rafted downstream to reinforce the walls of Fort Douglas. What could not be moved was burned. The burning, however, gave new flame to the smouldering fire in the breasts of the Métis and halfbreeds. Here, after all, was proof that the empire of fur and the buffalo hunt was to be swept away. The Métis were to be stripped of their heritage, the freedom of the plains, by these grubbers of the soil. That which was theirs by right of their maternal ancestors would be taken from them. As the spring of 1816 advanced into summer, they began to gather to the west of the Forks. Menace hung heavy in the air.

4

The Pemmican War

THE BURNING OF FORT GIBRALTAR, coming as it did so soon after Semple's seizure of Fort Brandon and Fort Pembina, convinced the Métis and halfbreeds that *les jardinières* had come, as Métis minstrel Pierre Falcon was to sing, *"pour piller notre pays."* In May, 1816, the North West Company appointed Cuthbert Grant "Captain General of all the halfbreeds in the country." Grant, a Scots halfbreed who had been educated at Montreal, entered the service of the NWC at eighteen. He was a natural leader, physically powerful and intelligent. Sir George Simpson described Grant as being "of great nerve and resolution" and a "generous warm-hearted man who would not have been guilty of the crimes laid to his charge had he not been driven into them by designing men." Alexander Macdonell, now called "the Whiteheaded," supported Grant in all of his actions. Back of Alexander Macdonell was William McGillivray at Fort William, and behind him, the *bourgeois* or the partners at Montreal who had been alarmed since Selkirk's arrival in the early winter of 1815 from New York.

At the time of the Red River tragedy, Selkirk was already at the Sault Ste. Marie with all the available men and arms he could muster to come to the aid of the settlement. Miles Macdonell, freed earlier by the Canadian courts, was already on his way to the Red River.

On June 16, 1816, Semple was visited by two Saulteaux Indians who told him that servants of the NWC were gathered at Portage la Prairie and were making no secret of their intention to attack Selkirk's settlement. This information did not worry Semple enough to cause him to post outlying pickets; but as a precaution, a lookout was stationed at the highest point of Fort Douglas. Fearing attack, the settlers armed themselves before they went to work their fields in the mornings as settlers along the St. Lawrence had done two hundred years before. At night, everyone stayed within the uncertain protection of the fort's walls. Meanwhile, Cuthbert Grant and Peter Pangman led a party of seventy armed and mounted NWC servants east from Portage la Prairie, ostensibly to supply the Athabasca brigades at Bas de la Rivière.

Early in the evening of June 19, 1816, the lookout at Fort Douglas sighted a party of horsemen moving to the northeast and apparently intending to pass within a half-mile of the fort. Semple called for volunteers to intercept the party. There were about one hundred and fifty people gathered behind the walls, half of them men and boys, the other half older men, women, and children. Semple chose twenty-seven men to accompany him. As the light faded, the men moved out of the fort; they were armed only with muskets and went on foot. Semple rejected, as unnecessary provocation, the suggestion that the field piece be hauled along. The horsemen had halted on Frog Plain (*la Grenouillere*) at a grove of stunted oak and willow known as Seven Oaks.

As Semple and his volunteers approached in a ragged line, more horsemen appeared from behind the screen of bush. There were now twice the thirty-five who had been seen from the fort. They wore feathers and war paint, some carried lances, and all had knives and guns. They were by no means all Indians, but mostly halfbreeds and Métis. Semple sent back John Bourke to bring the cannon. A few of Semple's men began to edge back toward the river. At this, the NWC men spread out and moved forward in a crescent, to prevent Semple's party from escaping to the fort or to the river. One of the horsemen, Francois Boucher, spurred his horse toward Semple, shouting something to which Semple replied. There is no record of what was said, but Semple grasped the bridle of Boucher's horse and the butt of his gun. While Boucher did not fire the first shot, one came immediately. Like the famous "shot heard round the world" at Concord Bridge, no one knows which side shot first.

The Nor'Westers advanced, firing on the settlers. Lieutenant Holte fell dead, and Semple was wounded in the thigh and later killed. Men fell, dying or wounded, as the horsemen milled around them. Four of Semple's men ran for the river and escaped by swimming away. John Bourke, returning from the fort with the cannon on an ox-drawn cart, turned the awkward vehicle to flee, and was grievously wounded in escaping. Bourke and John Pritchard were the only settlers who survived the battle. Young Pritchard threw himself on the mercy of one of the Métis, whom he had befriended in the west, and was thus spared injury. (He lived to become the grandfather of Samuel Prichard Matheson, first Anglican Archbishop of Rupert's Land and Primate of Canada.) Only one of the Métis was killed. Grant was unable to restrain his men from butchering the wounded. The bodies – stripped of clothing, many of them scalped or disembowelled, skulls smashed with rifles butts – were left to the wolves. After some days, the settlers' remains were buried by the local Saulteux.

On the evening of June 20, news of the massacre reached Alexander Macdonell at Portage la Prairie. He shouted to the NWC servants encamped there with him: *"Sacré nom de Dieu, bonnes nouvelles, vingt-deux Anglais de tués."* The Massacre of Seven Oaks may well have been a tragic accident, but the machinations of the NWC gave it a certain inevitability. Late on the night of June 19, Cuthbert Grant sent John Pritchard with terms of surrender to Alexander Macdonell, the Sheriff of Assiniboia, who was in command of the distraught settlers within Fort Douglas. The ultimatum demanded that the fort be surrendered at once and that its people depart for Lake Winnipeg under Grant's safe-conduct. If they did not leave, the settlers might all be slain. At first, Alexander Macdonell stubbornly refused to comply with the ultimatum, but Pritchard pointed out the helplessness of their position and their surrender followed. Within two days, all the surviving settlers had left the fort and were on their way to Jack River House. Again, the crops were trampled and the buildings burned. Alexander McLeod encountered the refugees on the Red River. He harried their York boats into Netley Creek and there he searched and interrogated the terrified settlers. John Bourke and a few others were held prisoners to be taken to Fort William, while the rest were sent on their way. McLeod and the Nor'Wester Alexander Macdonell met at Fort Douglas to celebrate their victory, and Cuthbert Grant's men received high praise and other rewards for their evening's work.

Miles Macdonell was far ahead of Selkirk's main party from Sault Ste. Marie and already descending the Winnipeg River when Indians told him about the massacre. He turned back to bring the tragic news to his employer, Lord Selkirk, who was still at Sault Ste. Marie preparing to move on behind his main party of recruits. Despite the lack of interest on the part of the governments of the Canadas and the Colonial Office in the fate of Assiniboia, Selkirk had secured the services of ninety trained soldiers, mercenaries of the de Meuron and de Watteville regiments of German-Swiss who had been in Canada for service in the War of 1812 after previous action against Napoleon. These men, French and Poles as well as German and Swiss, had agreed to serve, for pay and for land at Red River, under their captains D'Orsonnens and Matthey. At York, Selkirk had also obtained at least twelve boatloads of food, military supplies, and equipment of all kinds. He was armed, in addition, with a commission as magistrate issued by the Acting Governor General of the Canadas at Quebec and with much legal advice, which in the end served only to increase his troubles.

When he heard of the disaster at Seven Oaks, Selkirk quickly altered his plans. Instead of proceeding to Red River by way of Fond du Lac, he decided to go directly to Fort William, seize it, and thus immobilize the main base of the NWC. This was accomplished without bloodshed, but with considerable annoyance to the resident *bourgeois*. William McGillivray and John MacDonald suffered the indignity of arrest. When Selkirk's men searched the post, they found HBC furs and confiscated letters and other evidence of NWC depredations. Hearings were held, charges were laid, and the NWC partners were sent east for trial in the courts of Lower Canada. All the financial and political power of the Nor'Westers was brought to the aid of their own defence and that of their vast enterprise. The HBC stood behind Selkirk with considerably less solidity, but the company could not entirely dissociate itself from him. It had much to lose should the NWC emerge unpunished for the massacre of Seven Oaks.

Indeed, this act of criminal folly caused the contending parties to consider what the struggle between them had brought about. There had been much bloodshed in the Pemmican War; and Seven Oaks, the final tragedy, should have been foreseen and forestalled. Both great enterprises were being hard pressed by their increasingly expensive rivalry. Dividends of the HBC, suspended between 1809 and 1814, had been resumed at the low rate of four percent in 1815. The NWC was no better off, having been reduced to passing off its *voyageurs* as militia during the War of 1812, in which they did service only for the NWC, but at His Majesty's expense. Worst of all, from the North West fur-trader's viewpoint, Selkirk was not discouraged by all the setbacks. His grim determination to see that this colony was preserved was becoming an embarrassment to the HBC. Perhaps it was time to get together for the greater good of all. Union of the companies was being talked of in both camps as an eminently practical solution.

Selkirk stayed at Fort William for the winter of 1816, subsisting partly on the supplies of the NWC which he purchased, only to be later charged with their theft. He sent ahead to Red River some of the de Meurons under Miles Macdonell, whom he appointed governor in place of Semple. First, they seized Fort Daer from its unsuspecting occupants. Next, early in 1817, they descended upon the Nor'Westers in Fort Douglas. In the spring, the crops were planted. Selkirk himself arrived at the settlement early in June. During the four months that he stayed there, he was periodically disturbed by the zealous inquiries of Canadian commissioners, who were more interested in aiding the NWC and in trying to satisfy the first stirrings of Canadian western expansionism than in seeking after truth.

At Frog Plain, on July 20, 1817, Selkirk welcomed the exiled settlers, returning for the last time from Jack River House (by then known as Norway House). The "careful laird" went into action. There was much to do. The Merino sheep, oxen, cattle, sixty horses – all were gone, as were the buildings which had housed them and their masters. Other horses were bought locally and new livestock was ordered. Selkirk made a treaty with the local Cree and Saulteaux through Chief Peguis, who was a long-standing friend of the settlers. By this treaty, the first between Indians and whites in what is now western Canada, Selkirk secured a reinforcing title to a strip of land along both banks of the rivers from Netley Creek south to Fort Daer and from the Forks west to Poplar Point. The strip extended back two miles from the river on each side "as far as can be seen under the belly of a horse on a clear day." This treaty ensured that the NWC could not press the claims of the Métis and halfbreeds to the land on the basis of their Indian ancestry.

This done, Selkirk proceded to lay out his settlement in a manner which was generally approved, both then and later. Small lots across the Red, along the Seine, were assigned to the de Meurons so that they might be close to Fort Douglas in case of any attack. Practically all the lots granted outright by Selkirk and later assigned by the HBC were ten chains in width (i.e., 220 yards), stretching back one mile, with an additional mile as a hay lot. All lands located on the west bank of the Red had also a ninety-acre tract on the opposite bank which was to be used exclusively as a wood lot. To the north of Fort Douglas, land was set aside for a school, church, and burial ground. The present Cathedral of

St. John and its surrounding cemetery remain as memorials to the deed. Locations were also marked for a grist mill and an experimental farm. Roads and bridges were projected. Ten thousand acres on the east bank of the Red opposite the mouth of the Assiniboine were set aside for the Catholic Church. Appeals had already been made at Quebec and even Rome for a Catholic mission. Selkirk promised a suitable parson for the almost entirely Presbyterian Scottish settlers and land was set aside for a Presbyterian church, school, and cemetery north of St. Johns at Kildonan.

All too soon, Selkirk's idyll came to an end. His presence was required in Montreal. To avoid harassment by the NWC, he decided to proceed south by horse to the United States, down the Mississippi to St. Louis, and east via the Ohio to Pittsburg, New York, Albany, and, finally, Montreal. With him went a few mercenaries and their two captains, D'Orsonnens and Matthey. As he rode south, the Convention of London was projecting the boundary between Rupert's Land and the Louisiana Purchase along the forty-ninth parallel to the Rocky Mountains. Selkirk was apparently aware that a development of this kind was in the wind. During his sojourn at Red River, he had written William Coltman, the Canadian commissioner, of his fears regarding a revival of NWC aggression. He proposed to move his colony into American territory, perhaps seriously, or perhaps only to emphasize the dangers which still faced his people. He wrote: "It may perhaps be the most prudent course to allow people to seek asylum within the American lines, where at least they will not have to apprehend hostility from subjects of the same Government and where if they be liable to be attacked it will not be considered an offence to be prepared for resistance."

Selkirk spent the next year in Canada, going from court to court in the Canadas in a vain effort both to clear himself and to bring the NWC to book. His health was bad and was probably made worse by the mental stress which he endured. In the fall of 1818, he left Montreal for England, his Nor'Wester pursuers still in full cry. He went to the south of France to rest and to make plans for his settlement and for new settlers. He died at Pau on April 18, 1820. Selkirk's death hastened the reconciliation of the Hudson's Bay and North West companies. Legal expenses plus the costs of competition were becoming unbearable. Moreover, the articles of incorporation of the North West Company were due to expire at the beginning of 1822.

In the Athabasca country, struggle for monopoly in the fur trade continued. With the blessings of Selkirk and the HBC, Colin Robertson had re-established the ill-omened Fort Wedderburn on Lake Athabasca. This time, there were happier results for the HBC. The NWC retaliated by taking Robertson prisoner, but he escaped on the way to Fort William and made his way to England via New York. Ignorant of this fact, some twenty de Meurons from Red River ambushed the NWC brigade at Grand Rapids at the mouth of the Saskatchewan on June 23, 1819. Seven NWC partners were made prisoner and sent to England by way of York Factory. This was the last in a long series of illegal arrests made by both sides. The NWC *bourgeois*, Benjamin Frobisher, was not so fortunate. Though he escaped at the Grand Rapids, he was lost in the wilderness and died.

By the summer of 1820, the NWC conclave at Fort William expressed a willingness to call it quits. Similarly, the HBC was now open to negotiations. Lord Bathurst, the colonial secretary, had long since cried "a plague on both your houses." Finally, through the agency of Edward Ellice, the London agent of the North West Company, peace and union were arranged. A Nor'Wester of long standing, "Bear" Ellice had attacked the HBC and Lord Selkirk during the winter of 1815-16 in the Montreal *Gazette* under the pen name "Mercator." In his letters to the newspaper, he questioned the HBC's charter and the validity of its grant of Assiniboia to Lord Selkirk. He described the NWC as the heir of the French, the true discoverers of the "western sea" which their Alexander Mackenzie had been the first to reach through North America in 1793. Thus, the NWC had a claim to the discovery of a North West Passage, while the HBC had remained inert on the bay. Ellice had sought to purchase Selkirk's shares, both before and after the Earl's death, as a means of halting the mutually destructive conflict. Enlisting the active if reluctant assistance of William and Simon McGillivray of McTavish, McGillivray Co. of Montreal, the principal partners of the NWC, an agreement was reached with Joseph Berens Jr., governor, and John Henry Pelly, deputy governor for the HBC, on March 16, 1821. This was entitled "An Agreement Between the Governor and Company of the Hudson's Bay Company and Certain Partners of the North West Company." It brought peace to the fur trade and to Assiniboia.

The brothers McGillivray (together with Nicholas Garry, who became, in 1822, deputy governor of the new company) carried the argeement to Fort William. Here on July 10, 1821, it was presented in the NWC's Great Hall, together with the accompanying Deed Poll, to the winterers, who were assembled for the last time. The agreement itself was short and simple. Trade henceforth was to be carried on under the name of the Hudson's Bay Company and under the terms of its charter, which the *bourgeois* had envied even longer than they had attacked its validity! The charter of 1670 was to be reinforced by an Act of Parliament of 1821, giving the new company exclusive trading privileges for twenty-one years in those portions of western British North America outside the orginal charter provisions. Criminal and civil cases would now be tried within the company's territories by company-appointed magistrates. It was agreed that the sale of liquor to the Indians would be restricted, and ultimately eliminated. The two companies would supply equal shares of capital and would equally share profits or losses. Provisions for profit-sharing were made for Selkirk's heirs, who would continue to hold full title to Assiniboia under the grant of 1811. Management was to be by a joint board of six, with the HBC filling four seats at the outset. The Deed Poll was a more elaborate document which was not well-received by the assembled winterers. They were to retain their positions as partners, but in fact they would share less than before in the profits and not at all in the higher management. However, those who were not retired under the terms of the Deed Poll were to become chief factors or chief traders. To the HBC officers, it was welcome news. For the first time, they would have a proprietary interest in the profits and a least a nominal share in the management.

The territory of the company was divided into four departments, each with a governor and a council composed of the chief factors, which was to meet annually. Their powers were not defined, but in practice the councils were purely advisory. Assiniboia, still under the ownership and control of the Selkirk heirs, was to be part of the Northern Department of Rupert's Land. This department, extending from the Arctic to the forty-ninth parallel, and from the Rocky Mountains to Hudson Bay, was to be governed from Norway House. George Simpson, governor of this department, was appointed governor-in-chief of all the HBC territories in 1826. The "little emperor" ruled firmly and wisely until his death in 1860.

For Red River, the union provided an opportunity for rebuilding and growth. It meant the end of organized immigration as a means of adding to its numbers. After the union of the companies, retired servants of both the HBC and the NWC moved to Red River and settled there permanently. An immediate effect of the union was the abandonment of the Nor'Wester route to Montreal. Henceforth, goods and men moved in and out of Red River by way of Hudson Bay and later by way of the Red and Mississippi rivers. The route carved by La Vérendrye was left in primeval peace for more than a generation. Red River ceased to be a crossroads but remained a supplier of pemmican and agricultural products. It became what has been aptly termed an "island colony." Until the civilization of eastern North America began to reach out towards it, Assiniboia enjoyed a "golden age."

5

The Island Colony

THE PERIOD BETWEEN 1821, the year of the union of the fur companies, and 1869, the year of the coming of the Canadians as a political force, was not entirely idyllic. The resolution of the Pemmican War gave to the Red River settlement a security that was only rarely and fleetingly disturbed by threats from the Sioux. For some time during the 1840's, the stirrings of the doctrine of Manifest Destiny in the United States, prompted by the dispute over the Oregon Territory, caused a nervous Imperial Government and Hudson's Bay Company to send troops to Assiniboia. They wished to occupy the area in case the Americans developed more than simply a hunger for Oregon and "fifty-four forty or fight." Moreover, the security gained from the union of the warring fur-trading factions did not free Red River from the fur trade's general hostility to settlement. The Hudson's Bay Company was opposed to anything more than a natural increase of the population. Vagaries of the environment had also to be contended with; floods and crop failures, for example, were serious problems. An attempt at local industry based on the buffalo came to naught, although it did serve to introduce money to Red River, thus replacing barter as the principal means of exchange. Money brought with it concomitant difficulties, among them a disinclination on the part of the settlers to accept the HBC monopoly.

To all of these difficulties there came, if not solutions, at least amelioration and acceptance. In these, both Catholic and Protestant churches led the way. With them came education and a continuous if tenuous connection with the outside world. Within the settlement, strong social disparities caused some dissent. These disparities, however, tended to be reduced by the facing of a common lot in both joy and adversity. In time, the disparities became less significant and a gentle calm prevailed. This calm was, no doubt, part somnolence, but it was also in large measure the result of good sense and a feeling of common humanity.

Following Selkirk's departure, life in the colony continued in its usual grim pattern. The harvest of 1817 was unaffected by natural hazards, but it was small because there had been few farmers and they had had little opportunity for a spring sowing. As a result, the whole of their small crop was preserved for seed and they made the now-familiar trek to Pembina for another winter of buffalo-hunting. The winter of 1817-18 proved a more arduous season than previous ones, with the result that the settlers were reduced to near-starvation. On their return to Fort Douglas in the spring of 1818, they entered on a further season of discontent. At first, all went well; crops were planted and flourished, more houses and barns were built, and Red River appeared to be well on the mend. The North West Company remained hostile, but it was reasonably circumspect in its behavior. Then, at the end of July, there came a plague of grasshoppers which devoured the crops to the last stalk and leaf. Even the trees were stripped to the bare branches. All that the Selkirk settlers were able to save was a few ears of half-ripened barley. The trek to the Pembina refuge was again the only recourse for the winter of 1818-19.

What little seed remained was planted as soon as the frost left the ground in 1819. It made a fair start, but in June the new crop of grasshoppers hatched, only this time there were tens of millions in the place of the millions of the previous year. The new crop vanished. Even the bark of the trees was eaten, and dead insects lay everywhere, two to four inches deep, clogging the creeks and polluting the rivers to an extent unmatched until recent times. The winter of 1819-20 at Pembina was not so much a burden. Experience had made plainsmen of the Highland crofters. Their skill on snowshoes, their ability to track the buffalo, and their accuracy as marksmen, these talents served them well. Indeed, they were tempted to adopt the hunter's way of life; but their attachment to farm and hearth was not easily cast aside.

With the financial help of both the HBC and the Earl of Selkirk, the settlers sought seed grain far to the south. In the winter of 1819-20, an expedition set out on snowshoes to make its way overland to Prairie du Chien on the Mississippi, far south of St. Paul. The journey out took three months, but the journey home was eased, if not speeded, by the use of flat boats. The expedition returned to the Forks in June, 1820, bringing with it 250 bushels of wheat. The crop of 1820 was not a good one, but it did provide seed; and after 1820, the colony was never again without it.

In the meantime, seed of another kind was being planted at Red River, seed which was to flourish and the product of which was to form an integral part of Manitoba's history. In the summer of 1818, two priests, Fathers Joseph-Norbert Provencher and Sévère-Joseph Dumoulin, arrived at Red River and set about establishing the Roman Catholic Mission which was later to become the Archdiocese of St. Boniface. The two priests had been sent by Bishop Plessis of Quebec at the urgent request of Lord Selkirk and on the petition of the French and the Métis, as well as those Scottish settlers who were Catholic. The pair went to work quickly and, between baptisms and marriages, oversaw the erection of a chapel. On All Saints' Day, November 1, 1818, they conducted their first mass on the east bank of the Red, opposite the mouth of the Assiniboine, on land on which several churches were to rise, each grander than the last, over the next century and a half. Provencher dedicated the new chapel to St. Boniface, patron saint of the Germans, in order to strengthen the weakened faith of the German-Swiss de Meurons and perhaps in anticipation of the great missionary work that was to be done. Thus, the parish of St. Boniface came into being, and the name attached itself by association to the surrounding lands.

As the population of Assiniboia gradually increased, so too did the work of the St. Boniface mission. A school was established at the same time as the chapel, and Guillaume Edge, who had arrived with the priests, became schoolmaster. Provencher was created Co-adjutor for the Northwest in 1820, was consecrated Bishop of the Northwest and of Juliopolis, *in partibus infidelium,* in 1822, and finally was made Bishop of St. Boniface upon the creation of that diocese in 1848. In the meantime, more clergy and Grey Nuns came out to staff the school, which was later to become St. Boniface College. They also served satellite missions at St. Charles and Baie St. Paul on the Assiniboine, and St. Norbert and Ste. Agathe on the Red. A mission that had been set up at Pembina in 1818 was withdrawn when Pembina was found to be situated in American territory. The mission was moved and became the nucleus of St. Francis Xavier on the White Horse Plain. In the early 1840's, a mission was established at St.

Laurent on southeastern Lake Manitoba. Thus, the Catholic Church was soon an integral part of the life of Red River.

In terms of growth and expansion, the Church of England was not far behind that of Rome. In 1820, the Reverend John West was sent out with the financial support of the HBC and of the Church Missionary Society. He established St. John's Church on land that had been set aside for the purpose by the Earl of Selkirk and founded the Red River Academy (the precursor of St. John's College). The latter school was set up for the sons of HBC officers and for the training of Indian and halfbreed clergymen. In time, it was supplemented by Miss Davis' School for Young Ladies. Further down the Red, Archdeacon William Cochrane directed the building of the sturdy limestone Church of St. Andrew, which still presides in quiet grandeur over the broad river. Between these two was built St. Paul's – henceforth, Middlechurch.

North of St. Andrew's, on the edge of Netley Marsh, was constructed the Indian Parish Church of St. Peter, Dynevor. West on the Assiniboine there appeared the Church of St. James, just beyond Omand's Creek where its log chapel still stands, clothed now in white clapboard and hidden by the trees of its churchyard from Portage Avenue. Beyond St. James there sprang up several parishes: Trinity Church, Headingly; St. Anne's, Poplar Point; St. Margaret's, High Bluff; and St. Mary's, Portage la Prairie. All of these had their beginnings before the 1860's, and in fact the Church of England establishment had grown by 1849 to the point where it was elevated to the Diocese of Rupert's Land, with the Reverend David Anderson as its first bishop. As in the case of the Catholic Church, the Church of England labored beyond its own vineyard. Its communicants were largely the servants of the HBC, both active and retired, but its mission and educational efforts were directed to the Indians and halfbreeds alike – and to this extent were part of the general self-help and goodwill that prevailed.

The Church of England was host for a long period to a considerable number of more-or-less unwilling churchgoers. The promise of a Presbyterian minister made by Lord Selkirk to his predominantly Calvinist Scots was a long time in being kept. The Presbyterians' resources were slim and the contributions made by the HBC were confined almost entirely to the two established churches. In 1841, the Methodists set up missions to the north at the invitation of the HBC. Among these was the mission of James Evans at Norway House. Here, Evans devised the Cree Syllabics, an alphabet and a system of writing for the Indians of the area. He also became the first printer in the Canadian West, using moulds made from the lead lining of tea chests and paper made from birch bark. The Weslyan Missions, however, did not penetrate south to the Red River settlement.

The lack of a Presbyterian cleric was not borne with Christian forebearance. The Scots were long and loud in their demand for a man who could preach the gospel according to John Knox and who could deliver his sermons in Gaelic. These appeals to the HBC went unanswered, as did an urgent request to the Church of Scotland. Finally, the demands of the Scots were heard by the Presbyterians of Canada, who sent out the Reverend John Black in 1851. Black was joyously welcomed by some three hundred Presbyterians in the manse that had already been prepared for him. The manse and church were built at Kildonan, midway between St. John's and St. Paul's.

Alexander Macdonell, who had succeeded Semple after the massacre in 1816 was confirmed as Governor of Assiniboia in 1817 and continued in office until June, 1822. Macdonell's was rather a gay administration, marked by much roistering and feasting in Fort Douglas and accompanied by considerable laxity in accounting procedures, not to mention a lack of interest in the welfare of the settlers. Macdonell therefore came to be known as the "grasshopper governor," not because his regime coincided with the onslaught of that pest, but because his own depradations exceeded even those of the grasshoppers. Macdonell, however, soon felt the heavy corrective hand of George Simpson, the new governor-in-chief of Rupert's Land and surrogate for the Selkirk heirs. Macdonell was removed from office and replaced by Captain Andrew Bulger, a bluff and hearty soldier. Bulger served until the fall of 1823, being succeeded by Robert Perry Pell until June of 1825. Donald McKenzie succeeded Pell until June of 1833, and then Alexander Christie took his place to serve as governor through the transition of Assiniboia to direct company control in 1835.

During this period, several efforts were made, all equally inspired and all equally unsuccessful, to put the colony on a self-sustaining basis. George Simpson, soon to be knighted by the Queen for his services to the seekers of the Northwest Passage, was a careful steward for the HBC proprietors. The many dependents of the fur trade who had been moved to Red River at the time of the union of the companies still relied largely on the generosity of the HBC for a living and were therefore a drain on its profits. The only cash crop, so to speak, was the twice-annual Red River buffalo hunt.

To supplement this sole means of income, the colony resorted to several stratagems. The first of these was the Buffalo Wool Company, founded in 1822 and financed by the HBC under the patronage of Lady Selkirk. The original idea appeared sound. Buffalo wool was to be had for the gathering after the hunt. It could be carded, spun, and woven into cloth, which in turn could be made into shawls. It was expected that these shawls would be made fashionable when introduced in the United Kingdom by Lady Selkirk and her aristocratic connections. By 1825, however, the venture had failed, since in the English market the shawls brought no more than one tenth their cost of production.

The second stratagem involved a Tallow Company aimed at marketing this product of the now considerable local cattle supply. Land which had satisfactorily grazed buffalo for untold generations was equally well suited to grazing cattle. Unfortunately, the larger herds required for tallow fell victim to a series of extremely severe winters and could not survive in the open. Thus, in 1843 the Tallow Company followed the Buffalo Wool Company into bankruptcy. All was not lost, however, since the settlers continued to raise cattle in individual herds with considerable success, adding a welcome variety of dairy products to the meat diet of the settlers and fur traders.

There was also a series of experimental farms encouraged by the HBC through Sir George Simpson and the executor of the Selkirk Estate, John Halkett. These ventures were also unsuccessful, though they did contribute, temporarily, to the widespread growing of hemp and flax. A large-scale sheep-raising venture led to the search for and purchase of sheep as far away as Kentucky, with heavy losses among those which were purchased and unskilfully driven to Red River. Of the 1,471 sheep purchased, only 251 survived the long journey. As with cattle, sheep were henceforth raised only in small flocks for wool and meat.

The over-all result of these and other ventures was far from complete failure. To a greater or lesser extent, each venture added something to Red River's capacity to support itself. But nature remained a formidable adversary. Blizzards had helped to wreck the Tallow Company, and the inexplicable disappearance of the buffalo from its usual haunts in 1823, followed by widespread prairie fires in 1824, had speeded the ruin of the buffalo-wool venture. Grasshoppers came again and again, and were followed by a plague of field mice, their numbers greatly multiplied by an abundant diet of grasshoppers. Moreover, early and late frosts were as common as they were unpredictable. In some years, the spring was too wet for planting; while in others, the fall was too wet for harvesting. Growing seasons were often too dry, and just as often too wet. In short, the climate of Manitoba was as it always is.

In 1826, 1852, and 1861, there came another natural scourge with which the colony was ill equipped to deal. Flood proved the near-nemesis of the Red River settlement. In 1826, flood waters very nearly caused the complete abandonment of the settlement. Alexander Ross has reported that there was very high water in 1776, 1790, and 1809. He tells the story, related to him by Louis Nolin, of Nolin's having sailed from Red Lake (in what is now north-central Minnesota) in 1776, via Pembina, to the Forks of the Red and Assiniboine over the face of one vast lake. Samuel Pritchard Matheson, Archbishop of Rupert's Land, has left us an account of the flood of 1861. During this flood, Matheson paddled a canoe into the loft of the family barn to rescue a hen, and later paddled through the lower-floor rooms of his grandfather's home.

The flood of 1826, however, remains the most spectacular of any of which first-hand accounts survive. Ross discounts tales that the flood resulted from any unnatural diversion of the spring run-off from the Missouri or Mississippi drainage basins. It was, he says, an extremely wet summer in 1825 throughout the valleys of the Red, the Assiniboine, and their tributaries. The following winter was one of heavy snow and frequent blizzards. Spring came late in 1826, but when it did, it came with a rush. John Pritchard, who had survived the Seven Oaks massacre, reported in a letter of August 2, 1826, that the ice at the Forks did not move out of the Red River until May 1. Ross noted that the river rose nine feet on May 4.

On May 5, it overran its banks and spread across the adjacent plain with great speed. The same day, the settlers fled, either on foot or by boat, driving their animals and carrying such furniture as they had been able to rescue. They found refuge on high ground at Silver Heights, west on the Assiniboine, or further afield at the Stonewall Ridge (to the west) or at Pine Ridge (to the east). The river covered all of the seventeen miles of land between these two heights. Practically all buildings were swept away, with only the three churches and the grist mill being spared. Fort Douglas went with the rest. In his letter of August 2, Pritchard reported graphically: "The crashing of immense masses of ice was as loud as thunder; neither the tallest poplar nor the stoutest oak could resist its impetuosity. They were mowed down like grass before the scythe. Far as the eye could discover, the earth was covered with water carrying on its surface the wreck of a whole colony. Houses, barns, stables, fences, and in fact all that could float was a prey to the destructive element." The area of what is now downtown Winnipeg was covered in some places to a depth of fifteen feet. Pritchard says that the river rose thirty-five feet above "its normal level" which is twenty feet higher that it reached in 1809. It crested on May 22 and began slowly to recede when the ice jam at the estuary of the Red broke, thus allowing the water to disgorge into the southern basin of Lake Winnipeg.

It was not until after the middle of June that the settlers were able to return to the mud-encrusted sites of their homes. At this time, the settlers held a council to consider removal or abandonment of the settlement. Simpson wrote, perhaps half-hopefully: "This I consider an extinguisher to the hope of Red River ever retaining the name of Settlement." Some of the *Canadiens* returned to Canada; and over one hundred of the recently-arrived German Swiss pulled up stakes for Iowa, with the active help and fond farewell of the HBC. With a determination to succeed that is a tribute to their courage and doggedness the Scottish settlers began anew at the Forks for the fourh time in fifteen years.

The cheers with which the HBC saw the German Swiss on their way after the flood of 1826 rose not entirely out of hope that the colony was breaking up. A change had begun to take place in the company's attitude toward the colony. The HBC had taken the settlement on as an unwanted child, reluctantly assuming a responsibility which it had not sought when the death of the Earl of Selkirk removed his interest and control. Being stuck with the thing, as it were, the HBC tried to make the best of it. Together with the Selkirk heirs, the company had undertaken elaborate and expensive schemes and methods to make it able to support itself. But the flood of 1826 seems to have been a turning point. Following the flood, the grudging acceptance of responsibility was replaced, to a degree, by the pride of paternity. This analogy, however, should not be carried too far. The HBC, and particularly its North American viceroy, Sir George Simpson, were certainly pleased to see their foundling approach maturity after the flood and to encourage and reward its success as a self-sustaining community. The company, however, drew a sharp line when the settlers began to encroach on the preserve of its foster parent. The HBC would tolerate no interference with the fur trade on the part of the colonists. Thus, the story of Manitoba from 1826 to the coming of Canada at the end of the 1860's is largely the story of attempts on the part of the HBC to keep its Disrict of Assiniboia within what the company considered its proper sphere of activity, which was to supply the fur trade, not supplant it or even to compete with it.

The flood of 1826 seems also to have marked another sort of watershed. Henceforth, the colony prospered agriculturally and otherwise. Crops were good, cattle flourished, and a trade soon developed in the exchange of Red River cattle for American horses. The buffalo hunts were uniformly successful and Red River fishing produced ample return for no great effort. By 1830, Simpson was moved to write: "This settlement is in the most perfect state of tranquillity; 'peace and plenty' may be said to be its motto." The Scots and Orkneymen had settled in as effective farmers of the river valley, to the extent that experts sent over from England to instruct the settlers in farming found themselves being instructed. The English and Scots halfbreeds also settled reasonably well into the status of small-farm proprietors.

The settlement had already taken definite shape, one that it was to retain beyond the time of its admission as a province of Canada. The active officers of the Hudson's Bay Company were to be found at first in the vicinity of Fort Garry. This fort had been built in the early 1830's near the site of the flood-ravaged Fort Gibraltar and had been named in honor of Nicholas Garry, the man who had represented the HBC at Fort William at the time of union with the NWC. The officers later moved down river to Lower Fort Garry, below St. Andrew's. The Highlanders and the Orcadians (as the Orkneymen were called) were located on Point Douglas and northward through Middlechurch; the English halfbreeds were found at the Forks, south on the west bank of the Red and west on the Assiniboine; and the French and Métis were located on the east bank of the Red around their church of St. Boniface. Satellites both of English and French and of halfbreeds and Métis were found further west on the Assiniboine – at St. James, Headingly, St. Francis Xavier (Granttown), Baie St. Paul, Poplar Point, High Bluff, and Portage la Prairie. Further Métis settlements appeared south on the Red at St. Norbert and Ste. Agathe, on the Seine at Ste. Anne des Chenes, and on Lake Manitoba at St. Laurent.

All of these groups got along surprisingly well with one another. Differences in religion and background tended to preclude intermarriage, but did not prevent active friendship and co-operation in day-to-day activities. No man's hand was turned against his neighbor. Doors were not locked, and not merely because there were neither locks nor anything to steal. There was practically no theft or any other serious crime. Drunkenness was an occasional problem, but both the HBC and the local authority exercised reasonable control. John Palliser, reporting on the state of the colony in 1857, advisedly altered the old saw when he commented on the Métis: "They hunt during three months of the year and beg, borrow, and starve during the remaining nine."

Generally speaking, the Métis continued to regard the hunt as their main occupation. But they also continued the work of the fur trade in their various capacities: as *voyageurs,* boatmen, cart drivers, or fishermen, as well as being slayers of buffalo and purveyors of pemmican. Their work was seasonal and at all times precarious and it therefore tended to encourage their instinctive tendency to emulate the nomadic and fatalistic "feast or famine" mode of existence of their maternal ancestors. Regardless of its good intentions, the HBC was unwittingly the author and encourager of what has been described by Chester Martin as a "pampered providence." When the Métis were required as hunters or as transport workers, the company expected them to be available. For the Métis to be readily available, the company had to support them in the intervals between jobs. Charity was as cold then as it is now, and what was grudgingly given was resentfully received. Since they themselves were extremely generous and hospitable, the Métis could not understand the profit motives of the HBC. They therefore became a potential source of dissension, though not yet so apparent as to disturb the even tenor of the Red River settlement. Their resentment and hostility, moreover, found a periodic release in the excitement of the buffalo hunt.

With the help of a growing number of "free traders" (independent merchants both within and without the settlement), the Métis soon became the focus of an increasing threat to the monopoly of the HBC by dealing in fur and hides through sources other than the company. It was largely out of a desire to protect its fur-trade monopoly that the HBC initiated an arrangement with the sixth Earl of Selkirk to restore the Selkirk grant to the absolute control of the company. Things had been moving in this direction at least since the flood of 1826. The Council of Assiniboia dates from the administration of Governor Andrew Bulger in 1822. At the instigation of George Simpson, Governor Donald McKenzie widened the scope of the council in 1832, including in it James Sutherland, John Pritchard, and Robert Logan, all of whom were friendly to the HBC. When their advice was sought, Bishop Provencher and the Reverend David Jones, the Anglican incumbent, were invited to the Council. In 1834, the current Earl of Selkirk agreed to return the grant that had been given to his father by the HBC, his price being £15,000 in company stock plus accrued interest. This amounted, in 1836, to £84,111, not an excessive recovery by the Selkirk family, since its expenditures were estimated to have been not less than £100,000.

On February 12, 1835, the first meeting of the new Council of Assiniboia was held at Upper Fort Garry, under the presidency of George Simpson as Governor-in-Chief of Rupert's Land. There were fourteen councillors, including Alexander Christie who, as Governor of Assiniboia, would preside in the absence of Simpson. Bishop Provencher and the Reverends David Jones and William Cochrane sat by virtue of their ecclesiastical offices. Other members were HBC officers (including Alexander Ross as Sheriff of Red River) and local dignitaries (including Andrew McDermot, a leading merchant or "free trader"). Present also were John Pritchard and Cuthbert Grant, a striking case of the lamb and the lion come to lie down together.

The District of Assiniboia was now recognized as stretching over a fifty-mile radius from its center at Upper Fort Garry. The council exercised power therein subject to the ultimate authority of the Hudson's Bay Company vested in it by the charter of 1670. The council was empowered to make laws, both of a civil and criminal nature, to appoint justices of the peace, and to organize a police force and a militia unit. One of its first acts was to authorize the building of a jail adjacent to Fort Garry, a sure sign of encroaching civilization! The council was to act as a supreme court for Assiniboia, sitting quarterly and hearing appeals from the four lower courts, as well as cases referred to it by them. In time, the actual judicial work was entrusted to a Recorder of Rupert's Land who was appointed by the HBC. The first and most famous of the four consecutive recorders was Adam Thom. A Scot of legal training, Thom had been editor of the Montreal *Herald* at the time of the rebellions of 1837 in the Canadas and he was of a notorious anti-*Canadien* bias. He had worked with Lord Durham during the latter's famous mission of 1838, having been hired, it is said, simply as a means of procuring his silence. His eccentricity and irascibility were enough in themselves to make him an object of suspicion to the Métis.

One of the early district justices of the peace – that for White Horse Plain – was Cuthbert Grant, who already held an appointment from the HBC as "Warden of the Plains" at £200 per year. This sinecure (a sort of prairie equivalent of Commander in Chief of the Western Approaches) was given to him ostensibly to protect the settlement from Sioux raids from the west, but it was actually designed to keep him from trading in fur and to influence the halfbreeds and Métis to do likewise.

The law-making power of the Council of Assiniboia was the widest possible, greater even than that the of legislature of Upper and Lower Canada or of the Parliament of the Province of Canada which was soon to come into existence. This power was never exercised arbitrarily, since the members of the council, besides being men of good will, were also restrained by the distinct possibility that their decrees might be ignored by the more unruly elements of the local population or might be overruled by Sir George Simpson or the London Committee of the HBC. Though in theory the council's activities were to be financed by a 7½-percent duty on all goods imported into or exported from the area, practical difficulties and a distinct lack of any substantial legal export market meant that in practice the burden of expense was borne by the HBC. This cost the company was prepared to absorb if the council could be instrumental in preserving the company's increasingly-endangered fur monopoly.

Though entirely appointive and basically the tool of the HBC, the Council of Assiniboia was representative of the more stable elements of the community. The heads of the local churches sat as a matter of right and the English, Scots, Orcadians, halfbreeds, and local merchants were represented – as well as the company, through its local officers. At times its deliberations and even its decisions did not sit well with Sir George Simpson or with his London principals, but these men voiced little complaint. Some members, such as Alexander Ross (a retired HBC servant who was still employed by it as Sheriff of Red River) would oppose the company when they felt its actions were inimical to the interests of the colony. The council introduced the jury system and its justices of the peace rotated through the existing parishes, both Catholic and Protestant. This gave a somewhat democratic shading to the council's activities and caused residents to identify with their parishes more fully than they would have solely out of involvement with the church. This identification of parish with government was to have considerable importance at the time of the transfer to Canada.

Of even greater importance at that crucial time was the landholding system which was introduced by the company at the time of the founding of the Council of Assiniboia. All titles to land granted by Selkirk and his heirs were recognized by the company, and the company stood ready to sell land in the usual river-front lots at rates of five shillings per acre to seven shilling sixpence per acre contingent upon its being developed for farming and upon the declaration by the purchaser that he would not engage in the trading of fur or hides other than through the company. Most of the Métis did not bother about formal or "legal" titles. They were squatters, but were blissfully unaware of the fact. As far as they were concerned, the land was theirs by inherited right. Many were even unaware of their lot limits, or other such legalistic matters. And since land was by no means at a premium, indeed, it was the one thing that there was plenty of, neither the company nor the council ever made any effort to regularize its possession. When the transfer to Canada became imminent, this lack of title to land became a matter of great concern. Misunderstanding of the intentions of the HBC and an unreasoning (though not unreasonable) fear of the Canadians, led to the gravest consequences. For the moment, however, all was serene, and it was trade, not politics, which was next to disturb the relative harmony of Red River.

6

Winds of Change

IN THE NORTH of Rupert's Land, the HBC continued to enjoy its unchallenged monopoly of all commerce. In Assiniboia, however, the situation was completely different. The Buffalo Wool Company and the Tallow Company, despite their ultimate failure, had accustomed the settlers to money as a medium of exchange. Henceforth, the settlers showed greater interest in obtaining cash, not so much for its own sake but for the greater variety of goods which it made available. Simultaneously, there appeared avenues for obtaining and spending money other than through the HBC. Theoretically, the London Convention had drawn the American boundary along the forty-ninth parallel of latitude in 1818; it was surveyed, if inaccurately, shortly thereafter. This demarcation left the greater part of the buffalo grounds in American territory. For many years, this was no problem, since an imaginary line drawn through the vast empty plains was as meaningless to Indian, white, and halfbreed as it was to the buffalo themselves.

Few Americans penetrated the border regions before the middle of the nineteenth century and none of these came with the intention of setting up farm communities. Agents of the American Fur Company and a few independents made their way into the regions of the upper Missouri and the Red, and these were followed, in due course, by small American military detachments out of Fort Snelling. They hardly made a foothold, however, and were concerned only with watching the always dangerous Sioux. In 1861, even these corporal's guards were withdrawn for the more serious business that arose out of the firing on Fort Sumter on April 12. Before this, the American power, civil or military, was of no practical consequence at Red River.

The American trader was an entirely different matter. By the 1830's, regular trading posts were in operation at Pembina and at St. Joseph (now Walhalla in North Dakota), as well as at other points within relatively easy reach of Red River. A very considerable traffic in fur, buffalo robes, pemmican, and other buffalo products was soon being diverted to the Americans, rather than going to the HBC. To control this illicit commerce had been one of the chief motives behind the company's take-over of the direct government of Assiniboia in 1835. The offices of Sheriff of Red River and of Warden of the Plains, both of which had been designed as a curb to smuggling, brought little satisfaction to the HBC, and illegal trade became almost universal at Red River. Smuggling was so widely practised at Red River that it became quite acceptable, even respectable. All forms of restraint employed by the HBC proved ineffective. The company, however, continued to hold to its charter privilege and parliamentary licence to trade as a monopoly.

The principal American beneficiary of the settlers' refusal to comply with this authority was Norman Kittson, who had set himself up at Pembina and who was engaged in a regular ox-cart traffic with St. Paul by 1845. He was a pioneer of the route which was, by 1860, to supercede the traditional Hudson Bay route. "Commodore" Kittson and his associates, men such as Joseph Rolette and Charles Cavelier, provided a variety of goods that were not available from the HBC: chiefly rum and other spirits, which the company had stopped using as articles of trade but for which the demand was still high.

The HBC wanted to avoid trouble with the settlers. Incidents had pointed up the volatile nature of the Métis when they were slighted and their rights and privileges violated. There had also been some indication that the English halfbreeds would support the Métis in a crisis. In 1834 at Fort Garry, Thomas Simpson (at that time a junior officer with the HBC) had struck a Métis named Larocque in retaliation for an alleged insult. An angry crowd gathered, threatening violence against Simpson and all the men of the HBC. There were war dances outside the fort and the crowd threatened to burn it if Simpson were not delivered up to them. Governor Christie and Sheriff Ross appealed in vain for reason to prevail. Reverend Georges Belcourt, a friend and counsellor of the Métis, was summoned from St. Boniface and succeeded in persuading the Métis to calm down.

His task was no doubt made easier by the fact that the HBC provided tobacco and a ten-gallon keg of rum. Again, in 1836, Louis St. Denis was flogged for theft. The onlookers, both English halfbreeds and Métis, threw mud and stones at the man who wielded the whip and were only restrained from lynching him by the intervention of the company police. Incidents of this nature occurred often enough to cause the HBC considerable concern for its own safety and for the survival of the whole settlement.

Various methods were employed in the attempt to end or at least to curtail the flow of trade across the border. Between 1833 and 1846, a direct subsidy of £300 per year was paid to the American Fur Company, on condition that it confine its trading to the area south of the forty-ninth parallel. The HBC could not, however, prevent the people of Assiniboia from crossing the border. It offered higher than usual prices for fur and buffalo products, but with little success in deterring the illegal trade. Local free traders such as James Sinclair and Andrew McDermot were encouraged to bring in goods through Hudson Bay for private sale, charging them the low rate of £8 per ton for freight. That did not keep them from trading outside the HBC. When the company began to keep its stores open at regular hours and at all seasons, extending liberal credit, the free traders cried that they were being ruined by unfair competition. As the illegal trade continued, the HBC began to use harsher measures. Free traders were required to obtain bonds if they wished to import goods; a 20-percent import duty was put on goods from the United States; illicit furs were seized by force; merchants were obliged to take an oath to abstain from illegal trade or to submit their outgoing letters open to the company's post; and the police force was increased. All this was effected, however, without appreciably diminishing the illicit trade.

Recorder Adam Thom was of little help in calming matters. He came to Red River with a deserved reputation as being anti-*Canadien* and was soon regarded as being anti-Métis, anti-halfbreed, and anti-Indian. His salary of £700 per year was paid by the HBC and he could not escape the accusation of favoring its policies. Following the political turmoil in Canada in the late 1830's and early 1840's, a somewhat similar agitation began at Red River. The Métis and halfbreeds petitioned the Council of Assiniboia for a share in the government of the settlement and for a definition of their special status as natives of Red River. The concept of a "New Nation," a concept first advanced for them by the North West Company almost a generation before, was again made manifest.

The right claimed by the Métis to a share in the government was ignored. They were told that they had the rights of British subjects, but no special status. By 1845, the situation was becoming serious. A body of halfbreeds and Métis threatened to effect a jailbreak to liberate those of their fellows who were being detained for illegal trading. Overenthusiasm on the part of the HBC police had led to claims that not only trading goods, but personal effects had been taken from the halfbreeds and Indians. Once again, Father Belcourt prevented violence, though he recognized the existence of legitimate grievance.

In December 1845, Governor Christie appealed to Sir George Simpson for help, asking that the settlement be ringed with satellite forts to check all incoming and outgoing goods, that all furs be seized, and that there be provided "a body of disciplined troops to give still greater effect to our authority." Sir George had already anticipated this request. Considerations of Imperial policy came to the rescue of the HBC monopoly. The American presidential election of 1844 had been won by the ardent expansionist, James K. Polk, largely on the cry of "fifty-four forty or fight." This slogan aptly expressed the sentiments of the United States; they wanted full control of the Oregon Territory, which had been jointly shared since 1818 with the English. Oregon stretched from Mexican California to Russian Alaska, with its northern boundary set at 54°40′ north latitude. Such permanent settlement as existed in the region was predominantly American, while British activities were confined to trading posts of the HBC at the mouth of the Columbia River and on Vancouver Island. The American threat was very real. The Americans had already annexed Texas and were anxious to acquire more territory. The English naturally resisted, since their claim to the Pacific slope was a good one, based as it was on the rights of discovery and on a treaty with Spain in the late eighteenth century. The Americans threatened war. At the time, this was perhaps somewhat presumptious of them, considering their relative weakness when compared with the might of the British Empire. The English, however, were not looking for trouble. They were, moreover, already wedded to a general policy of conciliation toward the Americans. In any event, they offered a compromise which the arrogant Polk rejected out of hand. War seemed imminent.

Simpson was not concerned about Oregon, since HBC interests in that area were by no means vital. Rupert's Land, however, was a different matter and Simpson devoted his considerable talents to securing British help in protecting it both from without and from within. He appealed through the London Committee of the HBC for troops to protect Red River as a Crown colony. This appeal received short shrift. The English government replied that the HBC had always claimed special status under the Charter of 1670 and that defence measures were more its concern than they were those of Great Britain. Simpson and the HBC reluctantly agreed and, in their anxiety to get troops for Red River, offered to underwrite the costs. The English government finally agreed, though it caused Simpson some anxious moments, and prepared to dispatch 347 men: infantrymen, artillerymen, and engineers. This force assembled at Cork under Major John F. Crofton and sailed from Ireland for York Factory on June 26, 1846. On June 12, however, the United States Senate had ratified the Oregon Treaty with England, thus settling the dispute.

President Polk's defiance of "perfidious Albion" turned out to be just another ploy in American political gamesmanship. Polk's real interest lay in obtaining lands from Mexico. Early in the summer of 1846, he succeeded in provoking a war with the Mexicans, and had no desire to take on the English as well. When England renewed its earlier offer to split the territory along the forty-ninth parallel, Polk readily agreed. Thus, a stretch of Pacific coastline was preserved for the future Dominion of Canada and Simpson had gained his principal objective.

The British troops arrived at Red River to garrison both Upper and Lower Fort Garry, although the reason for their coming had ceased to exist even before they embarked. They continued to serve at Red River until 1848. On his arrival, Major Crofton found the people "disaffected," but the presence of his troops was enough to prevent trouble. They were not a police force in any sense; they did not patrol the settlement, nor did they enforce the decrees of the Council of Assiniboia. Their presence was, in itself, enough. Their task was made easier by a violent epidemic of measles in the spring of 1846, which took much of the fight out of the Métis and half-breeds. The epidemic took more than three hundred lives among the Indians, Métis, and halfbreeds, and the settlement lost interest in arguing.

The military also had a beneficial effect on the economy of Red River. The soldiers brought in a new supply of cash which they spent readily, in the way that soldiers will. Their needs in the way of foodstuffs and winter clothing also had the effect of stimulating business. Wemyss Simpson, a brother-in-law of Sir George, wrote from Red River in 1846 that "the people of the Settlement were never so well off, as the Government spends about £30 per day and the Company also spends a great deal, buying all the cattle, pigs, sheep, and grain." Thus, the military presence and ready money helped restore Red River to its usual tranquility, if only temporarily.

As the Oregon crisis was over before the troops had arrived, the Imperial Government was not impressed by HBC arguments for their retention as a bulwark against Manifest Destiny. Major Crofton was returned to the United Kingdom in 1847, and his troops followed in 1848. They were succeeded by a small corps of fifty-six Chelsea Pensioners, half-pay veterans who brought with them a total of ninety-nine dependent women and children. This was an economic disappointment to both the settlers and the HBC and a death blow to the company's pretentions of monopoly. In fact, it was under the looser control of the Pensioner force, that the issue of the trade monopoly of the HBC came to a head in Assiniboia.

In March, 1849, Guillaume Sayer and three other Métis were arrested by the HBC for illicit trading in fur. Reports have it that they resisted arrest, both giving and receiving serious injury. They were released on bail and called for trial on May 17, Ascension Day. Recorder Thom has been accused of purposely setting the trial for Ascension Day – an important day in the Roman Catholic calendar – as a means of getting through the trial while most of the Métis were engaged in their religious duties. If so, it was a serious miscalculation. The Métis attended an early mass at St. Boniface, so Ascension Day served only to provide for a ready-made place of assembly. After mass, the Métis did not disperse. They stayed to be harangued from the Cathedral steps by Jean-Louis Riel, "the Miller of the Seine." He was both father and forerunner, as a champion of his people, of the more famous Louis Riel; and as a miller, he was a person of some consequence at Red River.

At Riel's urging, the Métis surrounded the courthouse outside Upper Fort Garry. They numbered more than three hundred and most of them were armed. Riel demanded the acquital of Sayer and the three other accused. For good measure, he added an objection to the recorder's refusal to permit the use of French in court, an indictment of the HBC monopoly and a complaint at the Métis' lack of a share in the government of Assiniboia. Sayer admitted that he had sold furs, but added that he had been given permission to do so by an HBC officer. A jury, both French- and English-speaking, found him guilty but recommended clemency. Thom and his colleagues had no desire to provoke the Métis, with the result that Sayer was discharged and the charges against his companions dropped. The jubilant Métis interpreted this outcome as the triumph which it essentially was. The monopoly of the HBC had come to an end at Red River. With shouts of *"le commerce est libre"* and *"vive la liberté"* accompanied by numerous *feux de joie*, the armed crowd dispersed.

Both the Pensioners and the incompetent police had failed to act and, indeed, were not prepared to do so. Their inaction was prudent, as there could easily have been another Seven Oaks. The HBC, for all practical purposes, surrendered its trade monopoly. Import duties were cut to four percent and were seldom collected. Adam Thom was suspended and finally retired to England, while French interpreters were introduced into the Quarterly Court of Assiniboia.

For another twenty years, the HBC continued to rule in Assiniboia. The Council of Assiniboia continued to govern – its members, as before, selected by the company but still roughly representative of the people of the settlement. There was no oppression and a sort of tired paternalism prevailed which did not ruffle even the more rebellious elements. Red River enjoyed its last period of tranquility. There was a flood in 1852 and another in 1861. There were infrequent partial or complete crop failures. The buffalo hunt continued, but its heyday was gone. The Americans were moving steadily northward. Minnesota Territory was carved out of the Louisiana Purchase by the United States in 1849 and the state itself was erected in 1858.

An entirely new factor began to impinge on Red River before its people were well aware of its existence. The railway was destroying old concepts of time and space. In 1858, the railway reached St. Paul, while the steamboat appeared at Red River for the first time in 1859. The *Anson Northup*, out of Georgetown on the upper Red, was the first of a long series of vessels which were to continue until they in turn gave way to the railway. In 1859, the HBC began importing its trade goods by rail via Chicago to St. Paul and thence by Red River cart to Fort Garry. The solitude that had come upon the Montreal trade route after the union of 1821 now descended on the route to Hudson Bay. More and more native Manitobans sought, or were sent to seek, education in England or in Canada. Some, such as James Ross, Dr. John Bunn, and Louis Riel, returned to make their influence felt. In 1859, two former reporters for the

Toronto *Globe*, William Buckingham and William Coldwell, brought a printing press by rail and Red River cart to the settlement and published, on December 22, 1859, the first issue of the first western newspaper, *The Nor'Wester*. The name no longer roused memories of conflict, but the paper brought with it the new problem of the claims of Canada. Canadians such as Dr. John C. Schultz, Henry McKenney, and James H. Ashdown began to be seen and heard, as did Americans like "Dutch George" Emmerling, Frank L. Hunt, Robert A. Davis, and Alfred H. Scott. The old order was changing. At first, the change was gradual, even in part graceful, but before long it was to be quick, drastic, and complete.

The dawn of its Canadian age was long in coming to Manitoba; but when it did, it came up like thunder. There was an extensive period of preparation, however, with most events taking place far beyond the horizons of Assiniboia. Manitoba first entered history as part of the North American barrier to Asia; then it took its place as a crossroads and supply source for two fur-trade empires. In the latter process, it was, almost accidentally, provided with an agricultural nucleus. As the nineteenth century passed the halfway mark, Manitoba became once again coveted as a larder and a highway to the far west, though this time on a far grander scale.

The Province of Canada, crushed against the United States by the Canadian Shield, sought lands where its surplus farm population could find a future without losing a birthright. All of the colonial governments of British North America desperately needed a means of sustaining themselves without losing their identity, since all were victims of a squeeze between British free trade on the one hand and American protective tariff policy on the other. The United States had possessed itself of vast lands at the expense of Mexico; it had successfully manoeuvered the British Lion out of its share of the Oregon Territory; and Alaska was to become American by purchase in 1867. In spite of the diversion created by the Civil War, the United States still cast a predatory eye to the northwest. In the 1860's Rupert's Land drew attention to an extent that it never had before. It was the subject of earnest discussion in the new Canadian capital of Ottawa, in Washington, and especially in London.

It was all well and good to see the United States emerge from the Civil War with slavery abolished and the pre-eminence of the federal government assured. What advantage would the British gain, however, by letting the whole of the HBC territories fall into the hands of Washington? Could the rest of British North America, so closely hemmed in by geography, survive the imposing presence of the United States? Could the HBC continue to control its northern empire in the face of the irrestistible onrush of civilization? Indeed, was it even then controlling that empire?

The steamboat and the railway came on inexorably. A long delayed shift in men's fashions was depressing the beaver market as it had not been for two hundred years. Perhaps for the first time since the American War of Independence, the English were forced, in the 1850's and 1860's, to pay serious attention to the future of their North American possessions. Something had to be done about Canada and the Maritime colonies, which were now drifting without economic rudders. Similarly, the new Pacific colony of British Columbia needed support if it was to maintain its Britishness over such an immense distance and against so many American influences. There were many problems in British North America to preoccupy the Imperial Government and many solutions presented themselves for consideration.

Already, the enthusiastically expansionist senators Ramsey and Sibley of Minnesota had moved a bill in the American Congress to provide for the admission of Rupert's Land into the American Union. The Canadians had begun to lay claims even earlier. When the HBC's exclusive licence to trade came up for renewal in the English Parliament in 1857, Canadian representations were fierce against what they called the reactionary, unproductive, and entirely wrong-headed government of Rupert's Land by the HBC. The Government of Canada presented a petition signed by several hundred Red River settlers to the Select Committee of 1857 in which the petitioners requested union with Canada. The petition may well have been inspired by Canadian expansionists and accepted at Red River, where the HBC government was generally unpopular. Captain William Kennedy, who had gained a degree of fame in the search for Sir John Franklin and who was now resident of Red River, sponsored the petition. He was known to be close to George Brown of the *Globe*. The Canadians also claimed that Canada was the heir of the French, and of the Scots who followed them and thrust their way to the "western sea." John Palliser, Henry Youle Hind, and Simon J. Dawson had poked and pried about the southern regions of Rupert's Land and had gone home to Canada to report on the agricultural and other riches that waited there to be tapped. Their reports were echoed and re-echoed in the news columns and editorials of the Canadian press, especially in George Brown's Toronto *Globe*.

When the abrogation of the Reciprocity Treaty of 1854 became a possibility after 1861, and a reality after 1866, the economies of the British North American colonies began to grind to a halt. The machinery of government in the Province of Canada had already done so, the victim of unresolved biracialism and bilingualism. The British owners of the Grand Trunk Railway saw a line into the plains of Rupert's Land as a way out of their financial difficulties. The political leaders in Canada – John A. Macdonald, George Etienne Cartier, Thomas D'Arcy McGee, Alexander Tilloch Galt, George Brown, and others – saw a firm foundation for a new British North American political unit in the far-flung reaches of Rupert's Land and the Pacific slope. The acquisition of Rupert's Land by the new Dominion of Canada was implicit in its birth and essential to its survival. With Rupert's Land and British Columbia, the new Dominion stood a fair chance of holding out against American blandishments; without them, it would surely fail.

The beginning of the end of the rule of the HBC in Assiniboia is to be found in the Parliamentary Select Committee of 1857, which was set up at Westminster to examine the affairs of the company in the light of increasing complaints about its effectiveness and as a preliminary to the possible renewal of its exclusive licence to trade. When this licence was granted in 1838, provision had been made for the annexation to the Crown of all or part of Rupert's Land for the development of a colony. Dissatisfaction expressed both in Vancouver Island and in Assiniboia plus the interest that was being evinced by Canada prompted what was to be a very thorough inquiry.

The opinions of Hind, Palliser, and others were cited as evidence of the immense agricultural potentiality of the plains. On the other hand, the HBC used its ablest servants to testify to the exact opposite. Sir George Simpson, fighting to the end to preserve the fur trade and viewing these latest assaults as mere excuses for the establishment of a new North West Company, made statements which must have troubled his Presbyterian conscience. Rupert's Land, he said, was a potential desert hemmed in by swamps and precipitous mountains. Only grass grew there, and that only in patches. Opponents of the HBC, such as Alexander K. Isbister, a native of Red River and successful London barrister, described the country as another Garden of Eden. Both he and Simpson exaggerated, each in his own way, in order to serve his own ends.

The upshot was that the exclusive licence to trade was not

1 *York Factory, 1821*
(water color by Peter Rindisbacher)

2 *Fort Prince of Wales*, c. *1769*
(from a sketch by Samuel Hearne)

1

2

3 *Fort Gibraltar, 1804*
(water color by Rev. H. J. Robertson)

4 *Fort Douglas, 1817*
(from a sketch by Lord Selkirk)

3

4

5 *Thomas Douglas, Earl of Selkirk*

6 Chippewas at Fort Dufferin near Emerson, 1873

7 Métis and English and Scots halfbreeds employed as scouts by the Boundary Commission of 1873

6

7

8 *Red River natives of Scots and Indian origin*

9 Louis Riel, c. *1876*

9

10 *Provisional government,* c. *1870*
Riel is seated at center, flanked by
John Bruce (on his right) and
W. B. O'Donoghue (on his left)

10

11 Main Street, Winnipeg, looking south from Notre Dame, 1872

12 Upper Fort Garry, 1860 (photographed from the south bank of the Assiniboine)

11

12

13 Dog carioles, c. 1857, typical winter transport of the fur trade

14 Ox-cart train leaving Long River, 1873 The covered wagon was an advance over the two-wheeled Red River cart

13

14

15 York boats, carrying sail and sweep oars

16 Steamboat at Winnipeg, c. *1880*

15

16

17 Settlers arriving from South Dakota, 1891
An early example of the immigrant trains from the United States which passed through Winnipeg

18 Dutch immigrants at Winnipeg's Immigration Hall, 1893

17

18

19 Homesteader picking up supplies at the railhead, c. *1900*

19

20 Ukrainians completing a thatched and mud-plastered home, c. *1905*

21 Ukrainians harvesting, c. *1910*

20

21

22 *Typical Mennonite house barn built* c. *1890*

23 Steam threshing about to get under way, Crystal City, c. 1880

24 Ukrainian newcomers seeking employment, c. 1905

23

24

renewed, the HBC was left otherwise undisturbed in its possession of Rupert's Land, and a way was left open for Canada to expand westward through negotiation with the company. Thus, the handwriting was on the wall. As early as 1860, the HBC made an offer to sell its land and governing powers to the Imperial Government. It was an abortive effort. The Colonial Office, at first receptive, became cool after a change of government. England was not, at that time, anxious to extend its colonial responsibilities. Indeed, it was anxious to be divested of them.

Matters did not rest there for long. The Grand Trunk Railway, through its principal promoter, Sir Edward Watkin, became interested in the long-range prospect of rail communication with the Pacific. The Duke of Newcastle, a prime mover of the proposed scheme, approached Henry H. Berens, governor of the HBC, for a land grant from the company for this purpose. Aghast at the idea, Governor Berens made a final eloquent statement of the fur-trade position: "What! Sequester our very tap-root! Take away the fertile lands where our buffalos feed! Let in all kinds of people to squat and settle, and frighten away the fur-bearing animals they don't hunt and kill! Impossible. Destruction – extinction of our time-honoured industry. If these gentlement are so patriotic, why don't they buy us out?" Newcastle's reply was terse: "What is your price?" Berens, after a pause, replied: "About a million and a half." All was over but the mechanics of the transaction. Watkin, Newcastle, and others of the railway financiers organized the International Finance Society, a holding company, which in 1863 bought up the stock of the Hudson's Bay Company. A new committee was installed – one which was receptive to radical change.

The Imperial Government was now becoming increasingly concerned about the belligerence of the now victorious North in the American Civil War. The English were anxiously assisting at the birth of the new Dominion of Canada and had also to think about its future in the northwest. Moreover, the Canadians themselves were of little help. Before Confederation, they held out to have Rupert's Land presented to them by right and without reparation. It was not until after the passage of the British North America Act and its implementation on July 1, 1867, that negotiations began in earnest. England, fearing that the Americans would move to take over Rupert's Land, had entered into direct negotiation with the HBC. Canada expressed deep interest, coming to bargain late in 1868. Sir George Etienne Cartier and William McDougall made a final plea for the territory on the grounds of prior discovery and the doubtful nature of the charter of 1670. They stopped short, however, of offering to challenge that charter in the courts.

The Imperial Government backed the HBC in its claims for compensation and Canada yielded. The Hudson's Bay Company was to receive £300,000 in cash. It was to retain a stated acreage around each of its 120 posts, varying from one post to another from five to 3,000 acres, and was to retain ownership of one twentieth of the fertile belt. It was also to be permitted to carry on its trade without hinderance or "excepional" taxation. In addition, Canada would pay for several tons of material for the proposed telegraph which had already been shipped to York Factory.

On the face of it, the arrangement was a bargain for Canada. But the deal was not yet closed. Due to a temporary financial embarrassment on the part of the Government of Canada, payment had to be made by the Imperial Government, which would hold temporary title until Canada could afford to pay. The transfer to Canada was first set for October 1, 1869, but was later postponed until December 1 of that year. In the meantime, the Government of Canada obtained ratification for the agreement from its Parliament and prepared the way for the take-over with an "Act for the Temporary Government of Rupert's Land." This act provided for the government of the territory by a governor and council to be appointed by the governor-general-in-council.

The choice of governor was a natural one. William McDougall had long been interested in western expansion and had played a large part in the successful negotiations with England and the Hudson's Bay Company. All seemed serene as he departed with his party for his new domain. Whatever state of pleasant anticipation he may have enjoyed came to an abrupt end when he reached Pembina. Here he was refused admission into Assiniboia by an armed party which acted under authority of *Le Comité National des Métis de la Rivière Rouge.*

7

The Advent of Canada

THE FACT THAT FAR-OFF EVENTS would eventually have a direct effect on them was not lost on the people of Red River. Their island-like colony was fast losing its insularity. The steamboat whistle was now heard more often than the roar of the bull buffalo, and the excruciating shriek of the ungreased axles of a multitude of Red River carts signalled the approach of freight from St. Paul long before the slow-moving line hove into view. The railway crept slowly but steadily northward through central Minnesota and was soon to reach St. Cloud. The telegraph already extended as far as Duluth, from which point Jay Cooke was laying plans for a railway to the Pacific.

The *Nor'Wester* now carried regular news reports that were received from the head of the telegraph line. Thus did Red River first hear of the Confederate disaster at Vicksburg in 1863, of Lee's surrender at Appomattox in 1865, and of the stirrings among the British North American colonies now preparing to become the Dominion of Canada. The *Nor'Wester*, indeed, had become the voice of Canada in the West. From 1864 to 1868 it was owned by Dr. John Christian Schultz and was directed without restraint against the policies of the HBC and in favor of union with Canada. Schultz was a native of Amherstburg, Upper Canada, where he was born on January 1, 1840. He moved to Red River in 1860, having completed a course in medicine. He did not go west as a doctor, but rather to join his half-brother, Henry McKenney, in business. By local standards, Schultz prospered. He did practise some medicine, but he also operated a pioneer pharmacy, held an interest in more than one general store, traded in fur, and dabbled in real estate. Schultz, moreover, was no stranger to the Quarterly Court, often being party to civil actions. Schultz was an impressive man physically, over six feet in height, with broad shoulders and a leonine head; his voice, which matched his presence, was often heard in the Council of Assiniboia. Attempts on the part of both Schultz and his fellow Canadians, however, to secure his appointment to the council went unheeded by the council and the HBC.

Dr. Schultz was the unquestioned leader of the Canadian party at Red River. His unpopularity was not, however, due to this leadership. Schultz's assumed mantle of zeal in the cause of Canada slipped frequently to reveal his own self-seeking. In an age of sharp dealing and *caveat emptor* business practices, he was regarded as being outstandingly unscrupulous. This had made him unpopular with the local establishment, the Selkirk descendants and the Orkneymen, and with the English-speaking halfbreeds. Furthermore, he was most unpopular with the Métis, for whom he repeatedly showed contempt both in person and in print. A successful, boastful newcomer can expect to be disliked in almost any community, but Schultz seemed to go out of his way to court unpopularity.

Despite his universal unpopularity among the natives of Red River, Schultz rose to great heights of wealth and office in his adopted province. He was to serve as Member of Parliament for Lisgar from the admission of Manitoba until 1882, at which time he was appointed to the Senate. From 1888 until 1895, Dr. Schultz served as Lieutenant-Governor of Manitoba and on his retirement was made a Knight Commander of the Order of St. Michael and St. George. Through all this, he never sought to earn the respect or affection of his fellows. A generation after the events of 1869-70, Sheriff Colin Inkster, on reading the record of Schultz's achievements on his tombstone, remarked: "It is too bad we knew him."

A number of other Canadians seemed to have been cast from the same mold as Dr. Schultz. Walter Bown, a dentist, operated the *Nor'Wester* in the interest of Canada – and in the interest of Schultz, after 1868. John A. Snow and Charles Mair were two other Canadians whose activities did nothing to improve the image of Canada in the minds of those native to Red River. The scale was only partly balanced by such men as the farm expert, Kenneth McKenzie, and the later arrival, Dr. J. H. O'Donnell. In general, the impression given by the Canadians was not one which reassured the Métis and the halfbreeds as to what they might expect when the Canadian government assumed control of Rupert's Land.

There was no authority which could provide reassurance to the people of Red River. The only outside authority to which they could look for guidance was the Hudson's Bay Company, and the company was woefully silent. From the *Nor'Wester* and from such outside papers as found their way to Red River, the settlers could perceive that change was imminent; but they could do little more than guess at what that change might mean. Those to whom the natives might have looked for guidance were either unable or unwilling to help. The company's officers and retired servants were as much in ignorance as was Governor Mactavish. These worthies had hoped to share, through the Deed Poll which accompanied the union of the fur companies in 1821, in the financial benefits of any final settlement. Being uninformed, they sensed betrayal and had little heart for reassuring their fellows.

The general air of uncertainty which prevailed at Red River was not lifted in 1867 by Confederation. The HBC had been somewhat unpopular with the greater number of those at Red River since as far back as they could remember. The Sayer trial of 1849 had ended the HBC's efforts to maintain its trading monopoly, but had done nothing to alter its image. As buyer and seller, the company was still the local trade giant. It resisted all attempts to widen the already broad base of the Council of Assiniboia and turned a deaf ear to suggestions concerning an elective assembly. Governor Mactavish, increasingly affected by the tuberculosis which was eventually to claim him, could only hold the line and carry on as before, waiting on events far beyond his jurisdiction or control. He could give no sure answer to a question which increasingly troubled the Métis: Did they or did they not have any real claim to the land which they occupied?

In 1817, Selkirk had given his settlers titles for their land. The grants to the various churches were also protected by title. On the other hand, the lands of many of the HBC officers and servants were held by no formal title. In 1835, the company had established a system of land sale; but before the transfer to Canada, less than 12,000 acres had been sold. Other lots were simply entered in a company register and any transfer of occupany therein noted. For most of the Métis and halfbreeds, there was not even this formality. As Sir George Simpson put it before the Select Committee of 1857: "We point out the situations where they may squat, we do not give them titles unless they make some arrangement for the payment. . . . The majority of them have settled themselves down where they liked and we could not prevent them." After all, the land was as limitless as the horizon. To the average Métis, occupied with the buffalo hunt or with the task of transporting furs, land was only a place to rest from time to time. It had little or no value to him either as property or as a source of livelihood. He built a hut by a river and lived there when not otherwise engaged. As often as not, he would move when the local fuel supply was exhausted. The Métis' concept of land was more that of his Indian mother than that of his white father – land was there simply to be used. It was not something to be owned, to be parcelled out like sacks of flour, or ticketed like bales of fur and listed in a book. But this attitude began to change as civilization speeded up its relentless advance.

The Canadians at Red River openly denied the right of the Métis, or of any others without title, to occupy land. They even scorned HBC titles and murmured darkly of the changes that would soon be made. If local tradition is to be believed, Dr. Schultz marked out as his own much of what is now downtown Winnipeg – an area north of the Assiniboine and west of the Red. The HBC, as was coming to be expected, remained silent on the matter. There was no Canadian authority to contradict the claims or to quiet the rumors. The churches were reluctant to offer what would be, in any case, a false assurance. At no time did either the HBC or the Dominion of Canada contemplate any overturning of occupancy. The Canadian Act of 1869, which concerned the temporary government of Rupert's Land, provided that all local laws and regulations which were not inconsistent with the British North America Act of 1867 were to remain in force. But there was no specific reference to titles of land. The men in London who were now in the process of deciding the fate of half a continent were not even aware of – let alone concerned with – the few acres of some 10,000 people at Red River. They were not long to remain either unaware or unconcerned.

In 1868, Red River, already disturbed and harassed by uncertainty, suffered another blow at the hands of capricious nature. The entire crop was destroyed by a recurrence of the plague of grasshoppers. The buffalo grass of the plains was gnawed to the roots and the buffalo disappeared from his customary haunts. Hunters returned empty-handed and hungry. Even the lake fisheries failed, and neither rabbit nor prairie chicken was to be found. The plight of Red River aroused international sympathy. The HBC and the mother churches made generous contributions for the provision of relief supplies. More than £1,000 was raised in the United States and even more in Quebec. The gifts were not by any means a recognition of Red River's existence or of any particular concern for the problems of its people outside of their immediate need for sustenance. It was another shining example of man's humanity to man when his sympathies are aroused. Nonetheless, a contemporary hand noted in the Minute Book of the Council of Assiniboia opposite a reported promise of a cash gift for relief purposes from Ontario: "This money was never received."

The Government of Canada used the emergency at Red River to kill two birds with one stone. It had intended to build a wagon road, once the transfer had been effected, between St. Boniface and the northwest angle of Lake of the Woods. As a relief measure, the Canadian government sent out a party under John A. Snow to begin work on the road, starting at Red River and using local labor. Unfortunately, Snow, Charles Mair, and a few other Canadians fitted in well with the local concept of the Canadians. The party employed only a few natives and worked hand in glove with Dr. Schultz.

At the same time, William McDougall, minister of public works in the Government of Sir John A. MacDonald, decided that no time should be lost in instituting a survey of Red River lands, based, of course, on the square survey system that had long since been adopted in Canada from the American Northwest Ordinance of 1787. At best in ignorance and at worst in arrogance, McDougall ordered the survey without local authority and in complete defiance of the existing river lot system. In spite of the misgivings which he had already communicated to McDougall, Lieutenant-Colonel John Stoughton Dennis, the officer in charge of the survey, ordered it to proceed. Now, before the very eyes of the Métis, Canada was tramping on their rights. All the fears and suspicions aroused by Dr. Schultz and the *Nor'Wester* were now being realized.

On October 11, 1869, on the land of André Nault at St. Vital, west of the Red, Louis Riel brought the survey to a halt. At the head of a party of eighteen unarmed Métis, he calmly told the surveyors that they could not proceed, standing on the survey chain in order to reinforce his point. His statement reflected the concern of the Métis and others of Red River over their lands: "The Canadian Government has no right to make surveys in the Territory without the express permission of the people of the Settlement."

From the outset, the struggle was one for recognition of the ownership of land. It was not one of race, language, religion, or political allegiance. These factors were brought into the affair from outside, clouding the issue almost beyond recognition; so much so, in fact, that the clouds have not yet been entirely cleared away. Though the issues were obscured in the events of 1869-70, the fact of leadership was never to be called into question. The acknowledged leader, from the moment he stopped the survey, was Louis Riel, then just eleven days short of his twenty-fifth birthday. Riel was not a conspirator and he did not encourage the Métis or the others in their disaffection with events to that time. The movement was there, the grievances were real, and the organization of an opposition had already begun. Riel simply breathed life into that movement and, to a considerable degree, made it his own.

Louis Riel was born at St. Boniface on October 22, 1844, the son of Jean-Louis Riel, the "miller of the Seine." He himself had little Indian blood (only one eighth), but he always considered himself a Métis. As a child, he showed promise in the Grey Nuns' school and was chosen by Bishop Taché to be sent, along with three other Métis, for further schooling at Montreal, which, it was hoped, would lead to the priesthood. Young Riel was brilliant, eloquent, and argumentative; but he was also moody, resentful of discipline, and of uncertain temper, especially when crossed. From 1858 to March, 1865, Riel pursued his studies at the College de Montréal, "*le petit seminaire.*" In January, 1864, his father died; but apparently Louis' presence was not required at home in St. Boniface. In 1865, it was mutually agreed that he had no vocation for the priesthood; though the mystic if unorthodox devotion to revealed religion which he had brought with him from Red River remained with him for the rest of his life.

After leaving *le petit seminaire,* Louis went to work in the Montreal office of Rodolphe LaFlamme, a strongly nationalistic and anticlerical Quebec lawyer who had been an active anticonfederate as an ally of A. A. Dorion. While so employed, Riel became engaged to be married; but when the young lady's parents heard of the proposed match, they managed to put a stop to it, not wanting a Métis in the family. To what degree the association with LaFlamme and the blighted romance may have affected him can only be guessed at. From Montreal, Riel went to Chicago and thence to St. Paul. Here, he may have worked for one of the firms that were engaged in freighting goods to Red River. Again, this is conjecture and nothing is definitely known. It has been established, however, that Riel left the Falls of St. Anthony in early July, 1868, arriving by steamboat at St. Boniface on July 28. He moved into his mother's house, which still stands in St. Vital, south of St. Boniface, near the Red River.

He now remained in the settlement, and there can be no doubt that he observed, absorbed, read, and listened. He knew the situation and was ready to act when the time came. He was the son of a leader of his people and he had the education which so many of them lacked. Already he was becoming convinced that it was his mission to save his people, the "New Nation," from being disinherited and dispersed. It was a conviction which grew and intensified until it finally destroyed him.

By this time, there had been many serious failures in communication. Generally speaking, only Ontario seemed directly interested in expansion to the northwest, and there was no measurable Quebec balance to the Ontario element already at Red River. The *Canadiens* and Métis at Red River could see no prospect of any sizeable influx of their *co-religionaires* from Quebec. By mere inaction, the Catholic Church in Quebec indicated disinterest and thereby aroused the anxiety of its clergy in Assiniboia.

More directly, the Government of Canada evinced no understanding of the local situation, though it could not claim to have been kept in ignorance. The ailing Mactavish went to Ottawa in the summer of 1869 both to seek and to offer advice. He came away saying: "Those gentlemen are of opinion that they know a great deal more about the country than we do." Bishop Taché, summoned to the Ecumenical Council of 1870 at Rome, paused in Ottawa in June, 1869, to seek some guarantee of the use of the French language and of the Catholic position in education in the coming changeover. He left feeling both unassured and uneasy. Joseph Howe, at one time the erstwhile opponent of Confederation in Nova Scotia and now secretary of state for the provinces in the Government of Sir John A. Macdonald, journeyed west in October 1869. He spoke to many of the local people, assuring them that all would be well and that everyone would share in the new government no matter what his origin or background. There are no grounds for the belief that he encouraged the Métis to resist. Either the facts of the Métis' concern over their land were not presented well (or were not presented at all) or the Government of Canada was impervious to suggestion. The latter, in the light of the historical record, would appear to be the more likely.

The Métis and other inhabitants of Red River were perhaps also guilty of poor communication. They stopped the survey without having first enquired if the Council of Assiniboia had approved of its being carried on. Just the same, it is not surprising that they should have neglected to consult the HBC government, since it had not held their respect for many years. J. S. Dennis did ask Father J. M. Lestanc, administrator for the absent Bishop Taché, to approve the survey. Lestanc refused to say either yea or nay on the question, but did tell Dennis that if he could reassure the Métis as to the security of their title to their lands, all would be well. Dennis, however, could give no such assurance.

The HBC in London was not consulted after the transfer had been arranged, nor did it inform Mactavish or any other officers in Rupert's Land of the terms of the transfer. On July 10, 1869, the HBC governor, Sir Stafford Northcote, wrote Governor Mactavish to the effect that he should grant approval for a survey by the Canadians, passing on a request of the Canadian government which had been made through the Colonial Office. On August 16, Mactavish wrote in reply that such a survey would likely cause trouble. Mactavish received no other relevant communication from the HBC before the issue was joined, nor did he receive any enlightenment from Ottawa. Northcote did write from London instructing Mactavish and all of the company's servants to co-operate with the incoming Canadian authorities, but the letter was dated October 19, 1869. Riel had set foot on the surveyor's chain more than a week before.

After forming the provisional government of Assiniboia, Riel claimed that it was the legal as well as the actual authority at Red River. This claim was rather an extravagant one, since neither Assiniboia nor Rupert's Land were without government of any kind. It is true that the Government of Canada could not exercise power before the transfer was accomplished, and that the HBC had abdicated its authority on fulfilling its agreement with the English government. This government, however, had enjoined the HBC to maintain its authority until the power of Canada in Rupert's Land had been confirmed. Unfortunately, no one at Red River was aware of this fine legal shading. Thus, in the fall of 1869, there was actually no more practical power of government at Red River then there was in Antarctica. Riel simply moved into the vacuum which power, like nature, abhors.

On receipt of the news of William McDougall's rebuff, Sir John A. MacDonald moved quickly to put out the fire – or at least to contain it – and to put the responsibility of his Government at a minimum. He cabled London to stop payment of the £300,000 and to delay the transfer until such time as order had been restored. His political sagacity warned him against picking up hot bricks, though the Imperial Government reminded him that he had a legal responsibility to fulfil the contract. In its turn, the Imperial Government recognized MacDonald's right to tread carefully. Macdonald followed up with immediate remedial action. McDougall was sent an urgent message ordering him to hold at Pembina and to do nothing until he should be advised from Ottawa. An appeal went to Rome for permission to have Bishop Taché excused further attendance at the Ecumenical Council and to return to Red River. Taché set off at once. Then Macdonald set to work, albeit somewhat belatedly, to set matters right at Red River. He arranged for the quick departure of two emissaries, men known and respected at Red River, whose mission was to inform the people there of Canada's good intentions. They were to assure them that they need fear no abrupt change, that their rights and privileges would be undisturbed, and that they would soon have some share in the government of the colony.

For the carrying of a definite offer to placate Red River, Macdonald chose Donald A. Smith, successor to Sir George Simpson as resident governor for the HBC in Canada. Smith was armed with a firm offer of generous terms and was empowered to deal with the "people of Red River" and to state that "in granting titles to land now occupied by the settlers, the most liberal policy will be pursued." He was also to invite the people to send delegates to Ottawa should it prove necessary to do so. The choice of Smith was a good one. He was then rising fifty, had been in the service of the HBC since 1838, was married to an English halfbreed, and was a shrewd and able man. The latter fact was demonstrated in his later career, which saw him as a major figure in the building of the CPR, an MP for Selkirk and then for a Montreal riding, Governor of the HBC, Canadian High Commissioner in London, Imperial Privy Councillor, and Lord Strathcona and Mount Royal at the time of his death in 1914. Smith, moreover, was the embodiment of the HBC, which was the only governing authority with which the people at Red River were familiar. He could be trusted to convince the settlers that Canada was their friend, to place money and offers of employment where it would do the most good, and, above all, to give away no more than was absolutely necessary in securing the peaceful transfer of Rupert's Land to Canada.

In the meantime, Riel was consolidating his position. On October 16, he met with his activist sympathizers at the home of Father J. N. Ritchot, parish priest of St. Norbert. Here, they organized *Le Comité National des Métis de la Rivière Rouge* with John Bruce as president and Louis Riel as secretary. The basis of organization was that of the buffalo hunt; whatever his title, Riel was "captain of the hunt" and his orders were to be obeyed. Bruce was only an ephemeral figure; he was president by virtue of his greater age and perhaps because of his wider acceptance by the mass of the Métis. Riel, however, was the motivating force, while Father Ritchot was always at hand to give advice, very often exceeding what might be deemed his proper ecclesiastic function in so doing.

On October 21, a party of horsemen was dispatched to Pembina to await the governor-elect. His progress from St. Paul had been noted, as had the fact that he carried a quantity of arms. When McDougall reached Pembina on October 31, he was greeted with an order of the *Comité National* which forbade him entry without its permission. He blustered, flaunted his authority to the impassive Métis, and insisted on moving on to occupy the HBC post on the Assiniboia side of the line. On November 2, he was escorted back into the United States by an armed party led by Ambroise Lépine. Coincidentally, Riel had seen to the erection of a barrier across the trail to Fort Garry immediately south of Rivière Sale (now La Salle) at St. Norbert. At this point, all those who sought access to the settlement were stopped and interrogated. On October 26, Bruce and Riel were summoned before the Council of Assiniboia to explain their actions. When questioned as to his intentions, Riel did not equivocate. He and his committee would allow no Canadian governor to enter Assiniboia until terms and conditions had been arranged with the settlers. He was acting in the best interests of all. Unmoved by the council's warning of "disastrous consequences," Riel would agree only to inform the council of his committee's views.

Riel's armed followers provided comforting strength, but they had to be fed and otherwise maintained. Fort Garry was a supply center and could therefore solve Riel's logistical problem. Fort Garry, however, was far more than a storehouse. It was, in fact, the nerve center of Red River; it had sturdy walls, cannon, and an armory, and it controlled access by land and water. If the master of Paris was the master of France, then even more so was the master of Fort Garry the master of Red River. On November 3, without prior warning, Riel's men quietly entered and took possession of the fort. The move was made quickly and peacefully, and Riel promised to respect all private property. Such inroads as were made on the resources of the HBC were carefully noted and in the end the company was reimbursed by the Dominion of Canada. Having achieved physical control of Red River, Riel now turned to the more difficult task of achieving assent to his course by the inhabitants of the area.

On November 6, Riel issued a call from Fort Garry to the English parishes to send twelve representatives "in order to form one body" with the Métis in discussing the future of Rupert's Land. The English-speaking whites and halfbreeds were far from being of one mind. They feared trouble, even violence, both from within and from without. They did, however, in the hope of a peaceful solution, send the delegates as requested. These were chosen by parish meetings and were roughly representative – more so, indeed, than was the Council of Assiniboia.

The delegates met on November 16. Riel presented a first List of Rights, upon which union with Canada could be accepted. The list was quickly forgotten in procedural wrangles. The English-speaking delegates demanded that a new president and secretary be chosen, but were turned down on the grounds that such a change would have to wait upon a decision as to a common course. James Ross, who came to be regarded as spokesman for the English-speaking delegates, deplored the barring of McDougall and the seizure of Fort Garry as smacking of rebellion. Riel replied, saying in French:

> If we are rebelling against the Company which is selling us and wishes to deliver us, and against Canada which wishes to buy us, we are not rebelling against English supremacy which has not given its approval for the final transfer of the country. . . . Even more we are faithful to our homeland. . . . We wish the people of Red River to be a free people. Let us help one another. We are all brothers, all kinsmen, says Mister Ross and this is true. Do not let us separate. See what Mister Mactavish says. He says that from this assembly can come incalculable good. Let us unite. The evil that he fears will not take place.

On this basis, the assembly continued to sit, Ross and the English settlers insisting that McDougall be admitted, Riel and the Métis adamant that he should not.

Riel now decided that he must take all authority into his own hands. After an all-night debate, he persuaded the Métis to accept the idea of a provisional government. Many were reluctant; their faith made them shy from rebellion against the state, even if individually they were rebellious against all forms of authority. Riel's proposal was put to the assembly on November 24. The English settlers demurred; they must consult their home parishes before going so far. They did not, however, reject the proposal of a provisional government out of hand. The assembly stood adjourned until December 1.

December 1, 1869, was the day officially set down for the transfer, which was now indefinitely postponed. At Pembina, a raging blizzard confirmed the early onset of winter. In spite of the warnings that he had received from Ottawa, McDougall entered Assiniboia and read into the howling wind the proclamation of his authority to govern in the name of the Queen. The winds scattered McDougall's words, but captured on paper they were posted on walls and trees in the settlement.

This was a challenge that Riel could not ignore. If the pretended authority of Canada could be made to prevail, his moves in defence of his people had all been made in vain. He did not wait upon events. On December 7, he moved against Schultz, who, in enthusiastic response to Dennis' call to arms, had barricaded himself and forty-five volunteer Canadians in his store. The store, situated on Main Street in the hamlet of Winnipeg, was surrounded by Métis, and two cannon were brought from the fort. Schultz was given fifteen minutes to surrender and promptly did so, whereupon he and his men were imprisoned in the fort. On the same day, Riel suppressed the *Nor'Wester* and its new-born rival, *The Red River Pioneer*. Then, on December 8, Riel issued the following declaration:

DECLARATION OF THE INHABITANTS
OF RUPERTS' LAND AND
THE NORTH WEST

It is admitted as a principal of morality that public authority exists of indubitable right; as it is also acknowledged that a people which has no government is free to adopt one form of government rather than another; to accept or refuse that which is proposed for it: it is on the ground of these two principles that the people of Rupert's Land and the North-West were content to suffer in silence, and to bear the kind of servitude in which the peculiar circumstances which surrounded their cradle had placed them.

A company of adventurers, known under the name of the Hudson's Bay Company, and vested with certain powers by His

Majesty Charles II had established themselves in Rupert's Land and in the North-West to carry on the fur trade. That Company consisted of an aggregation of men who had need of a constitution. But as the chief concern was trade that constitution was largely confined to it. As there was then, however, no government which was concerned with the interests of the people already established in the country, need was for that people to resort, in matters requiring judicial settlement, to the officers of that Company: such was the origin of the government which has ruled the country to the present time.

This government, so accepted, was far from meeting the needs of the population actually resident, which in virtue of its energy and devotion developed, grew and rose to the point at which it deserved, because of its numbers, its civilization and its commerce, a place among the nations.

Always moved by the principles set out above, the people of Rupert's Land and the North-West supported loyally the above mentioned government and obeyed it faithfully; when contrary to the law of nations in March, 1869, that government abandoned them and transferred to Canada, by certain negotiations, which it did not even deign to communicate to its people, all the rights which it had, and those it claimed to have in the country.

Now as it is another principle conceded by all publicists that a people becomes free, and can henceforth govern itself as it judges fit, when the sovereign to which it was subject abandons it, or subjects it against its will, to a foreign sovereign, and that, moreover, it transfers no right to the sovereign to which it subjects that people.

We, the representatives elected by the people, assembled in council at Fort Garry, after having invoked the God of Nations, relying upon these fundamental moral principles, declare solemnly, in the name of our constituents and in our own names, before God and before men:

1. That from the day on which the Government, which we have always respected, has abandoned us in transferring to a foreign power the sacred authority which had been entrusted to it, we are of right free and released from all obedience to it, and that the sole legitimate authority today in Rupert's Land and the North-West is the authority accorded provisionally by the people to us their representatives.

2. That we refuse to recognize the authority of Canada which pretends to have the right to come to impose on us a form of government still more contrary to our rights and to our interests than the government to which we have submitted of necessity until now.
3. That on the first of November last, when we despatched a delegation to conduct beyond the limits of our country His Honour William McDougall and his companions, who were advancing on our territory in the name of Canada without prior warning on his part, and in spite of a prohibition intimated to him by us, to come and govern here as an autocrat, we have only acted in conformity with the sacred right of all citizens to oppose themselves vigorously to the subjection of their native land.
4. That we continue and will continue to oppose Canada with all our energies, and the entry of the Canadian government in our country, under the form announced, and in case of persistence on its part to come to trouble us with warlike incursions, we protest beforehand against these unjust acts and declare it to be responsible before God and before all people for the incalculable misfortunes which would be the result of its ambitious rashness. Let it know that before seeing our country enslaved, we shall contrive to use the means of defence that Providence has put in our hands, and it is not to see it invaded by strangers that we have so often defended it, at the price of our blood, against the hordes of barbarians today become our friends and allies.
5. That notwithstanding the Dominion of Canada will always find us ready to enter with it on negotiations favourable to its enlargement and to our prosperity.
In support of these declarations, relying on Divine Providence, we commit by oath our lives our fortunes and our honour.

Given at Fort Garry December 8, 1869.

John Bruce, President
L. Riel, Sec.

Riel's legal grounds were not sound, no more than had been those of McDougall in his proclamation of December 1. Riel thus took power, but it was power based solely in his small band of Métis followers. Consent would follow if he managed to persuade his fellows at Red River that his was the proper course. In effect, Manitoba was born in December 8, 1869; the formalities of May 12 and July 15, 1870, were but the christening and baptismal rites.

8

Provisional Government

DECEMBER 8, 1869, THE DAY ON WHICH Riel issued his declaration, was also the day on which Donald A. Smith arrived at Fort Garry. Though restricted to the fort, Smith was able to talk with whomever he pleased and he soon achieved a following among those Métis and halfbreeds who opposed Riel. His principal support came from Charles Nolin and Pierre Leveillé, whom he convinced that being pro-Canadian did not necessarily entail working with the local Canadians. Riel insisted that Smith deal with the provisional government, but Smith would only discuss his mission with all the people. Rather than provoke a breakdown through the use of force, Riel reluctantly agreed to the mass meeting which Smith requested.

The first meeting was held on January 19, 1870, in the open square of Fort Garry before the governor's house. Though the temperature stood at twenty below zero, there was a large attendance from throughout the settlement. Smith had already gained a sympathetic following through his judicious use of words and money, and he now proceeded to describe himself to the assembled settlers as their friend, their relative through marriage, and the messenger of good will from Canada. For five hours, the crowd stood, stamped their feet, shivered, and filled the air with their frosty breath as the various documents were read by Smith and translated by Riel. Riel confined himself entirely to the function of interpreter and performed it well. The meeting adjourned as the brief daylight waned. It had gone well for Smith and for the Canadian cause. He apparently succeeded in convincing many of those present that Canada and the HBC would treat them well, and Riel now stood in some danger of being rejected by his own people.

During the night of January 19, Reverend J. M. Lestanc, the administrator of the diocese of St. Boniface, and Father Ritchot persuaded the Métis to stick with Riel. The clergy felt that a divided Métis were a danger to civil peace. Together, the Métis could more readily come to an understanding with the other inhabitants of Red River and thus achieve a better bargain with Canada. In the end, Rev. Lestanc and Father Ritchot successfully thwarted Smith's attempt to divide and rule.

On January 20, with the weather unchanged, the remainder of Smith's communications were quickly gone through and the crowd took special note of the specific assurances in Governor-General Lord Lisgar's letter to Governor Mactavish: "And the inhabitants of Rupert's Land, of all classes and persuasions, may rest assured that Her Majesty's Government has no intention of interfering with, or setting aside, or allowing others to interfere with the religions, the rights or franchises hitherto enjoyed, or to which they may hereafter prove themselves equal." This was spelled out even more clearly, for the particular concerns of Red River, by the reading of Joseph Howe's letter of December 7, 1869, to William McDougall: ". . . in granting titles to land now occupied by the settlers, the most liberal policy will be pursued."

Riel now took the platform. Smith had convinced his audience that Canada meant well toward Red River, but it was Riel who could translate that good intent into action. Donald A. Smith could spell out the way, but Louis Riel would command the progress of events. Smith had brought from Ottawa the basis on which the French and English of Red River could co-operate; but this co-operation could continue and strengthen only under Riel's leadership. Riel proposed, amid cheers, that an elected convention of forty representatives, twenty English-speaking and twenty French-speaking, be assembled to consider the proposals brought by Smith and to determine a course of action. The proposal was accepted, again amidst cheers, and the meeting adjourned in a welter of good feeling which even the weather could not chill.

Representation in the second assembly, as in the first, was based on the parishes. The number to be elected by each parish was based on population and was determined by a committee composed of men of both languages. Parish representation ranged from one to four members. Winnipeg objected to being included with St. John's and on

March 5 was granted separate representation. (This was only the first in the city's long litany of demands for a more adequate voice in the councils of the province.) The elections were duly held, formally and in accordance with the methods of the time. Riel's candidates were opposed in many of the French parishes, but only three anti-Riel candidates were returned: Charles Nolin, George Klyne, and Thomas Harrison. Riel was annoyed, since he had hoped for a united front among the Métis. The English-speaking delegates, including James Ross, Thomas Bunn, and Dr. C. J. Bird, were mostly moderates. The Canadian, Kenneth Mackenzie was returned for St. Mary's, Portage la Prairie; the Irish-American W. B. O'Donoghue was elected in Riel's interest in St. Boniface; and the American, Alfred H. Scott, won in Winnipeg over A. G. B. Bannatyne.

The convention met on January 26, a day later than had originally been planned. Riel showed no inclination to force issues or to arbitrarily assert his authority. He moved that Judge Black be chairman, though Black was by no means pro-Riel. Rather, he was highly respected by all elements. Riel also agreed to put aside the original list of rights. A new list was to be drawn up by a committee of six members of the convention (three French and three English), including James Ross, who was becoming more and more sympathetic to the provisional government, and Charles Nolin, who was not. The committee set to with a will and on January 29 the new list was presented to the convention. It paralleled the first in its demands for the recognition of land titles; money for schools, roads, and bridges; recognition of local rights and customs; and so on. It sought direct "steam communication" with Lake Superior, as well as a rail connection with the United States. There was to be a temporary, territorial-type government, borrowed from the example of the United States, to be replaced in a short time by provincial status. The territorial legislature would control all lands within a radius equal to the distance from Red River to the American border. This list was debated at length, clause by clause, and relatively amicably.

So things went until, on February 3, Riel proposed, in amendment, that the immediate grant of provincial status be sought. This was a token of Riel's essential lack of confidence in the intentions of Canada. As a province of Canada, Red River would, in the nature of things, control such matters as Crown lands and education. It was better that these be placed in local hands at the outset, rather than wait on the good will and good time of Canada. The convention would not go along with Riel in this matter. It was too much to undertake the complexities and expense of the provincial apparatus starting from scratch. The motion lost. The division was on a language basis and carried against Riel by the votes of the Métis opposition: Nolin, Klyne, and Harrison. Riel was displeased, but not yet enraged. His bitterness was increased by the Métis defectors, two of whom were his relatives. Riel then moved that the agreement between Canada and the HBC be set aside and that it be replaced by direct negotiation between Canada and Rupert's Land. This also was voted down. Riel gave way to his too-ready temper and railed against those Métis who had opposed him. Nolin answered to the effect that he was his own master and that they all owed the HBC much for past kindnesses. Riel shouted that the measure would pass no matter how the convention might now vote. The confused session was hastily adjourned.

Riel continued to act in anger. He was justly suspicious that Smith was working against him by putting Métis and halfbreeds on the HBC payroll. He placed the almost moribund Mactavish under guard and accused him also of plotting against the provisional government. Dr. Cowan was jailed, as was the sympathetic Bannatyne, whose continued presence in Fort Garry Riel viewed with suspicion. Tempers cooled, and on February 7 the convention met again in calm deliberation. Riel behaved well. The Canadian commissioners were heard in turn. It was learned from Smith that he had power from Ottawa, though only he new how much. Riel questioned him closely as to the demands in the list of rights, forcing Smith to reveal that he had little real power of negotiation but that he could invite the sending of delegates to Ottawa. All of the convention now saw that they were in a position to deal with Ottawa through their own representatives, and not through Smith.

On February 9, the convention agreed to the concept of the provisional government as already established. The lingering doubts of a reluctant few being quieted by the statement of Mactavish that they should "form a Government, for God's sake, and restore peace and order in the Settlement." With one change in personnel, the committee that produced the List of Rights was struck off to write a constitution for the provisional government. On February 10, it recommended an elective council of twenty-four, twelve from the French-speaking parishes and twelve from the English-speaking parishes. The executive was to consist of a president, a French and an English secretary, and a treasurer. The existing HBC quarterly court would be continued and James Ross would assume the chief justiceship. Riel was president, Thomas Bunn and Louis Schmidt were secretaries, and W. B. O'Donoghue was treasurer. Riel's name was proposed as a delegate to Ottawa, but he insisted on the presidency as of right. Charles Nolin agreed to accept Riel and the whole Provisional Government, provided that Mactavish, Cowan, and Bannatyne were released. The triumphant Riel at once agreed and promised the release of the remainder of Schultz's party, who were still locked up in Fort Garry. Agreement on the provisional government was reached at 11:00 P.M. and was greeted with cannon salutes and a display of fireworks (the latter being obtained from the Schultz store where they had been kept in anticipation of the advent of Governor McDougall). The usual austerity of the fort was relaxed, and everyone, with the exception of Riel, enjoyed a "revel" until the early hours.

On February 11, Riel, with the concurrence of the convention, named delegates to carry terms to and to negotiate with the Government of Canada at Ottawa. These delegates were: Father J. N. Ritchot, Judge John Black, and Alfred H. Scott. The choices were made so as to provide representation for French, English, and American interests. Ritchot had been at the center of events since the beginning and Riel had full confidence in him. Black, the last HBC Recorder of Rupert's Land, had held this position since 1862 and had a lifetime of service behind him. He held the confidence of all factions. Scott had been a bartender in Bob O'Lone's Red Saloon and was, no doubt, familiar with many local problems. It may be that the choice of Scott was made advisedly, as Riel had cast off such small influence as the Americans may have had. He no longer needed them as a counter in the game for recognition by Canada. The delegation, then, was made up on February 11; but its departure for Canada was delayed for more than a month as incipient success turned to genuine tragedy.

On January 9, Thomas Scott, Charles Mair, and ten other Canadian prisoners made their escape from Fort Garry. Riel's men conducted a house-to-house search and recaptured several of the escapees. Scott and two companions managed to struggle through the drifts and biting winds to Headingly, where they found refuge, proceeding to Portage la Prairie on January 15. Here, Scott helped raise some of the local people against Riel. On January 23, John Schultz made a lone escape, letting himself down from his cell by rope of buffalo hide which he fashioned with a knife that had been smuggled to him in a cake by the ever-resourceful Mrs. Schultz. The rope broke and Schultz seriously injured his ankles in the fall. In spite of his injuries, he crawled out of the fort as far as Kildonan – and this in February –

where he was hidden and treated by Robert MacBeth, a Councillor of Assiniboia and no friend of Schultz. Partially recovered, Schultz went on to Lower Fort Garry and there tried to raise a force against Riel.

Meanwhile, about one hundred men, under the reluctant command of Major Charles A. Boulton, assembled at Headingly en route to the "liberation" of Fort Garry. Here, they were delayed by a two-day blizzard and by admonitions from Kenneth Mackenzie and W. F. Lonsdale of the convention. Having suffered defections, the party carried on to the fort, after promising Boulton that they intended no more than to free Riel's prisoners. At the lower fort, Schultz had little success. The predominating sentiment there was a feeling of neutrality, largely the result of Riel's steady release of prisoners on their promise not to oppose the provisional government. Schultz did assemble a party of over a hundred, which he conducted as far as Kildonan. Here, he was stopped by desertions prompted by Riel's evident moderation, the pleas of the Protestant clergy, and the emptying of the cells at Upper Fort Garry.

The insurrection against Riel finally collapsed as the result of a deplorable accident. On February 16, a young and somewhat mentally-handicapped Métis named Norbert Parisien had been arrested by Schultz's men on suspicion of espionage. In escaping, he shot and killed Hugh Sutherland, son of John Sutherland of the convention, who came upon Parisien unexpectedly while crossing the ice of the Red. Parisien was recaptured and badly beaten; he died some days later. This gave pause to the would-be liberators of Fort Garry. The bereaved mother pleaded for peace, and Schultz's force melted away. With only one companion, Schultz departed overland to Duluth to bring the truth as he saw it to Canada. The Portage party decided to return home in a body, forced by heavy snow to take the trail through Winnipeg, where they were apprehended by Riel's men – filling, once again, the so-recently emptied cells. Boulton, as their leader, was charged with treason against the provisional government, tried, and condemned to be shot. Donald A. Smith, the parents of Hugh Sutherland, and others appealed to Riel and Boulton was reprieved, though still held in custody. Riel used Smith's intercession on behalf of Boulton to bind him to a promise to do nothing to impede the forthcoming negotiations with Canada. The threat of violence receded – but only momentarily.

There remained Thomas Scott. An Ulsterman, Scott had come to Canada in his late teens, had served in the Hastings County militia, and had moved west in 1869 with J. A. Snow and the road-building party. A man of pronounced Orange sentiments and of youthful bluster, he was of the same age as Riel. The two men also shared a violence of temper. Like Riel also, Scott was firmly wedded to the vociferous defence of his rights as he saw them. He had been a prime mover in the Portage expedition and was second only to Schultz in his loud support of the Canadian cause and in his denunciation of the Métis. As a prisoner, he did not learn the virtue of silence. His behavior was unrestrained and his language was vicious against his captors and their leader. Scott had viewed Boulton's caution as cowardice and Riel's conciliation of Boulton as more of the same. Scott, however, was wrong on both counts.

Riel, urged by some of his Métis advisors, determined on drastic punishment for Scott. His violent temper came into play together with a desire to dispel forever his own lingering doubts that his was the accepted power at Red River. On March 3, Scott was tried before a summary court on a charge of insubordination. It was the method of the buffalo hunt in dealing with malefactors, though the penalty was extraordinarily harsh. By a majority vote, Scott was found guilty and sentenced to death. The proceedings and the verdict, delivered by the president of the court, Ambroise Lépine, were explained to Scott, who understood no French, by Riel himself. As in the case of Major Boulton, appeals were made to Riel for clemency. Donald A. Smith, Reverend George Young, and Father Lestanc entered their pleas; but to no avail. Riel was adamant. The authority of his government must be respected and Scott must die. He was shot outside Fort Garry at noon, March 4, by a Métis firing squad.

There was no excuse for the murder. It put a blot on all of Riel's achievements, and it served to deprive him, for the better part of a century, of his proper place and title as "the father of Manitoba." This mad act – the result, perhaps, of his own incipient madness – pursued him for the rest of his tortured life. Riel's execution at Regina on November 16, 1885, was as much vengeance for the shooting of Scott on March 4, 1870, as it was for the treason of the Northwest Rebellion.

In Ontario, the drums of racial and religious bigotry had already been sounding a tattoo. The shooting of an Ontario Orangeman by a French Catholic brought the drumbeat to a crescendo. The Yahoos were loosed and the tragic division of Canada's founding races and religions was played out against the verdant background of the valley of the Red River. The only blood shed was that of Scott, but had words been bullets, hecatombs would have fallen on either side. Macdonald had already put in hand plans for a military expedition to Red River. Now it was to take on all the aspects of an Orange crusade. Even before the Red River delegates set out on their mission of peaceful union, the small military power of Canada, and especially of Ontario, was being mobilized.

At Red River, the shooting of Scott caused little more than a ripple of concern. If the execution had been necessary to ensure the acceptance of Riel's power, then it was successful. The great tragedy was that it was not necessary. All outstanding difficulties had been resolved; the people were united behind Riel and remained so. Those of the Canadians and Americans, even of the Métis, who did not accept the fact of provisional government either left the settlement or remained silent. Peace reigned until the arrival of the Wolseley Expedition in August. In Canada, there was no peace, and ripples from the East were to become deeply disturbing to Riel as spring turned into summer.

The elective council provided for by the convention was duly elected. The elections were conducted by public meetings, all males over twenty-one being entitled to vote. Nineteen of the twenty-four met as summoned at Fort Garry on March 9. Most had been members of the convention, but there were some new faces, particularly among the English. These included A. G. B. Bannatyne and William Fraser, for Winnipeg, and John Norquay, the future premier, from St. Anne's High Bluff. Riel addressed the council on the state of affairs in Assiniboia without mentioning the Portage la Prairie adventurers or the Scott affair. He did note the return of Bishop Taché, referring to him as another commissioner from Canada and warning that what Taché might have to say should be weighed carefully. His remarks were well received and the council adjourned until March 15.

On March 9, Taché had returned to St. Boniface in the company of Fathers Lestanc and Ritchot, having spent the previous night at St. Norbert. The bishop had spent some days in Ottawa, as requested by the Government of Canada, on his return from Rome. He had conferred with Sir John A. Macdonald and with Sir George Cartier and had left the capital on February 17, carrying letters from Macdonald and Joseph Howe promising amnesty for any incidents that may have been of doubtful legality. As the bearer of official tidings, Taché was not welcome to Riel, though the bishop had been his mentor and was much loved and respected by the Métis. Riel made no effort to restrain Taché, but he did post a guard at the episcopal palace. He also remarked of Taché: *"Ce n'est pas Monseigneur Taché qui passe, ce n'est pas l'Evêque de Sainte Boniface, c'est le Canada qui passe."* Louis did his best to keep the bishop isolated, fearing a further assault on his power and on the provisional government. His actions were already becoming somewhat aberrant.

Taché, whose sole interest seems to have been the welfare of his flock, went to Riel at Fort Garry on March 11. He told Louis that a general amnesty had been promised and that though the promise had been made prior to the shooting of Scott, he was sure that it would be honored by the Government of Canada. Taché also advised the immediate despatch of the delegates to Ottawa. Louis answered that he was no rebel against the Crown and that he had no other aim than "to arrive at an understanding with the Canadian authorities before entering Confederation." On the following Sunday, Taché preached in the cathedral to a packed congregation which included Riel and his soldiers. Taché asked for unity and moderation, promising that Canada would do all that was right.

Riel was for a time reassured and took steps to assert his and Assiniboia's loyalty to the British connection. The newspaper, *New Nation,* successor to the suppressed *Nor'Wester,* had begun to appear in January under the editorship of Major Robinson. From the outset, it was stridently annexationist, parroting the doctrines of the Minnesota expansionists. Even its advertisements were replete with eagles and the stars and stripes. It supported the provisional government, however, this being a condition of its being permitted to publish. Riel now took over the paper himself, installing Thomas Spence of Portage la Prairie as editor. The *New Nation* became as excessively pro-British as it had been pro-American. In April, the *fleur de lis* and shamrock flag of the provisional government was joined on a companion staff by the Union Jack, to the considerable discomfit of the Fenian, O'Donoghue.

The convention reassembled on March 15. The first order of business was to hear Bishop Taché tell of the promised amnesty and to read a telegram from Howe indicating the general acceptability of the terms of the second List of Rights as adopted by the convention in February. At the bishop's request, Riel released all prisoners within twenty-four hours. He also indicated his willingness to step aside for a Canadian governor on the achievement of satisfactory terms. The council then turned to other matters. A resolution denouncing England, Canada, and the Hudson's Bay Company for neglecting the rights of the people of Rupert's Land, and a resolution concerning loyalty to the Queen were debated and passed. A committee was named to draw up a constitution and code of laws for the "Provisional Government of Rupert's Land and the North-West Territory." This task kept the council gainfully employed for some time in spelling out the details of local ordinances and in revising those which had been carried over from the Council of Assiniboia. It is difficult to resist the suspicion that Riel deliberately kept the council occupied with these worthy diversions while he and the executive edited quite extensively the instructions that were to be carried to Ottawa by the designated delegates.

Together with Schmidt, Bunn, and O'Donoghue, all of whom he dominated, Riel drew up a third List of Rights. This list placed provincial status as the first necessary condition of union with Canada. Riel thus included the proviso which the convention had rejected. The new list also contained a demand that the Métis and halfbreeds be given grants of land as their share of the Indian title which still prevailed in Rupert's Land outside of the narrow limits of the Red River settlement. These additions were the result of Riel's increasing conviction that Métis land claims must rest on something more substantial than Canadian promises. Provincial status, which carried control of Crown lands under the terms of the British North American Act, was an ideal guarantee. This third List of Rights was again amended to form a fourth and final one which was carried east by Ritchot, Black, and Scott. The further amendments were most probably made at the suggestion of Taché and would provide the new province with a two-chamber legislature and a constitution similar to that of Quebec with a legally recognized bilingualism and, most important, a guarantee of the existing parochial school system. Article 7 demanded "that the schools be separate, and that public money for schools be distributed among the different religious denominations in proportion to their respective population according to the system of the Province of Quebec." The new province's French and Catholic population was to be protected against the possible overturning of the existing balance between the two major languages and religions by any migratory movement from Ontario.

This final List of Rights was accepted by the delegates to Ottawa without any comment being recorded – if any comment there was. Judge Black had objected for a time to being the emissary of the provisional government (his HBC blood ran strong in him), but apparently neither he nor his fellow delegates raised any objections to the changes that had been made by Riel and the executive. Riel also asked Ritchot to see that the new province bore the name "Manitoba" rather than "Assiniboia," since he visualized a much greater territorial limit to his creation that that of the HBC district. Riel's choice of name stood, though the suggestion may have come from Bishop Taché. The name "Manitoba" was more acceptable to Macdonald, since it was relatively unknown and had not figured in the recent difficulties – thus having none of the unpleasant associations of defiance and insurrection carried by the name "Assiniboia."

Armed with the fourth List of Rights and with formal commissions from the provisional government, the three delegates departed for Ottawa on March 22. Judge Black, travelling separately from the other two, arrived at the Canadian capital on April 17. The journey of Father Ritchot and Alfred H. Scott, however, had a more dramatic conclusion. They were arrested when they reached Ottawa on a warrant which had been obtained by Hugh Scott and which charged them with the murder of his brother, Thomas. Hugh Scott's action was taken at the inspiration of those who were aroused against Riel by the speeches and writings of Charles Mair and John Schultz, late of Fort Garry, and of Col. George T. Denison of the Canada First movement. Father Ritchot and A. H. Scott were held under house arrest in the palace of the Bishop of Ottawa until released through intervention of the Canadian authorities on April 23.

By this time, the Orange clamor in Ontario had become so great and so widespread that Macdonald and Cartier dared not receive the delegates openly or as representatives of the provisional government. Since Smith had invited them in his official capacity as an agent of the Dominion of Canada, Macdonald and Cartier had to accept them as representatives of the people of Rupert's Land. The two first Fathers of Confederation had to move carefully, not only to secure the safe birth of their new child, but also to prevent a family rupture between the two senior provinces, Ontario and Quebec. The extremity of the Orange reaction had produced a further reaction in Quebec. Its people came naturally to the defence of their French-speaking *co-religionaires* in the West. If, in the course of helping out their western friends, they could thwart the erection there of a new Ontario – or alternately, if they could encourage the erection of a new Quebec – so much the better.

Macdonald and Cartier determined to settle the matter without risk of further thunder from the West. The Red River delegates were received on April 25 and a satisfactory result obtained on May 2. This agreement, which received royal assent on May 12 as the Manitoba Act, was both a triumph and a disappointment to Riel and the provisional government. Provincial status was obtained, but the province was restricted to the settled areas of the valleys of the Red and Assiniboine. Rightly, it was called the "postage stamp province." Nevertheless, it was a province. The fifth province of Canada was to stretch from the American border to the present Boundary Creek, north of Winnipeg Beach, east to a line running just beyond Beauséjour, and west to thirty miles beyond Portage la Prairie. The vast and empty remainder, the Northwest Territories, was to be administered by Ottawa as its unquestioned fief. Manitoba was to have control of education, to have a responsible government with a bicameral legislature, courts, and other provincial institutions, plus the subsidies given other provinces. It would be represented in the Senate by two members and in the House of Commons by four. In the same way that it was truncated in area, so too was Manitoba cut down in power. Control of Crown lands, enjoyed by other provinces, was to be retained by Ottawa, "for the purposes of the Dominion." Macdonald wanted a Pacific railway and he did not wish any impediment, such as a contrary-minded provincial authority, to stand in its path.

The vexing question of Métis and halfbreed lands, which had been the root cause of the whole resistance at Red River, was settled to the initial satisfaction of the new Manitobans. Existing holdings within the province would be recognized and titles issued. In addition, the Métis were granted a share in the new Northwest Territories, where the Indian title had yet to be extinguished. The Métis were not to be regarded as Indians and made wards of the state. They were to receive 240 acres for each child of a halfbreed head of a family. They were to be given lands as settlers and as descendants of the aborigines. They could farm or do as they pleased with their land. The hope was that they would settle down on the land, become farmers, and, in due time, form part of a thriving western agricultural society.

Their work done, Black and Scott left the scene. Judge Black went to England in well-earned retirement and Alfred Scott settled in New York. It was left to Father Ritchot to carry the Manitoba Act back to Fort Garry for the approval of the provisional government. He had sought a written amnesty for all irregularities, including the murder of Scott, but had been put off. Cartier, filling in for the ailing Macdonald, made verbal gestures and ended by saying that it was a matter for the Imperial Government to decide, since Canada had no jurisdiction. Sir John Young, then governor-general and soon to be elevated to the peerage as Lord Lisgar, had no instructions from London and could say only that he believed that an amnesty would be forthcoming and that it would reach Red River before Ritchot did. The aroused state of opinion in Ontario made the question of an amnesty a very hot one politically. Any premature announcement would have been considered as coddling of treason and would have heaped hot coals on the heads of the Canadian government.

Father Ritchot reached Fort Garry on June 17, to be greeted by an enthusiastic crowd of 1,000 and a 21-gun salute. On June 24, the legislative assembly of the Provisional Government met in the fort. Riel introduced Ritchot, praised his work, and translated his statement of the terms of the Manitoba Act into English. Ritchot also repeated what he had been told about the amnesty being an Imperial matter, adding that it was well in hand. Immediately thereafter, on a motion by Louis Schmidt and Pierre Poitras, it was unanimously carried that "the Legislative Assembly of this country do now, in the name of the people, accept the Manitoba Act."

Even before the Manitoba Act had passed all stages in the Parliament of Canada, the Wolseley Expedition to "restore order" at Red River was en route. It was a regretted but necessary move on several counts. Had an official military mission not been sent, there was the danger that Ontario hotheads such as George Denison would raise and lead a force of irregulars to the west to punish the "traitors." The Manitoba Act was regarded in many quarters, and especially in Ontario, as rank submission to the *Canadiens* and the Catholic Church. A full-scale military operation would show that Canada was not truckling to treason. The force itself consisted of about 1,000 men drawn equally from regular Imperial forces and from Quebec and Ontario battalions. The ranks of the Second Quebec Rifles, however, contained only 77 men of *Canadien* origin out of a total of 362. The infantry force was augmented by a battery of the Royal Field Artillery, a company of engineers, a supply column, and hospital corps personnel. It was assembled at Toronto, went by rail to Collingwood, and from there by steamer; after a delay at Sault Ste. Marie, imposed by American reluctance to pass military supplies and personnel through their canal, they were debarked at Prince Arthur's Landing at the western end of Lake Superior. From here, the men struggled through the inhospitable rock, brush, and muskeg to Lake Shebandowan, where a stockaded base camp was constructed. Then they proceeded along the route that had been pioneered by La Vérendrye and developed by the North West Company through Rainy Lake, Rainy River, Lake of the Woods, Winnipeg River, Lake Winnipeg, and the Red River, arriving at Lower Fort Garry on August 22.

As the Wolseley Expedition made its mosquito and blackfly infested way, it lost neither its Orange fervor nor its desire for revenge for the murder of Thomas Scott. Wolseley himself began to sound more like an avenging Roman proconsul than a restorer and guarantor of peace. Manitoba's first Orange Lodge was formed as the force moved westward. At Red River, Riel was alternately apprehensive and enthusiastic about the coming of Canadian power. Taché was uneasy about the amnesty and went to Ottawa, receiving no more assurance than had Ritchot. Failing here, he sought the early departure of the lieutenant-governor to ensure the establishment of a civil administration before the advent of the military. Here also, he failed. Delay, and the political necessity of the lieutenant-governor's entering his domain via Canada, meant that Wolseley would arrive first.

Still uneasy, Taché returned to Red River. He did not communicate his uneasiness to Riel. The bishop did not have any quarrel with the choice of lieutenant-governor. He was Adams George Archibald, a Nova Scotian and a veteran of the Confederation movement who had served at Charlottetown, Quebec, and London in the formation of the Dominion of Canada. He was, as a maritimer, tarred neither with the brush of Ontario nor that of Quebec. He bore a deserved reputation as an able administrator and a just and compassionate man. He amply sustained that reputation in his two years as lieutenant-governor of Manitoba and the Northwest Territories.

The progress of the Canadian troops did not go unobserved by Riel; his scouts reported as they passed each lake or portage. With these reports came rumors that Riel's life and those of the members of his government would be endangered, even forfeit, when the troops arrived. The Fenian O'Donoghue urged Riel to make a fighting stand at Rainy Lake, at Rat Portage, or on the Winnipeg River. His peculiar logic saw a new day for Ireland in any and all reverses to British arms. His proposals, most unchristian for a former Christian Brother, were thrust aside. Riel wanted, as always, a peaceful transfer. He had made plans to send a welcoming delegation of some hundreds of his men to meet Archibald at the northwest angle of Lake of the Woods and then, for reasons unknown, abandoned them. The return of Taché was anxiously awaited. While Riel waited and fretted, his uneasiness was communicated to those around him and to the settlement. It was not the dread of the unknown that had existed in the fall of 1869; but the oncoming Canadian power was not viewed as an unmixed blessing. There was a general air of disquiet. In this period, July 15, 1870, came and went; Manitoba was now a province of Canada. This fact, if known, went unnoted at Red River. Louis Riel remained in control, but he was increasingly racked by indecision.

Taché reached St. Boniface on August 23, just as Wolseley was moving upriver from Lower Fort Garry. Riel went to the bishop's house at once and was there told that the Canadian government had agreed to the amnesty, though not in writing. That night, the troops camped within six miles of the fort in a driving rain which persisted throughout the night and into the morning. Louis was disturbed at his breakfast by a horseman from Kildonan who warned him that the troops were advancing on the fort, deployed for a fight and swearing to lynch the president and his government. As the thin red line advanced from the north, Riel, O'Donoghue, and two others fled through the south gate and took the ferry to St. Boniface. Wolseley cautiously entered the empty fort, raised the Union Jack, and fired a salute to his victory. Riel paused at Taché's home and informed the the bishop that he had deceived him. He then proceeded to the home of his mother at St. Vital. As the Canadian troops began to search him out, he slipped away to St. Joseph, in Dakota Territory. The executive faded away, as did Louis, and most members of the legislative assembly of the provisional government remained discreetly out of sight.

Wolseley took charge. He did not wish to impose martial law and carried no civil power. He asked Donald A. Smith to act as temporary governor until the arrival of Archibald. Smith's only recorded act was to issue a warrant for the arrest of Riel. Before the lieutenant-governor arrived, the long-deprived soldiery, the volunteers especially, made the best of such amenities as Winnipeg had to offer. The Red Saloon, Monchamp's, and Dutch George Emmerling's did a roaring business. Bob O'Lone of the Red Saloon died in a barroom brawl, a martyr to both Manifest Destiny and Fenianism. André Nault was ambushed, beaten, and left for dead. Elzéar Goulet, who had been a member of the Scott court martial, was recognized on the street in Winnipeg and was pursued by a crowd of Canadians; he drowned while attempting to escape by swimming the Red. The soldiers felt cheated of their prey. Anti-Riel and anti-Métis sentiment was high and Wolseley was unable to contain it. More blood was shed in the nine days between the arrival of Wolseley and that of Archibald than had been shed in the nine months of the provisional government. Archibald arrived on September 2, taking over from Smith the same day. The organization of the new province could now begin.

9

The Formative Years

THE CONVENTION OF THE PROVISIONAL GOVERNMENT had balked at seeking provincial status because there was nothing on which to build – no treasury, no system of local government, and no body of educated or experienced men to undertake the tasks of administration. In spite of these and even more substantial political obstacles, Manitoba was, thanks to Louis Riel, a province of Canada and its problems had to be faced and solved. Lieutenant-Governor Archibald did very well with that little with which he had to work. He created and set in motion the machinery of government, guiding it closely at all times and avoiding indentification with any group, including those of Schultz and Riel. In forming a government, Archibald was assisted by some of the natives of Red River, men such as A. G. B. Bannatyne, John Sutherland, William Fraser, John Norquay, Pierre Delorme, Patrice Bréland, and James McKay. The Britishers and Canadians were represented by Alfred Boyd, Thomas Howard, and Henry J. Clarke. More important to the initial organization of the Government of Manitoba was a group of *Canadiens,* known collectively as "Cartier's young men," though their average age in 1870 was thirty-four. This group moved west in 1870, abetted by George Etienne Cartier. In this, Cartier acted at the urgent solicitation of Bishop Taché, who was anxious that French Canada share in the launching of Manitoba. Chief among these *Canadiens* were Joseph Royal, A. A. C. Larivière, Marc A. Girard, and Joseph Dubuc. These men, all lawyers, had great influence on the framing of Manitoba's constitution. The constitution, in fact, is modelled on that of Quebec.

On September 20, 1870, Alfred Boyd and Marc Girard were appointed by Archibald to be executive councillors and Manitoba's first government. As senior executive councillor, Boyd is regarded as being Manitoba's first premier; but for all practical purposes, both Archibald and his successor, Alexander Morris, were their own first ministers. The new executive saw to the taking of a census. Then, on the strength of that census, it laid out constituencies and conducted the election of a legislative assembly. The census indicated a population of 558 Indians and 11,405 whites and halfbreeds. The halfbreeds consisted of 5,757 Métis and 4,083 English halfbreeds. Of the 1,565 whites, 747 were natives of Red River, 294 had been born in Canada, and the remaining 525 were of British or American birth. As to religious denomination, the population was almost equally divided, there being 6,247 Catholics and 5,716 Protestants. The constituencies followed the same parish lines as had been used in the selection of the Provisional Government. There were twelve French-speaking and twelve English-speaking parishes, and the members who were elected represented a fair cross section of the population in these areas. Included were men such as Norquay, Bannatyne, Schmidt, and Delorme, who had been members of the assembly of the Provisional Government, and even Donald A. Smith, who was returned in Winnipeg-St. John's over Dr. Schultz. Of the twenty-four members, some seventeen could be considered sympathetic to the former provisional government and its leader.

In January, 1871, the executive council was enlarged to include the following members: H. J. Clarke, a Montreal Catholic, as attorney-general; Thomas Howard, a Quebec Protestant, as provincial secretary; and James McKay, an English-speaking halfbreed, as president of the executive council. Clarke's administration, as it was commonly called, summoned the second chamber of the legislature into short-lived existence. Manitoba's legislative council was representative of the groups of people within the province, but it soon proved redundant and expensive and was prevailed upon to vote itself out of existence in 1876. Colin Inkster, its last speaker, served with distinction as sheriff until the mid-1920's.

The legislature held its first session, beginning March 15, 1871, in the home of Bannatyne. The council chamber of Fort Garry was not used (perhaps because of its association with Riel and the provisional government), but the tradition of Red River was maintained. The mace, symbol of royal power, was carved from a portion of the flagstaff of the fort and the hub of a red river cart. Joseph Royal was elected first speaker of the legislative assembly and James McKay of the legislative council. The session lasted six weeks and produced a tidy crop of forty-three bills, which, on receiving royal assent through Archibald, provided the province with the sinews of government. A system of public schools was set up on the model of Quebec's separate schools, a system of courts on the British model, and statute law on the model of Ontario. The constitution of Manitoba may have been based on that of Quebec, but the law of Manitoba was to be English, not French – nor would it be developed out of the local forms of the Council of Assiniboia or the provisional government.

A few settlers came from Ontario in 1871, but not in the numbers that had been hoped for by Ottawa. The lure of free land served by railways caused many to remain in Iowa, Minnesota, or Dakota Territory, as was to be the case for decades to come. Land surveying was begun again, after the long delay occasioned by Riel, but this time the surveyors were instructed to respect the river-lot system wherever that system existed. Gilbert McMicken established the Dominion Land Office, Métis titles were cleared, and land grants were made.

The generally even tenor of affairs was disturbed by the appearance of a Fenian threat from the United States in the fall of 1871. The Fenian Brotherhood, an Irish-American organization, was dedicated to freeing Ireland, a function which they equated with attacking English power wherever and whenever they had the chance. They were possessed by a sense of dedication as great as that of the Orange Order, though directed, of course, in the opposite direction. W. B. O'Donoghue, erstwhile treasurer of the provisional government, had never despaired of striking a blow for Ireland by delivering Red River into the hands of the Americans. Rebuffed by Riel and the Métis, he got in touch with a group of Fenian "generals" in order to arrange a raid into Manitoba – which province, he assured them, would rise up in the American cause. The province rose, all right, but in support of Canada and the British connection. Riel himself returned to St. Boniface and, together with Ambroise Lépine, organized a force of some four hundred, which he offered to Archibald. Archibald accepted gratefully and thanked Riel personally, over the highly-vocal opposition of Schultz, Denison and Orange Ontario. The Fenian raid was a fiasco. Warned by American Consul James W. Taylor, Captain Wheaton of the United States Cavalry expelled the Fenians from the HBC post on American territory at Pembina, dispersing them without firing a shot.

It had been piously hoped in government circles at Ottawa that the whole Riel-Scott business would be quietly forgotten, but the Fenian Raid brought it again to the fore. Archibald was reviled in the English press for courting the "traitor" Riel; at the same time, he was praised in the French newspapers for his far-sightedness and good common sense. The incident helped to reinforce good relations among those native to Red River, but it roused more racial and religious trouble in the East. The promised amnesty to Riel and the others of the provisional government became a political impossibility. Taché, who was elevated to be archbishop in September, 1871, insisted that a full amnesty had been promised. However, both Macdonald and Cartier, alert to the political danger of further antagonizing Ontario, assumed an air of injured innocence and lied through their teeth. Archibald took no direct action to apprehend Riel, Lépine, or any other of the "criminals" of 1869-70. His successor, Morris, finally issued warrants for their arrest in 1874. Lépine was captured, tried for the murder of Scott, and sentenced to hang. After much popular clamor, both for and against carrying out the sentence, the governor-general, Lord Dufferin, commuted the sentence to two years' imprisonment, or five years' banishment and loss of political rights.

Meanwhile, Louis Riel was harassed in mind and sick at heart. His was the great disappointment of the rejected hero. He was not rejected by the Métis, to whom he was always the *non pareil*; but he had hoped, in spite of many indications to the contrary, that he would be taken for the great man he felt himself to be. Instead, the Province of Ontario put a price of $5,000 on his head, and many citizens of that province vowed that they would do the job without the reward. Riel was twice returned to the House of Commons for Provencher, and twice expelled – the second time as an outlaw. Like the Biblical David, he had to flee from his enemies, and he assumed the name David in addition to his own. He drifted between mental hospitals in Quebec and the homes of friends in New York and New Hampshire, finally settling as a school teacher at St. Peter's Mission on the Sun River in Montana Territory. Here, he married and became an American citizen. He did not, however, forget his people, the "New Nation," or his hopes for their greatness. When they called him for help from the Saskatchewan River in 1884, he went to their aid. He died a traitor's death at Regina, a victim of mental breakdown and the harsh realities of Canadian politics. He spoke the simple truth when, in the course of his trial, he said: "I know before God, that I am the father of Manitoba."

Well before Riel's final departure from his province, his people had been slipping away to the north and west to new Métis settlements on the Saskatchewan. They preferred the life of the plains hunter to that of the farmer. Their Red River environment was confining and their livelihood was gone. The day of the buffalo hunt was over even before that of Canada had begun. After the complete failure of the hunt of 1868, the buffalo had never returned to the Red River hunting grounds in their former numbers. The biannual hunt continued to be mounted until after the province was created, but there was much more hunting than finding. For a variety of reasons, the buffalo were rapidly approaching extinction. Only small and scattered remnants of the once mighty herds were reported in the 1870's, and the last report of an unconfined buffalo in Manitoba was made in November, 1883, on the outskirts of the town of Souris, where a lone bull was sighted.

Manitoba now began to develop an identity that was far different from the old role of Red River as the source of sustenance for the fur trade. The province turned to the more prosaic but nonetheless precarious occupation of agriculture, though it did not depart from its historic role as a crossroads and distribution center. In fact, these functions were to increase to an unprecedented degree in its new Canadian context. The junction of the Red and the Assiniboine was still the focus of affairs. The routes into the West from the south and east converged there, and settlements fanned out from the new city of Winnipeg. Winnipeg became the source of supplies and the market through which the products of the farm were sent to eastern Canada and to the world at large. Imports rose from just under $1,250,000 in value in 1872 to just over $2,250,000 in 1874. Exports were not as high, but showed healthy increases. In October, 1876, the first shipment of wheat to the East was made by Higgins & Young, erstwhile dry goods merchants. After some difficulties, 857 bushels of wheat were gathered from the adjoining farms of Kildonan, Springfield, and Rockwood and forwarded by steamboat and rail to Duluth and by lake boat to Toronto. It may be noted, in this regard, that the initial price of the grain was eighty cents a bushel while freight charges were thirty-five cents a bushel. From the outset, the ratio of freight costs to grain price was to be the subject of acrid comment.

From the very start, Winnipeg tended to outgrow the West that sustained it. The new city enjoyed a prosperous birth based on a wave of immigration which transformed Manitoba out of all recognition. This coincidence of prosperity and immigration was to be a feature of Winnipeg's continuing development. (Although the city became a firm believer in the virtues of immigration, it did not easily reconcile itself to the resultant polygot population.) In 1870, there were less than three hundred residents and the town's thirty-odd buildings, were scattered along the wide muddy tracks which were later to become Main Street and Portage Avenue. By 1875, the city boasted a population of 5,000 and more than 1,000 buildings. Its citizens were occupied with a multiplicity of things, and the somewhat "wild west" atmosphere of 1870 was rapidly giving way to a sophistication more worthy of what was already being heralded as "the new Chicago." The streets remained quagmires during wet spells, but there were a few stone pavements to supplement the boardwalks. Real estate offices outnumbered both churches and saloons by far. The Red River, as yet unbridged, was crossed by several ferries, including one that was powered by steam. The steamboat docks by Fort Garry on the Assiniboine, and at the foot of Water Street on the Red, were kept busy all summer with freight moving in from the south and out to the west. Steam-powered grist mills and lumber mills, breweries and bakeries, banks and insurance offices, hardware and harness shops – all pointed to the inevitability of progress.

Winnipeg achieved corporate status late in 1873, having previously had no formal existence. There was some opposition to the move in the legislature and this was not overcome until after an unfortunate contretemps in which Mr. Speaker Bird was tarred by some irate would-be city fathers (who somehow spared the feathers). The mayor and council were elected and assumed office in January, 1874. Only one councillor, Alderman Alexander Logan, was a native of Red River – though two of his colleagues had arrived before the troubles of 1860-70. The mayor, Francis Evans Cornish, was an Ontario man who presided over council and magistrate's court with an easy grace and insouciant manner.

Immigration to Manitoba in the 1870's was not great when considered in relation to that which was to take place at the end of the century; nor did it compare with contemporary settlement in adjoining areas of the United States. It was, however, revolutionary in its impact on a community which had so recently been isolated in the fastness of North America. The population of the province more than tripled, with the accompanying increase in business activity which we have already noted. Towns appeared where trading posts and missions had been, or arose *de novo* on the rivers or the plain. Of greater importance, however, was the proliferation of farm communities. The initial policy of the Dominion, had been to set up a series of reserves for various groups. The Métis and halfbreed reserves were established first and proved far from successful, since the plainsman resisted the burden of the plow. There were also reserves of land for *Canadiens* from Quebec or for those induced to return to Canada from the temptations of the mill towns of Massachusetts and Connecticut. These reserves, located along the east bank of the Red at Letellier and St. Jean Baptiste, attracted all too few settlers in view of the expectations of the promoters and the investment made by the federal government. The reserve system of block grants for specific groups was soon abandoned as a general policy, though it did prove successful with two particular groups of people.

The Mennonites had long farmed successfully in the Russian Ukraine. However, under Alexander II, the Tsar Liberator, they were persecuted as a result of their devout resistance to military service. Firm in their faith, they sought a safe refuge for its preservation. With the help of the Ontario Mennonite, Jacob Shantz, they chose land in Manitoba. In 1873, the Dominion of Canada set up the so-called Eastern Reserve, to the east of the Red, centering on what is now Steinbach. The Mennonite pioneers arrived at Winnipeg in August, 1874, exciting comment with their strange language, outlandish dress, and Yankee-like hard bargaining. There were one or two instances of open violence against the unwelcome strangers, but the Mennonites paid in gold, and money is welcome everywhere. Thus, they were quickly accommodated with equipment and animals, and were soon busy building their closely-knit villages and setting an example of diligence which should have been a lesson to other Manitobans. They did set one example that was eagerly, if not gratefully, followed. They were the first to farm successfully on the open prairie. They knew the techniques of dry farming from their Russian experience, and that knowledge placed all prairie farmers in their debt. In 1876, a second or Western Reserve was established, centering on Morden; by 1879, there were close to 7,000 settled on the two reserves. In time, they were to give up their old ways if not their old faith, and to mingle with the general community.

Icelanders arrived coincidentally with the Mennonites, but entered more quickly into the diversity of the life of Manitoba and Canada. In 1873, an eruption of the volcano Hecla had covered their Icelandic pastures with lava and volcanic ash, thus destroying their means of existence. They first sought land in Ontario, but were unimpressed with the land they saw at Muskoka. They then moved west, where, under the aegis of Jon Sigurdsson, they chose land on the west shore of Lake Winnipeg, just north of the then northern boundary of Manitoba. Here, they hoped to find an ideal combination of farming and fishing. The Icelandic Reserve, or New Iceland, centered on the town named Gimli – the Icelandic word for "paradise." In the fall of 1875, the first party of 285 arrived at their new home. They rivalled the Mennonites in their hardihood and self-sufficiency, and surpassed all in their devotion to learning and in the speed with which they mastered English. By 1881, they numbered just over seven hundred and no group in Manitoba has had a greater and more beneficial influence in proportion to its initial numbers.

Until the mid-1870's, immigrants arrived quite steadily from Ontario and, to a lesser degree, from the United Kingdom and the United States. Their numbers then began to decrease as the world-wide economic depression made itself felt. Initially, the depression had begun to exercise a stifling effect on all economic activity as early as 1872, but it was not discernible in Manitoba for some four or five years thereafter. Come it did, however, and its blight remained until almost the end of the century. The new province had benefited from the coincidence of agricultural expansion and the disappearance of the buffalo hunt. It profited also by the techniques of farming the open plains which had been introduced by the Mennonite. In time, the province was to gain even more by the introduction of new grain varieties, milling techniques, and methods of grain handling. All these things, however, were to lie in abeyance for some years as the world waited out the long period of economic gloom.

It was also during the 1870's that the milling industry was revolutionized by the introduction of chilled-steel rollers in the place of millstones. Thus, for the first time, hard spring wheats such as Red Fife could be easily milled and a high-grade flour obtained. Since it is early maturing, Red Fife promised a fair chance for a successful crop and was so much in demand by millers as to make Manitoba No. 1 Hard a universal standard of excellence. At the same time, the handling of grain, particularly in the United States, began to undergo a great change. It was observed that in vast quantities grain could be handled as though it were a liquid; it was easier to pour grain from farm cart to box car to ship's hold than it was to bag it and manhandle it. Thus, the system of line and terminal elevators was constructed. All of this, however, pivoted on transportation, and transportation meant the railway. Only a national rail line could give Canada the central nervous system which would make a transcontinental dominion viable. Only rails could bring men in large numbers to the West and give them reason to remain there to raise grain and other crops. Railways had been fundamental to the politics of Confederation, and railways were to loom large in the affairs of Manitoba until well into the twentieth century.

At first, the prospects for rail connection with the eastern provinces appeared excellent. In 1872, the Government of Sir John A. Macdonald entered into a contract for the construction of a Pacific railway. In 1873, however, the whole deal went awry with the revelations of "the Pacific Scandal." It was revealed that during the election of 1872, Macdonald had accepted campaign contributions from Sir Hugh Allen, head of the Pacific railway syndicate. The situation was by no means unusual, nor was it confined to Sir John and his Liberal-Conservative Party. In this case, however, the complicity of his Government was so obvious that Macdonald resigned in order to avoid its defeat in the House of Commons. His Liberal successor, Alexander Mackenzie, was returned in a general election in 1874. Already, the general economic distress had weakened the far from robust Canadian financial structure, and Mackenzie determined that such an ambitious project as the Pacific railway was too much to undertake under the circumstances. A policy of piecemeal construction, on a "pay as you go" basis, was therefore decided upon.

This was a disappointment to Manitoba, but not a shattering one. Donald A. Smith had joined with James Hill, an Upper Canadian, and the two, with the help of Norman Kittson and George Stephen, had purchased the assets of the bankrupt St. Paul & Pacific Railway from its Dutch bondholders. They renamed it, more modestly, the St. Paul, Minneapolis & Manitoba, and began a line northward from Glyndon, just east of Moorhead. This line was intended to connect with a line running south to the border from the junction of the Red and Assiniboine. Financial delays on both sides of the boundary held things up until 1877, and the line from St. Boniface, connecting with the St. Paul, Minneapolis & Manitoba at St. Vincent, was not completed until December 3, 1878. The first train arrived at St. Boniface December 9, 1878. The lack of a bridge over the Red to Winnipeg had to wait on events, but its absence was no insurmountable obstacle. From late in November until mid-March, a line of track supported by double-length ties was laid on the ice of the Red River. By this means, trains crossed freely to connect with the lines built by the Mackenzie Government.

Before the American rail connection was made, the political wheel had turned and Macdonald was once again at the head of affairs at

Ottawa, where he was to remain until his death in 1891. His victorious appeal to the Canadian electorate was based on the "National Policy." Macdonald was determined that the railway to the Pacific be built in order that the nation might exist independent of the American transportation system. To make the Pacific railway an economic asset, it was to be coupled with the settlement of the West and with the establishment of Canadian industry in the East under the protection of tariffs. The story of the successes and failures of the National Policy is largely the history of Manitoba and of western Canada in general. With a rail connection to the East by the beginning of 1879, and with the sure promise of rails west to the Pacific, Manitoba embarked on its first great period of enthusiastic overexpansion – the boom of 1880-82.

This period was an intensification of the expansion of the mid-1870's on a scale which was unprecedented in Canadian history. For a short time, the sky was the limit. Winnipeg was again "the new Chicago," and speculation drove the prices of lots on Portage Avenue or Main Street above the going rate for similar frontage on Michigan Avenue or State Street in the "windy city." Emerson and West Lynne, its long-since devoured twin across the Red, were touted in local and eastern papers as improved versions of Minneapolis and St. Paul. Crystal City, Rapid City, Nelsonville – a long list of metropolises-to-be – clamored for the attention of settlers and received that of speculators. Winnipeg was prompted by the speculation fever to move heaven and earth in order to secure the crossing of the Red River by the new Canadian Pacific Railway. In 1881, Winnipeg ratepayers voted the sum of $200,000 for the building of a bridge for the new line, plus a perpetual exemption from local taxation. The bargain, quickly made, has long been regretted – though never entirely remedied. The price, though, was perhaps not too high, since the railway assured Winnipeg of retaining its pre-eminence as the distributing center for an agricultural West.

The boom was purely speculative; there were no solid economic bases for it. The heavy immigration which might have sustained or justified it was still twenty years in the future. While it lasted, the boom was spectacular, and land occupied the attention of the people as gold had done during the California gold rush. Values on paper doubled or trebled overnight, and land on townsites far into the Northwest Territories was eagerly snapped up. In mid-April, 1882, the whole house of cards collapsed. Many were ruined, including the pioneer merchant and respected political elder, A. G. B. Bannatyne, and the collapse left a chastened province upon which the long night of economic depression descended for the rest of the century. The CPR was built, but the people who were to settle the province and its hinterland did not come in the hoped-for numbers. The setback, however, did not crush Manitoba's spirit, nor its faith for the future. There was still much work to be done, and much more to be gained.

The transient boom was not without its beneficial results. The "postage stamp" province had never been reconciled to that title, nor had its government been able to function adequately with the limited assets which had been placed at its disposal. Urgent representations by the new premier, John Norquay, begun on his assumption of office in 1878, led in 1881 to the extension of Manitoba northward to the fifty-second parallel and west to 102° west longitude. The eastern boundary remained undecided pending the settlement of a dispute between Ottawa and Toronto as to where the western boundary of Ontario should be drawn. Toronto sought to have the province reach as far west as Lake of the Woods, while Ottawa would have preferred to establish a western limit in the vicinity of Thunder Bay. In the end, the Judicial Committee of the Imperial Privy Council decided in favor of Toronto's claim. The northern and western extensions, however, added very considerably to the area of Manitoba and increased its population at a stroke by some 16,000.

The boundary extension made peremptory the recognition of a situation which had in fact existed since the mid-1870's. The province was now overwhelmingly English-speaking and Protestant. The old dual system of French and English representation, which had existed since the days of the Provisional Government, finally crumbled. English Protestant ascendancy became an obvious fact. Joseph Royal had attempted to institute a form of the "double majority" system which had been used in the old Province of Canada prior to Confederation, but he failed to secure the necessary alliance between the French- and English-speaking elements of the old settlers. As a result, he and Pierre Delorme retired from the government. Norquay went to the people in December, 1879, in the last election in the "postage stamp" province and received all but three of the votes of the new legislature on its first division. The old order had been submerged in the new immigration and the fact was no longer in dispute.

While the long-awaited CPR was being slowly and arduously strung through the vast rock-and-muskeg barrier to the east, the boundary dispute with Ontario came to a ludicrous climax. Manitoba agreed with Ottawa's contention that the western boundary of Ontario be drawn north and south through Fort William, but Oliver Mowat, perennial premier of Ontario, would not settle for such a line. He increased Ontario's demands to include all of the land to the western shore of Lake of the Woods. The issue was academic until the building of the railway and the discovery of gold at the northern end of Lake of the Woods brought promises of provincial revenue. Both governments quickly established their police forces in the disputed area and set up premises licensed under the liquor laws of their respective provinces. The police occupied themselves with arresting one another, while the bootlegging element operated without hindrance among the thirsty miners and railway workers. In 1883, the Rat Portage region became an electoral division of Ontario, and a member was elected to sit at Queen's Park. Manitoba, in its turn, had erected the County of Varennes, and within it the electoral division of Rat Portage, which duly returned the Hon. J. A. Millar. The voting for both seats took place on the same day and involved the same electorate. The farce finally ended in 1884 with the judicial award of the disputed territory to Ontario. Manitoba's eastern boundary was then drawn along the ninety-fifth meridian, north from the northwest angle of Lake of the Woods to 52°50′ north latitude.

The antics of the two police forces at Rat Portage formed the one light moment in an increasingly-darkening western scene. The sure promise of the CPR and its rapid construction westward had brought initial joy and short-lived boom. The expected rush of settlers had not materialized; branch lines had been built neither to the extent nor in the directions that had been hoped for; grain prices remained low and freight rates levied by the CPR were exorbitant. These things, plus the high price of manufactured goods, were laid at the door of Macdonald's National Policy and the concomitant monopoly of rail construction held by the CPR. The resultant distress was aggravated by the collapse of the boom, which, when coupled with killing frosts in 1883, led to the formation of the first farm protest movement – the forerunner of many ritual denunciations of Ottawa which were to become a familiar part of the western Canadian scene.

The Manitoba and North West Farmers' Union was formed at Winnipeg in December of 1883. The union was in no sense a revival of the agitation of 1869-70. The vast majority of its members were of Canadian or British origin and it contained a large force of transplanted Ontarians. Their position was that taken by several similar groups in the future. They wanted free trade in all farm commodities, including those which were used on the farm as well as those which were produced by it; custom tariffs for revenue only, and not for the protection of industry; provincial control of public or Crown lands; provincial freedom to charter railways whenever and wherever needed; municipal freedom to build and operate grain elevators and flour mills; uniform grain inspection and grading; and the immediate consideration of the construction of a railway to Hudson Bay. The union deliberately put aside any direct political action, hoping to impress the authorities with the force of its logic. Its hopes were in vain. The demands of the Manitoba and North West Farmers' Union went largely unheeded, and though its voice continued to be heard for some years, its effectiveness faded as the movement came to be identified with the Liberal Party. However, at least two of the points of the Farmers' Union program were to have more than a passing hold on public attention in the West. These were the Hudson Bay railway and the monopoly of rail construction enjoyed in the West by the Canadian Pacific Railway.

A railway to Hudson Bay would be a renewal of the oldest of Manitoba's and western Canada's connections with Europe. It was to the bay that the first explorers had come in the search for the "western sea" more than two hundred years before, and it was through the bay that the country had had its main connection with the outside world until the railway began to encroach from the south. Proposals for such a line were heard even before rails began to inch northward from St. Paul in the 1860's. All were considered highly visionary, and, indeed, the engineering problems alone were enough to make even the most optimistic give pause. The CPR had shown, however, that muskeg could be filled and that rock as old as time could be blasted out of the way. After all, a line 700 miles to the north was less difficult than one 1,000 miles to the east, and the latter was already well under way. The terrain was much the same. So was the crushing cost – in both cases unrelieved by any hope of local traffic to help bear the expense of operating the lines. If the example of the CPR had shown that construction of the Hudson Bay line was possible, it was also that railway's monopoly in the West which gave the northern line its first hope of being realized. Clause 15 of the CPR charter, enshrined in the Statutes of Canada, 1881, gave that company a twenty-year monopoly of all rail construction in the West, south of its main line. The intent was to prevent American lines, such as the Northern Pacific or the Great Northern, from tapping the traffic of the CPR to the south. For if such tapping took place, it could bleed the CPR white with the great expense of maintaining the long and unproductive line north of Lake Superior.

By 1883, the monopoly clause was being blamed for high freight rates and for the dearth of branch lines to serve country points. The Macdonald Government held its agreement with the CPR: the monopoly was necessary to keep American lines at bay. A Hudson Bay railway, on the other hand, presented no such problem. It would provide shorter and more direct access to world markets, without infringing on the legal position of the CPR. It would also provide that competition which, it was devoutly believed, would reduce freight rates. Plans were discussed and prospectuses issued. The Hudson Bay line was debated formally and informally in both public and private forums, in legislative halls and barrooms. Surveys were made of the bay and of Hudson Strait. The estuaries of the Hayes, Nelson, and Churchill rivers were explored as to their merits as ports, and the rivers themselves were explored for the possibility of inland navigation. A Hudson Bay railway became a persistent western plea that continued for many years. The great stumbling block was the lack of funds, and not until well after the turn of the century did it become a matter for actual construction. Meanwhile, it served as a chimera for those Manitobans and other westerners who were increasingly concerned with the high level of CPR freight rates.

The Manitoba farmer and his fellow in the Northwest Territories were no less Canadians in their efforts to find a solution. The Hudson Bay railway remained a distant dream, but the locomotives of the Northern Pacific Railway of Minnesota and Dakota were almost within earshot, and their owners were far from averse to sharing in the hoped-for carrying trade of the Canadian West. In spite of the CPR monopoly, the legislature of Manitoba began, as early as 1881, to charter railways in order to form links with the American railway system. These charters were uniformly disallowed by the federal government on the grounds that they were in violation of the charter of the CPR and thus contrary to the settled policy of the Dominion of Canada. In addition, the lines of railway proposed by Manitoba clearly infringed on the exclusive power of the Government of Canada to regulate interprovincial and international means of communication under Section 91, Subsection 10, of the British North America Act. The Norquay Government, under increasing pressure from its constituents, persisted in its efforts to obtain rail-rate competition. The ingredients for a first-rate political storm were brewing.

Before Manitoba's railway problems could reach attention-getting proportions, a more immediate and dangerous confrontation developed in the Northwest Territories, a confrontation which caused the province to forget its local woes and to play a role as an active partner in the Dominion of Canada. In 1884, the old order of the West made a last convulsive effort to avoid extinction. Many of the Métis of Assiniboia had moved westward when their former hunting grounds became the Province of Manitoba. They strung out along the Saskatchewan River, with their principal settlement situated at Batoche on the South Saskatchewan, about eighty miles east of Battleford and forty miles south of Prince Albert. Here, they attempted to carry on the buffalo-hunting life which they had once enjoyed at Red River. So did their cousins, the Plains Indians, who were settled on reserves in the same general area. But time had run out for their way of life – just as it had for the buffalo. Both Indians and Métis, unable or unwilling to become farmers, began to starve. A preoccupied Canadian government had neither the resources nor the inclination to provide a permanent remedy – indeed, it had none to provide. As the 1880's advanced, the cries of distress from the Saskatchewan rose higher, only to fall on deaf ears. The few white settlers, the Indian Agents, the HBC servants, and even the relatively new North West Mounted Police all offered their warnings of trouble to come. Ottawa, however, would not be hurried. These were no United Empire Loyalists to whom the Crown was indebted. They were but the remnant of a group which had been a sore trial in 1870, and one which it was felt had already been more than amply rewarded.

In the summer of 1884, Louis Riel, then teaching at the St. Peter's Mission on the Sun River in Montana Territory, was summoned home by his people. He set up at Batoche as their universally-recognized leader and pledged himself to the peaceful settlement of their grievances. His petitions and appeals were ignored, as had been those previously forwarded. The only reaction from Ottawa was the provision of reinforcements for the NWMP. Being ignored by the national government was too much for Riel's unsteady mental balance; it tipped irretrievably. He now gave way to his messianic complex, calling for a general Indian and Métis uprising to establish the "New Nation" in its hereditary homeland. With the aid of his lieutenant, Gabriel Dumont, Riel attempted to rouse the Indians as far west as the foothills of the Rocky Mountains. The result was the Northwest Rebellion of 1885.

In March of that year, the Métis clashed with the police at Duck Lake, and twelve policemen were killed. When the news of this event was flashed eastward by telegraph, the West was no longer ignored. The fury of Ontario was unleashed in a hundredfold increase over that of 1869-70. Manitoba reflected the Ontario position. The denigration of Ottawa, and of the Canadian East generally, was a part of western Canadian life; but it did not extend to acts of war. Manitoba quickly marshalled a battery of field artillery, a troop of cavalry, and three battalions of infantry. These joined the forces of Major General Frederick Middleton in the brief campaign which culminated in the assault on Batoche in May and the surrender of Big Bear and his Cree in July. The subsequent trial, conviction, and execution of Louis Riel were reflected in Manitoba – as they were in Canada generally – by a widening of racial, religious, and language divisions. Riel was not remembered with gratitude as the founder of the province, except by the rapidly-diminishing number of his fellow natives of Red River. The unanimity of opinion against Riel in the Manitoba of 1885 was proof enough, if proof was needed, that the old order had indeed passed away.

Manitoba met its returning troops with a tumultuous welcome before shifting its attention to local concerns. The rebellion had been instrumental in proving to a doubting country that the CPR could provide quick and certain communication over its far-flung distances. Parliament proved willing to underwrite the spiralling costs of the railroad, and, on November 7, 1885, the last spike was driven by Donald A. Smith. The first through train to the Pacific coast passed through Winnipeg on July 1, 1886, adding to the joy of the celebration of the national holiday.

The transcontinental line was a great and necessary national achievement, but what of the growing need for branch lines to serve the farm communities and the clamor for a reduction in rail rates? Railway problems now dominated the Manitoba scene almost to the exclusion of all other topics. With the possible exception of a series of poor crop years, all the ills to which the province was heir were laid at the door of the CPR. All locally-chartered railways which might interfere with the CPR monopoly were struck down by the federal disallowance power. Norquay had made the all-too-familiar trek to Ottawa in 1885, and again in 1886, to seek "better terms." To the standard plea for the control of Crown lands, the standard refusal was given. To Norquay's request for relief from the railway monopoly, Ottawa answered that the monopoly would remain in effect at least until the line north of Lake Superior was in full operation. The subsidy in lieu of Crown lands and the per capita subsidies were increased, while swamp lands would be turned over to provincial control.

Norquay's report was not well received by the legislature. He had some difficulty holding his support in line during the session of 1885 and avoided a possibly embarrassing vote of nonconfidence by proroguing the House. The nonconfidence motion was offered by Thomas Greenway of Crystal City, member for Mountain, who had been in the House since 1882 and who had grouped an opposition around him which, with its emphasis on "provincial rights," rapidly assumed a Liberal hue. Norquay found himself in trouble again in the session of 1886 when news came of two further acts of disallowance. He regained the support of the House for a motion which called for the dropping of the CPR monopoly as soon as the railway was in full operation. Meanwhile, he urged that railways be built under the terms of existing legislation. This session also saw a redistribution of seats which raised the number to thirty-five and placed them more realistically in relation to the existing state of settlement.

An election followed which gave Norquay twenty-one of the thirty-five seats. This result was in no way indicative of the true state of provincial opinion on the disallowance question. All candidates, without exception, had pledged themselves as being in favor of the immediate construction of rail lines wherever necessary, in spite of the federal prohibition. Norquay led the van of this opinion in the electoral campaign. His break with Macdonald was now complete. Norquay's position was dictated by his loyalty to his province rather than to the Liberal-Conservative Party, to which he had become, at best, a reluctant adherent.

The extent of the split between Manitoba and Ottawa became evident as soon as the new House assembled in 1887. One of the first bills passed was "An Act Respecting the Construction of the Red River Valley Railway." Its purpose was to provide for the construction of a line southward along the west bank of the Red to West Lynne, whence a connection could be made with the Northern Pacific at Pembina. The act received the assent of Lieutenant-Governor James C. Aikins on June 1 and was disallowed, with a speed worthy of a better cause, on July 4. Despite federal disapproval, Norquay decided to proceed with the building of the line under the provisions of the Public Works Act, 1885, which, since it had been in force for more than one year, could not now be disallowed. Norquay's decision found wide support in Manitoba. The Winnipeg Board of Trade had denounced the CPR monopoly in no uncertain terms and had even threatened, in an excess of enthusiasm, to consider the withdrawal of the province from Confederation if railway disallowance did not cease forthwith. The Board of Trade's position smacks of throwing out the baby with the bath water, but it had the support of such solid members of the business community as James H. Ashdown and Mayor Lyman M. Jones. There was, in this, a harkening back to the days of the purchase of the West by Canada and a restatement of the belief that Canada, having bought the West, seemed bent on doing its will there without regard to the interests of westerners.

The building of the Red River Valley Railway was made the occasion for a series of displays of defiance, mostly of a good-tempered even enthusiastic nature. On July 2, 1887, the first sod was turned at what is now Pembina Highway and Parker Avenue on the southern edge of Winnipeg. It was a full-scale social turn-out, with Premier Norquay and Mayor Jones wielding spades with a will. The general attitude of the province was one of genial defiance of Ottawa to do its worst, and a sort of thumb-to-nose lightheartedness prevailed. Financing the new line, however, was difficult. The province's credit was very low, and this fact was by no means understated to the bankers of Montreal, New York and London by the CPR and the Government of Canada. Such small local capital as was to hand was cheerfully made available, but the enterprise was at best shaky.

Continued defiance of the policy of the Canadian government and its chosen instrument, the CPR, was beginning to have an effect. Before long, the CPR was reduced to desperation measures. President George Stephen had threatened in May, 1887, to remove the railway's principal maintenance and repair shops from Winnipeg if active resistance to the monopoly continued. Neither the province nor the City of Winnipeg were dismayed. If anything, their hostility was increased by this gratuitous threat. Were the shops removed, the CPR would thereby forfeit its exemption from taxation in a city which was already beginning to regret its hasty bargain of 1881. The CPR then built a spur line easward from its Gretna branch to cut across the projected route of the Red River Valley Railway and an injunction was secured to prevent the RRVR from crossing this spur. The Manitoba authorities ignored this action and went ahead with construction on other parts of the line. In September, the minister of justice, John Thompson, obtained an injunction in the Court of Queen's Bench forbidding further RRVR construction on the grounds that the line was being built on land which belonged to the Canadian government. Norquay was not intimidated. Supported by almost unanimous public opinion, he announced that a contract had been let to complete the line by June 1, 1888, "unless prevented from so doing by legal or military force."

Already in the bad books of the prime minister, Norquay damned himself still further by actively participating in the interprovincial conference at Quebec in October, 1887. He was the only Conservative premier to do so. This conference of provincial governments, the first of its kind, was thoroughly snubbed by Ottawa. The conference was attended by the premiers of Ontario, Quebec, Nova Scotia, New Brunswick, and Manitoba; all but the last being Liberal and all resentful of Macdonald's strong stand for the primacy of the national administration. The interprovincial conference did nothing but rehearse the particular prejudices of the disaffected provinces and enter a plea for wider provincial powers. Nevertheless, Norquay's attendance sealed his political fate.

Existing federal legislation provided for substantial land grants for railways under construction on the basis of so many acres per mile of line actually laid down. On this basis, the Winnipeg & Hudson Bay Railway was entitled to a grant of 256,000 acres, having laid down forty miles of rail. The land grant, when received, was to go to the province under the terms of its charter. A. A. C. Larivière, the provincial treasurer, received verbal assurance from Sir John in Ottawa that the transfer of 256,000 acres would be made. Larivière telegraphed this information to Norquay at Winnipeg, and Norquay thereupon issued $300,000 in Manitoba bonds, secured by the land grant, to be used to finance the construction of the RRVR. The land transfer, however, was not made; it was held up by Sir John A. Macdonald. Norquay thus found himself in the unenviable position of having issued bonds without collateral. This lapse was soon made public by E. P. Leacock, member of the legislature for Russell, hitherto a close ally of Norquay and a promoter of some note. Leacock demanded of the lieutenant-governer that the legislature be summoned to deal with this defalcation. Larivière returned posthaste to Ottawa to seek the redemption of the "old chieftain's" pledge. Macdonald denied that he had ever made any such promise. As Larivière put it later: "He endeavored to convince me that I had never been in Ottawa at all." With the ground thus cut from beneath them, Norquay and Larivière had no choice but to resign, which they did to the government caucus on December 22, 1887.

Norquay continued to sit as a private member until his untimely death in 1889 at the early age of forty-eight. No reflection was ever made on his personal integrity. Manitoba's first native-born premier marked the full transition from the old to the new in Manitoba. He had been a member of Riel's provisional assembly and had carried on to become a victim of Canadian politics. He was the victim of the party system, whose introduction into the province he had resisted. His loyalty to Manitoba always stood before his loyalty to party or faction.

Norquay was succeeded by Dr. D. H. Harrison, of Minnedosa, who chose Joseph Burke as his provincial secretary. Burke sought election in St. Francis Xavier, where he was opposed by the Liberal F. H. Francis. Francis won. The defeat of his new minister decided Harrison's course. He met the legislature on January 12, 1888, and resigned with his Government on January 19, being succeeded by Thomas Greenway who formed Manitoba's first Liberal administration. The new premier was equally pledged with his predecessors to complete the RRVR and to bring the monopoly of the CPR to an end. Macdonald, having put "Paid" to the treason of Norquay, was willing to compromise. He was by now aware that the use of the power of disallowance to advance the policy of the Canadian government was not always one which paid politically. He henceforth restricted the use of this power to cases of flagrant unconstitutionality and left mere controversy to the courts. Greenway was the first to benefit from this change of policy. He adjourned the legislature and set off for Ottawa with his attorney-general, Joseph E. Martin. They went, pointedly, at the invitation of Macdonald and were speeded on their way by numerous resolutions of local Conservative bodies warning Macdonald of mass desertion from the party if his railway policy was not immediately altered.

On his return, Greenway was able to report success. The CPR had been persuaded by Macdonald to give up the monopoly clause of its charter in return for a federal guarantee of $15,000,000 in CPR bonds, the money to be used for branch lines and the purchase of rolling stock. The reconvened legislature quickly passed an amended Red River Valley Railway Act which empowered the line to build not only to the border, but also from Winnipeg to Portage la Prairie – indeed, in any direction where branch lines might be needed in order to break the existing monopolistic position of the CPR. In addition, the legislature authorized, and the government quickly floated, $1,500,000 in bonds to underwrite the necessary cost of construction. Greenway also implemented changes which he had promised on taking office. Manhood suffrage and vote by ballot were instituted, these being reforms which had already been instituted at the federal level by the Liberal Government of Alexander Mackenzie. The electoral map was redrawn, and three seats were added, including an additional one for Winnipeg, thus doubling its representation.

The CPR had lost its monopoly but not its capacity for retaliation, nor its unscrupulousness in the exercise of corporate power. While the House was still sitting, William Van Horne offered to lease the uncompletted RRVR line to West Lynne for $50,000 a year on condition that the provincial government drop the whole RRVR project. Should this offer be rejected, stated Van Horne, the CPR would not extend its southwestern branch to Souris, nor would it build any other feeder lines in southern Manitoba. Greenway rejected the offer out of hand, dissolved the House, and went to the people further armed by this blundering power play of the CPR. Greenway's supporters carried thirty-three of the thirty-eight seats. Immediately after the election, Greenway and Martin made a bargain with the Northern Pacific Railway whereby the RRVR was to become the Northern Pacific & Manitoba Railway. The new line, besides operating the border connection, would build from Morris to Brandon and from Winnipeg to Portage la Prairie within one year. The complicated deal was designed, so Greenway and Martin thought, to prevent the NPR and the CPR from coming together and fixing rates. The CPR tried a counter offer through its close ally, the St. Paul, Minneapolis & Manitoba Railway, but it was rejected because of the known relationship of the two lines. A special session of the new legislature promptly ratified the NP&M project, though not without some misgivings due to the proven ability of the CPR to cause mischief.

The CPR had more mischief in mind. To build its Portage la Prairie branch, the NP&M would have to cross the tracks of the CPR's southwestern branch at what is now Fort Whyte, immediately southwest of Winnipeg. The CPR now pulled out all the stops in an effort to prevent this crossing from being made. Their efforts provided a climax to the railway issue which finally degenerated into farce, but it was a climax which could easily have been serious considering the determination of the people of Manitoba to be thwarted no further in this matter. The long-burning temper of the people had been fired with the additional fuel of a complete crop failure in 1888, and they were in no mood to be trifled with. Knowing the CPR's hostility, the construction crews of the Portage branch put in a diamond crossing at night. The CPR had it ripped out the following day. In addition, the CPR's western superintendent, William Whyte, had a locomotive ditched across the path of the oncoming NP&M tracks and manned the site in the expectation of trouble. The CPR's position was that permission to make the crossing must be obtained from the Railway Committee of the Canadian Privy Council. Attorney-General "Fighting Joe" Martin, who was also a vice-president of NP&M, made application for such permission in his capacity as a railway officer; but in his capacity as attorney-general, he had three hundred special constables sworn in to put in the crossing by force should this prove necessary. The authority to swear in the constables was given by none other than Dr. John Christian Schultz, the new lieutenant-governor of Manitoba. The Railway Committee of the Privy Council referred the matter to the Supreme Court of Canada. In the meantime, both the CPR men and the special constables remained at the site of the disputed crossing, warming themselves against the November blasts by the same fire of ties and exchanging nothing more lethal than insults. Finally, the Supreme Court ruled that the crossing could be made. The tension ceased and the potential combatants dispersed, scarred only by the inclement weather. Today, the white plumes of cement plant chimneys waft peacefully over what once might have been a battlefield, and the citizens of Fort Whyte go about their business largely unaware of the events that gave their hamlet its name.

10

Troubled Times

THE MANITOBA WHICH THOMAS GREENWAY came to lead in January, 1888, was a far cry from the settlement from which Riel had fled in the early 1870's. The American frontier had by now advanced to the forty-ninth parallel in Minnesota and was rapidly spreading westward through Dakota Territory. The Province of Manitoba, already once enlarged, rested astride a Canadian transcontinental railway to which was attached an all too thin fringe of settlement all the way to the Rocky Mountains. Winnipeg had assumed the proud title of "Gateway to the West" – which indeed it was. It was, however, a gateway through which few were to pass for the next decade. Over 60,000 persons came through Winnipeg to settle in Manitoba and the northwest in 1882; but only 21,000 came in 1887. Some who had already settled in Manitoba lost heart and left for the south or the farther west; some even returned to the east. The railways, whose absence or expensive presence were sources of discontent, took some extra blame for causing land to be excluded from settlement while owners awaited a rise in price; but the general economic stagnation of much of the Western world persisted. Good free land was still available in the American West and its amenities proved more appealing to those who emigrated from Europe. A number of Icelanders, for example, abandoned the stony, easily-flooded fields of the west shore of Lake Winnipeg for better land in Dakota. Manitoba's hour of great expansion was yet to come.

In the meantime, much was done to draw Manitoba into the mainstream of Canadian civilization. The railway was an omnipresent fact, and the accompanying telegraph kept the province in close touch with the rest of the world. Winnipeg boasted two, and sometimes three, daily papers. In the rest of the province, daily and weekly sheets proliferated; Brandon, Portage la Prairie, Emerson, Crystal City, Minnedosa, Russell, Killarney, Gladstone, Morris, and a score of other towns supported papers. In the mid-1880's, telephones were installed in Winnipeg and typewritten letters began to appear. For street lighting, gas began to give way to electric arc lamps in 1882, at the same time, the first stone pavements were laid. Horse cars appeared on Winnipeg's streets, to be replaced in 1892 by electric trams. Water was piped from the Assiniboine at what is now Cornish Avenue and Maryland Street in 1882. This supply, which suffered from a surfeit of mud in the springtime, was taken over by the City of Winnipeg in 1899 and replaced by water which was piped from artesian wells located in the northwest of the city and which continued to be used until the Shoal Lake aqueduct became operative during the First World War.

Organized theatrical performances were not unknown in old Red River and plays had been staged by the troops of the Wolseley Expedition during the winter of 1870-71. Such theatricals flourished on an amateur basis throughout the settled areas from the very beginning and were in time supplemented, at least in the larger centers, by travelling groups of professionals. Curling, rowing, hockey, lacrosse, baseball, and other sports were well organized during the 1880's. The hunting of game was in the process of passing into its sportsman's phase, though it was to remain a source of sustenance to many a homesteader until well into the twentieth century.

Commercial progress was by no means neglected. Brandon organized a board of trade in 1883; settlers created Dauphin in 1885; and the Torrens System of land registration was first introduced in the same year. The grain elevator, soon to be ubiquitous, began to poke skyward to relieve the monotony of the plain and its operation became organized into line elevator companies as railways and a flow of grain became a matter of course. The organized marketing of grain became the function of the Winnipeg Grain Exchange, which opened its doors in 1887. Winnipeg, Brandon, Portage la Prairie, Emerson, and other places began to boast a local society based on the wealth of commerce and of land. Crenellated brick monstrosities, in which even large families rattled about, appeared on Assiniboine Avenue in Winnipeg and its approaching streets. On the corner of Assiniboine and Kennedy was built Government House, first occupied in 1884 and still doing service as the residence of the lieutenant-governor. Social events – from wedding breakfasts through luncheons, teas, formal dinners, and balls – were reported in detail in the local press. Settled Manitoba was a microcosm of the Victorian world of solid virtue. The "wild west" atmosphere of the Winnipeg of the 1870's was gone, but a fair substitute was available on Main Street. The Indian bore the full brunt of the rough edges of civilization, but got little sympathy and even less help.

The echoes of the near-battle of Fort Whyte had hardly faded before railways again held the center of the stage, and Mr. Greenway and his Government soon found themselves in need of help. The local journals, particularly the *Manitoba Free Press,* had never accepted the deal made with the NP&M. Their opposition was by no means motivated by any softening of their attitude to the CPR; it was inspired, rather, by their continued championing of the Hudson Bay railway, which had been all but abandoned by Greenway. The *Free Press* charged both Greenway and Martin with accepting bribes for electoral purposes from the Northern Pacific Railway and made much of the fact that Martin was an NP&M vice-president, though this was far from unacceptable to the mores of the time. The charges against Greenway and Martin were never substantiated, and there is no reason to believe that the charges were founded on anything other than the usual "no holds barred" political tactics of the day. Nor is there any reason to believe that the public took the charges seriously.

The Government was embarrassed, however, by the fact that even though the Portage la Prairie and Brandon branches of the NP&M went into operation, the promised reduction in rail rates did not materialize. Regions which thus received direct rail service were pleased, but the province as a whole received no benefit in the way of rail-rate reduction. Effectively, the CPR and the NPR split the traffic and maintained the rate structure, even increasing rates on incoming goods. Finding himself thus deluded, the Manitoba taxpayer gave way to a righteous wrath directed at the authors of his continued misfortune. The unfortunate Greenway had been thoroughly taken into camp by the cleverest operators in the business. Fuel was added to the fire by the effective stoppage of the Hudson Bay railway project, which had promised freedom from the thraldom of both the CPR and its American counterparts. A desperate situation called for a desperate remedy, and, fortunately for Greenway, there was one at hand.

Both Protestant suspicion of Catholic and English suspicion of French had received some preliminary cultivation in Manitoba over the years and both were now ripe to harvest. Racial, religious, and language bigotry have a long and dishonorable history in Canada, as they have in many another civilized state. They can be traced back to the Plains of Abraham, and well beyond that to the fierce border wars between the French Catholics of Quebec and the English Protestants of New England. Bigotry is seen in an even earlier day when Huguenots were expelled from the almost moribund New France so that it might be as religiously pure as Cardinal Richelieu wished it to be. Mutual suspicion between language and religious groups figured in the rebellions of 1837 and in the discussions of Confederation in the Parliament of the Province of Canada. The greatest contribution of Macdonald and Cartier lay in their surmounting these suspicions and burying them in a broader national hope. But such suspicions would not remain buried. Manitoba had been born in a welter of religious and language conflicts which were imposed on Red River from Canada. That there was little logic on either side has never hindered the conflict, neither then nor later. The Northwest Rebellion and the subsequent trial and execution of Louis Riel had once more brought the French versus English and Catholic versus Protestant issue to an angry head. The Protestant Equal Rights Association came on in full cry, concerned neither with equality nor with rights. Their Catholic counterparts were no more enlightened in their views.

The execution of Louis Riel shattered the Conservative Party in Quebec and produced a nationalist-oriented Liberal Government led by Honoré Mercier. Mercier aggravated the situation with the Jesuit Estates Act of 1888. This measure was designed to compensate the Society of Jesus for its loss of property at the time of the conquest in 1759-60. Jesuit lands had passed to the Crown in the right of Lower Canada and, in due course, to the Province of Quebec in 1867. The act of 1888 provided compensation to the amount of $400,000 to the Jesuit order, with $60,000 more to go, as a balancing contribution, to the Protestant schools of Quebec. The wording and operating mechanism of the act were such as to bring shouts of rage from the ranks of organized Protestantism. It referred to the Pope and to the *Curia Romana* in respectful terms and made the Pope arbiter in any dispute concerning the distribution of the $400,000. All of this was but a red flag to the Protestant bull. The whole matter of the Jesuit Estates Act was properly of concern only to the people of Quebec, and they alone paid the sums involved. Nevertheless, it smacked of subservience to Rome in the eyes of the Orange Order and especially in the eyes of its Grand Master for British North America, D'Alton McCarthy, a prominent Conservative MP and a friend of Sir John A. Macdonald. Pressure was put on Macdonald to disallow the measure. However, once bitten twice shy, and Macdonald could see that Quebec required careful handling in the wake of the execution of Riel. There was also the fact, overlooked by McCarthy, that the matter was entirely within the competence of the Province of Quebec.

With regard to population, Manitoba was, to all intents and purposes, an Ontario in miniature – with some relieving features that were not universally apparent. Thus, the province was by no means immune to the bacillus of bigotry. A deep suspicion of all that was French and Catholic was endemic throughout the English-speaking and Protestant population. These suspicions had little to feed on once the *Canadien* and Métis community had been overwhelmed numerically, but the suspicions remained and from time to time made themselves manifest – with or without apparent cause. The efforts of the small French-speaking community to maintain a duality in the administration of the province even after the first major Ontario immigration had alerted many local Protestants to a possible danger. On October 4, 1876, the Protestant section of the Board of Education, echoing the sentiments of both the Winnipeg School Board and the Manitoba Teachers' Association, passed a resolution asking the Manitoba government to enact a new school law providing for a single, nonsectarian school system. They also asked for other changes: the use of English-language textbooks only; a system of school inspection; and a system of teacher certification. These measures would be administered by a single board of education without religious division. The only change to come out of these requests was that the equal division of school funds among Protestant and Catholic schools was altered to a proportionate division based on numbers of students.

In 1879, an effort to end the printing of public documents in French had passed the legislature under the innocuous-sounding title: "An Act Respecting Public Printing." Ostensibly, the act was proposed as an economy measure – and certainly it was true that the province was then, as so often in its history, sorely pressed for money. The bill, however, was unanimously opposed by French-speaking members, who justly feared that its motivation was more anti-French than pro-economy. The measure, Bill 25 of the session of 1879, was reserved by Lieutenant-Governor Joseph Cauchon. He refused Royal Assent on the grounds that the measure was a possible violation of the Manitoba Act and it was dispatched to the Minister of Justice for comment and disposal. It was not disallowed, but neither was it permitted to go into effect – it simply vanished into the limbo of politically embarrassing legislation. It is possible that Norquay agreed to forget the matter in return for an addition to the annual subsidy sufficient to pay the costs of printing in French. This would have been a small price for Macdonald to pay in order to be kept from such a politically sensitive decision.

The related issues of the duality of the school system and the official use of the French language became quiescent during the 1880's. The hopes and disappointments of the railway, the grand diversion of the Northwest Rebellion, and the Disallowance Question took prior place in the public mind. The school and language issues remained, however, and began to assert themselves even before Greenway took office. During the Assiniboia and St. Francis Xavier by-elections of January, 1888, which brought in the Liberal Government, they were again heard. The Conservative candidates accused the Liberals of intending to tamper with the school system and the use of French. The Liberals, including Greenway and Martin, were reported to have heatedly denied this. Later, when the School Question was in open dispute, they even more heatedly denied that they had ever made such denials. The whole business of these alleged pledges by Greenway and Martin was the subject of much debate at the time of the School Question and later. To sum up: it is apparent that such pledges were made in early 1888 by the Liberal leaders, but the binding nature of the pledge depends entirely on the memories of those who took part – all of whom had reason for vastly different remembrances.

By 1889, therefore, the time was ripe for the raising of the religious and language bogey. What better way to divert attention from the failure of the Greenway Government's railway policies? The groundwork had already been laid for educational reform on a broad scale. Apparently motivated by the Protestants' growing dissatisfaction with existing conditions, changes were planned which would increase the quality and efficiency of primary and secondary education. These plans would have involved the dismantling of the existing dual system. They were announced in public speeches made at Souris and Clearwater on August 1 and 2, 1889, by James A. Smart, Minister of Public Works. Economy and efficiency were the reasons given and there was no press reaction to indicate that the motivation was based on language or religion. The heat developed by McCarthy and the Equal Rights Association had already begun to spill over into Manitoba from the East and had been reflected in some grumbling editorial comment on the privilege enjoyed by the Catholic minority in education.

The whole thing flamed quickly with the appearance in Manitoba of McCarthy himself, who delivered a series of speeches well calculated to alert the always-receptive Protestant and English majority to the Catholic and French danger. The most significant of these speeches was delivered at Portage la Prairie on August 5, with Attorney-General Joseph E. Martin sharing the platform. McCarthy recited the all too familiar charges against the iniquitous Jesuit Estates Act and the evils of state-supported Catholic schools and the official use of the French language. The Portage audience reacted with great enthusiasm. Martin moved a vote of thanks to McCarthy and, in so doing, gained for himself an even more enthusiastic cheer. He announced that the Government would, in the next session of the legislature, abolish the official use of French and would seek the establishment of a single school system without a religious division.

This came as a surprise to Greenway, who telegraphed from Winnipeg to ask what Martin was up to. Martin replied that here was an issue which would give them the solid support of the majority of Manitobans. If the new policy was unsatisfactory to the provincial secretary, *Canadien* J. E. P. Prendergast, he could resign. The other members of the Cabinet accepted the new policy with few if any qualms of conscience. Prendergast resigned at the end of August, 1889. He and A. F. Martin of Morris led a gallant battle in the House and on public platforms to preserve both the French language and the Catholic schools, but they were little heard and less heeded. What came to be called the "Manitoba School Question" soon engaged the attention of the whole province and then of the country, to the exclusion in fact, of matters more worthy of note. The contemporary historian, Alexander Begg, wrote at the height of the national agitation: ". . . unfortunately for Manitoba, and unfortunately for Canada, any question that involves a conflict between race or creed is eagerly seized upon by unscrupulous politicians to stir up the spirit of bigotry that unhappily underlies the surface of our social and political fabric." The School Act of 1890 has been described as a contrived issue manufactured out of whole cloth to cover the Government's nakedness in its railway policy. It has also been called, too charitably, an aspect of the province's coming of age and of that striving for full provincial status so long denied it.

Having determined on a "root and branch" approach, the Greenway Government wasted no time. The printing of the *Manitoba Gazette* in French was halted by order-in-council and the first English-only issue appeared in early September, 1889. The abolition of the use of French as a language in the legislature or the courts of the province, as well as in public printing, was accomplished by statute early in the session of 1890. Another early statute of 1890 removed Catholic *fête* days from the calendar of public holidays; the right of a French-speaking defendant to a jury which is at least one-half French-speaking was also removed. These petty acts would indicate that the Government was not moved solely by an interest in improving the quality of education.

The assault on the separate school system was made in the legislature in February and March, 1890. Attempts to fend off the legislative attack were mounted not only by political leaders such as J. E. P. Prendergast and A. F. Martin, but also by the Roman Catholic Church itself. Here, the fight was carried by the *doyen* of western Canadian ecclesiastics, Archbishop Alexandre A. Taché of St. Boniface. Taché had helped write into the Manitoba Act guarantees of the French language and of the Catholic Church with respect to education, had worked to keep those guarantees operative, and now stood to see them swept away. We owe much of our knowledge of the circumstances of Manitoba's birth to his speeches and his letters to the newspapers of the winter of 1889-90. However, all of Taché's knowledge and eloquence went for naught. The general respect for the venerable prelate was undiminished – indeed, it was enhanced – but the majority would not be denied. In a democratic society, there was room for only one publicly-supported school system; and if the Catholics, or any others, wanted different schools, they would have to go it on their own.

Two measures were used to dismantle and rebuild the school system. The first of these, "An Act Respecting the Department of Education," placed control of education in the hands of a committee of the executive council. This cabinet committee was empowered to appoint inspectors of schools and the faculties of normal schools, to define their duties, and to fix their salaries. The act provided for an advisory board of seven: four of which were to be appointed by the lieutenant-governor-in-council, (two of these in consultation with the school trustees); two chosen by the teachers; and one appointed by the council of the university. The advisory board was to make regulations regarding the certification of teachers, set standards of admission to high schools and of matriculation, authorize textbooks, and determine the nature of religious exercises. The schools were to be nonsectarian, though not open to the charge of being "Godless." In practice, religious exercises tended to be of a Protestant nature, possibly due to the proliferation of Protestant divines in the advisory board. The first chairman was Robert Machray, Archbishop of Rupert's Land and Anglican Primate of Canada.

The second statute, "An Act Respecting Public Schools," abolished the former Catholic and Protestant schools and school boards. All public schools were to be nonsectarian, subject to the same regulations, and responsible for teaching the same curriculum through teachers who were uniformly qualified. There was provision for limited religious exercises which were to be conducted by the teacher just prior to the end of the school day in a manner to be set by the advisory board. These religious exercises were only to be conducted if the local trustees so decided, and any student might be excused attendance if his parent indicated this to the teacher. Schooling was to be free, but there was no provision for compulsory attendance. The latter provision was designed to permit parents to send their children to a privately-operated separate school if they chose to do so. It also helped those parents, unfortunately numerous, who preferred to spare their children the dangers of an education by keeping them more usefully employed on the farm.

Both bills were subject to long and bitter debate. R. P. Roblin and A. F. Martin vainly attacked the Department of Education Act as placing the schools under political control. The Public Schools Act received the most attention and the unanimous opposition of all the French and Catholic members. On one occasion, A. F. Martin spoke for nine and a half hours against the bill. Among other things, it was attacked as being unconstitutional. Joseph Martin replied that he doubted it was, but if so, the constitution would simply have to be changed. Even Prendergast, who made up in eloquence what he may have lacked in long-windedness, made no impression with his appeal for justice and his arraignment of bigotry. The Government, its majority in the House, and the mass of the English and Protestant population were implacable. The separate schools must go, and go they went by a final vote of twenty-five to eleven.

Lieutenant-Governor Schultz had already expressed his concern at the effect of the two bills as they moved through the legislative machinery. Macdonald told Schultz not to reserve them and stated that he would not disallow them. The veto was in the discard for provincial legislation which was not clearly unconstitutional. Macdonald counselled Schultz and the representatives of the aggrieved Catholic minority that the courts were the place to seek a final answer. But the appeal to the courts was forced to wait on politics. Archbishop Taché was convinced by Macdonald not only that his best hope lay in the courts, but that he would be well advised to wait until after the impending federal election. In return, Taché was promised financial help for the appeal. The election of 1891, Macdonald's last campaign, was fought on issues far removed from the schools of Manitoba. It was "the old man, the old flag, and the old party" which carried the Conservatives to victory on March 5, with but slight losses in Ontario and Quebec and with all but one of Manitoba's seats. Sir John, however, worn out by the cares of office and by his cure for those cares, died on June 6, 1891. He was universally mourned. Canada was not to look upon his like again.

Manitoba's Catholics took action soon after the election. Dr. J. K. Barrett of Winnipeg sought a ruling in the Court of Queen's Bench to quash by-laws of the City of Winnipeg which would require him to pay taxes for the upkeep of the new public schools. Mr. Justice Killam found no grounds for action, declaring the Public Schools Act to be within the power of the Legislature of Manitoba. The full Court of Queen's Bench sustained his ruling, Mr. Justice Dubuc dissenting. This decision was reversed by the Supreme Court of Canada and the matter then went to the final court, the Judicial Committee of the Privy Council at London. Here, the case was coupled with that of *Logan versus Winnipeg*. Alexander Logan, an Anglican and a former mayor of Winnipeg, sought redress for his own church. This case was referred directly to London by Manitoba in the hope that, if Barrett was sustained, all barriers would then be down and all denominations could claim public funds for their schools, or, conversely, could choose to pay their school taxes to the schools of their own churches. This Machiavellian manoeuvre was the brain-child of the new and brilliant attorney-general, Clifford Sifton of Brandon. The law lords ruled against Barrett and Logan. The point of the appeal lay in Section 22, Subsection 1 of the Manitoba Act, which forbade the legislature to pass any law that "shall prejudicially affect any right or privilege with respect to Denominational Schools which any class of persons have by law or practice in the Province at the Union." Since the only schools in existence in 1870 had been those supported by the churches through voluntary gifts, their Lordships decided that no right had been infringed and Manitoba was justified in setting up a nondenominational tax-supported system of public schools.

In the meantime, Greenway had dissolved the House and gone to the people on his record. The opposition did not contend with him on the school issue. Indeed, it was not an issue. It was settled as far as the majority of Manitobans was concerned and would remain so though the heavens fall. The Conservatives took a "me too" position and extended it by stating that should the Catholic position be upheld, the Manitoba Act should be amended to permit Manitoba to operate its schools as the province saw fit. Legislative seats had been increased to forty and redistributed in the Government's interest. Even this did not prevent the usually highly vocal as well as greatly underrepresented City of Winnipeg from giving all three of its seats to Greenway's supporters. The Liberals took twenty-six seats to twelve for the Conservatives, with two Independents who could be expected to support the Government.

The Catholics of Manitoba were dismayed by the privy council decision, but they were not yet defeated. They determined to make an appeal to the governor-general-in-council under Subsection 2 of Section 22 of the Manitoba Act. This subsection stated: "An appeal shall lie to the Governor-General-in-Council from any Act or decision of the Legislature of the Province . . . affecting any right or privilege of the Protestant or Roman Catholic minority of the Queen's subjects in relation to education." In November, 1892, this cause was taken up by a group of Manitoba Catholics and delivered to the new prime minister, Sir John S. D. Thompson, himself a Catholic. Thompson was as anxious as Macdonald to avoid the issue. He referred the matter to the Supreme Court for an opinion as to whether the right to appeal existed. The Supreme Court decided by a three to two vote that no such right did in fact exist. Once more, the scene was transferred to London and in January, 1895, the judicial committee of the privy council decided that certain rights of the Catholic minority had indeed been infringed and that the right of appeal for redress to the governor-general-in-council did exist. The judicial committee did not suggest how the redress of the Catholic grievances was to be brought about, nor was this any of its concern. The matter was discussed in cabinet at some length and submissions were heard from the Government of Manitoba delivered by D'Alton McCarthy and from the Catholics by J. S. Ewart. On March 21,

1895, the Government of Canada issued a remedial order requiring Manitoba to restore to the Catholic minority the right to their own schools, the right to share proportionately in public funds for school purposes, and the right to be exempt from taxation for schools other than their own.

The remedial order advanced the Manitoba School Question to the status of a national issue and it began to transcend the bounds of the relatively simple matter of public support for sectarian schools. This support was the general rule in any event, even in Orange Ontario. The remedial order did not change this aspect of the struggle other than to intensify it. It brought into the picture, however, the whole question of provincial rights, long a festering sore on the Canadian body politic. Could a province be coerced by Ottawa into a course of action contrary to that which the highest court had declared to be within its proper powers? The issue now became entirely political.

The Conservative Government of Canada, in office since 1878, had been badly weakened by the loss of Sir John A. Macdonald. It had begun to lose heavily in Quebec with the election of 1887, when the furor over Riel reduced its majority there to one seat. (In the election of 1882, the Quebec Conservatives had taken 51 out of 65 seats.) Quebec had already elected a Liberal provincial government under Honoré Mercier in January, 1887. Thus, the Conservative Party could no longer claim to be the sole protector of the rights of the *Canadien,* and this fact was reinforced by the choice of Wilfrid Laurier as national Liberal leader in June, 1887. In spite of this, the Conservatives showed great strength in by-elections, doubling their majority by 1895. The Conservatives were first plunged into disarray by the sudden and unexpected death of Sir John S. D. Thompson at Windsor Castle in December, 1894. The disarray continued until turned into chaos by the emergence of the Manitoba School Question onto the national scene. The onus of decision on the remedial order lay with Thompson's successor, Sir MacKenzie Bowell, whose divided and unruly Cabinet he was once moved to characterize as "a nest of traitors." If Bowell refused to act on the unsought power to coerce Manitoba, he would draw down upon himself all the wrath of the Catholic hierarchy. If he temporized, he stood to lose votes from both sides and in all parts of the country. Only a year remained before an election must be held. The Conservatives chose to move quickly in the vain hope that once having coerced Manitoba, they could then excuse themselves on the ground that in so doing they were only obeying the injunction of the privy council. In Quebec, meanwhile, they could claim credit for their courageous action in defence of Manitoba's Catholic minority.

On the other hand, delay served the interests of the Liberal Government of Manitoba. They were firmly entrenched at home and would prefer to deal in any eventual showdown with a Liberal administration in Ottawa. Furthermore, delay was as advantageous to the Federal Liberals as it was dangerous to the Conservatives. Laurier and his principal strategist, J. Israel Tarte, refused to take a definite stand; they decided to give the Conservatives enough rope to do the job. They had the active aid of the brilliant and ambitious Sifton, who was calling the tune in Manitoba. The Liberals were traditionally the party of provincial rights and could be expected to support Manitoba against federal coercion. That Laurier was a Catholic, as were the great majority of his fellow *Québecois,* was merely another example of the continuing dilemma of Canadian politics. An additional oddity existed in the fact that Mackenzie Bowell was a high-ranking Orangeman and N. Clarke Wallace, his Controller of Customs, was Grand Master of the Order. This strong Orange tint in a government pledged to relieve Catholic disabilities was a factor in Laurier's favour. When he considered the almost rabid anti-Catholicism of Ontario Conservatives, the *Canadien* of Quebec was suspicious of their sincerity in the case of Manitoba. The *Québecois,* therefore, were more inclined to side with Laurier and a possible compromise through "sunny ways."

Greenway and Sifton dawdled with efficiency and effect. The legislature was adjourned in order that a reply might be considered by the Government. There was considerable movement between Ottawa and Winnipeg, and a number of possible solutions were discussed in vain. Manitoba was in no mood to compromise. Even the governor-general, Lord Aberdeen, took an informal and probably improper hand in the discussions – but to no avail. After a three-month delay, Manitoba replied to the remedial order on June 24, 1895. The reply comprised a lengthy defence of the new school system as being more efficient and less expensive than the old system and as being better suited to the sparse population of Manitoba. The danger of a multiplicity of school systems for Mennonites, Icelanders, Anglicans, Methodists, and other races and creeds was pointed to as a possibility should the old system be re-established. Legal complications over the use of public funds and the levying of school taxes were envisaged. Much more deliberation was required for a mutually-acceptable solution. The solidity of opinion in favor of the existing school system was stressed. The reply ended with strong protestations of loyalty to the Queen.

Ottawa moved more quickly than Manitoba had done. On July 27, 1895, Bowell's Government issued a further order-in-council asserting that Ottawa, having once intervened, would have full jurisdiction and that Manitoba's arguments were specious. Details could be discussed, but if Manitoba did not comply, Parliament would be called on January 2, 1896, to consider remedial legislation. Manitoba remained immovable. A reply was not made for almost five months. On December 20, 1895, the Manitoba Government stated that Ottawa's position was "positively and definitely rejected." Manitoba could only be checked if there was "clear and unmistakable proof of flagrant wrong-doing on the part of the Provincial Authority." As Manitoba's position had been upheld by the highest tribunal, there was no such proof. To add emphasis, the legislature was dissolved coincidentally with the reply to Ottawa and polling was set for January 15, 1896. The election campaign was short and decisive. Greenway and Sifton directed their electoral thunder at Ottawa's "tyranny' and characterized Manitoba as a David standing against the federal Goliath. The Conservative opposition in the province had no alternate policy. Indeed, ex-Premier Harrison, Norquay's ephemeral successor, urged his fellow Conservatives to let the election go by default so as to emphasize provincial solidarity. Manitoba was even more united against federal encroachment than it had been in the case of railway disallowance in 1888.

The voting resulted in the election of thirty-two Liberals, five Conservatives, one Independent Liberal, and two Patrons of Industry. (The Patrons were a farm protest movement imported from the United States and were opposed on principle to separate schools. They were "the cloud no bigger than a man's hand" which was to grow through time and transformation into the Progressive Movement of the early twentieth century.) A. F. Martin, staunch supporter of *Canadien* and Catholic rights, went down before the Orange past grand master, Stewart Mulvey, a Liberal. *Canadien* representation in the House was thus reduced from four to three. The Conservatives still had no alternate policy on schools, while the *Canadiens* were content with a modest proposal that they be permitted to pay taxes to Catholic schools and not be taxed additionally to support the public school system. For all practical purposes, thirty-seven of the forty members stood behind the school settlement of 1890.

The Bowell Government which summoned Parliament to meet on January 2, 1896, fumblingly determined to pass a remedial bill and to pit the whole weight of the Canadian state against the intransigent Manitobans. A desperate call for help – from the Conservative Party, not from Bowell – brought the venerable but vigorous Sir Charles Tupper from his post as High Commissioner to the United Kingdom to rally the faltering ranks of the Government. He was quickly elected to the House of Commons in February and assumed full leadership of the fight for the remedial bill. He was prime minister in all but name, and he became so in fact on May 1, 1896. Tupper strove mightily and well, but his efforts were in vain. Eighteen Conservatives deserted the party on second reading of the bill. Time was now running out. Parliament would expire when its term ran out on April 25. The House was kept in continuous session, at one time for more than one hundred hours. In the meantime, D. A. Smith – now Sir Donald and a Montreal MP – and two cabinet ministers were sent to Winnipeg in a last-ditch effort for compromise. Smith had none of the success that he had enjoyed in 1869-70, and he and his companions returned empty-handed. Tupper withdrew the remedial bill as being impossible to pass in the time remaining and carried the issue of the Manitoba School Question to the people of Canada.

The electoral campaign of 1896 was a loud and rowdy one by Canadian standards. The Catholic bogey was paraded in Ontario, and the Protestant menace was touted throughout Quebec. Clerical interference in politics in Quebec reached unprecedented heights. Everywhere there was great excitement – everywhere, that is, except Manitoba. Voting took place on June 23, 1896. The Liberals won with 118 seats against 88 for the Conservatives. The parties split evenly in Ontario and Nova Scotia; the Conservatives took Prince Edward Island three to two and lost British Columbia four to two. In Quebec, *Canadien* hopes for Laurier and suspicion of Conservative *bona fides* gave the Liberals 49 of the 65 seats. Manitoba was an apparent paradox. Four of the seven seats went Conservative, so that Manitoba appeared to have voted for a Government that was determined to coerce it. This was hardly the case, however. The Manitoba School Question which so disturbed the rest of the country, was not an issue in Manitoba. It was a settled fact, having been determined in two provincial elections. Manitoba was so convinced of this that it gave the Conservative Party 57 percent of its popular vote. True, D'Alton McCarthy, the arch anti-Catholic and anti-*Canadien* had been returned in Brandon as well as in his home riding of Simcoe North. But Brandon was Sifton territory and McCarthy had a hearty assist from Manitoba's attorney-general, whose eyes were already on wider horizons and who was therefore content to let McCarthy keep the seat until a settlement of the School Question could clear the way to Ottawa.

The settlement was not long in coming. In the fall of 1896, Laurier sent Israel Tarte to Winnipeg. Here, negotiations were conducted, with Sifton acting for the Greenway Government. Laurier had no mandate to ask drastic concessions from Manitoba, no more than Manitoba had the desire to grant them. Sifton's elevation to the federal cabinet was assured and good will prevailed between the representatives of the governments. It was not so, however, with the local Catholic clergy. Archbishop Taché had died in 1894 and his successor, L. P. A. Langevin, was characterized by Tarte as "rigid" and his clerical colleagues as "fanatics." The Catholic Church was thus largely ignored by the negotiators, and if the settlement was acceptable to most of the Protestant clergy and to McCarthy himself, it was because few concessions were made. That concessions *were* made was a source of constant rumbling from the Orange lodges. The so-called Laurier-Greenway Compromise was announced on November 19, 1896, just two days after Clifford Sifton was named Minister of the Interior and Superintendent of Indian Affairs in the Laurier Government. Sifton thus began a new phase of his career in which he was to become closely involved with Manitoba and the West as the organizer of the great era of prairie settlement.

The compromise, entirely the work of Tarte and Sifton, did of necessity involve some concessions to the Catholic position. Religious teaching could be conducted between 3:30 and 4:00 P.M. by a clergyman or his deputy if authorized by the local school board or if requested by the parents of ten pupils in a rural school or of twenty-five pupils in an urban school. The children were to be separated by faith only for religious instruction and any child might be excused if his parent so requested. In rural schools where there were twenty-five pupils of the Roman Catholic faith, and in urban schools where there were forty pupils of that faith, one properly-certified Catholic teacher was to be employed. Where the Protestants were in a minority, a Protestant teacher was to be employed under the same conditions if requested by the minority. There was also a concession in the matter of language instruction which was to have repercussions which its authors could not have dreamed of. The settlement read: "When ten pupils in any school speak the French language or any language other than English, as their native language, the teaching of such pupils shall be in French, or such other language, and English upon the bilingual system." The intention here was to avoid the charge of favoritism to the *Canadien* and also, to an extent, to open the way for Mennonite schools and to encourage these stolid sons of the soil to a wider acceptance of education. The end results, with the great rush of eastern European immigration at the end of the century, was to produce a number of Ukrainian-English and Polish-English schools among the French-English and German-English. The general laxity of school administration led to situations where students achieved university entrance standing without having even a practical knowledge of English or French. By 1912, there were 1,436 school districts in operation. Of these schools, 125 were French-English, 43 were German-English, and 65 either Ukrainian-English or Polish English. This was one reason why the school system was again to come under close scrutiny.

It was also understood in the compromise, though not spelled out in detail, that the Catholic interest should be given fair representation on the advisory board, on panels of examiners, and in the ranks of school inspectors. Throughout most of the province, the new system was quickly accepted. Most rural parochial schools moved into the public system – though there were some exceptions, notably in the city of Winnipeg, where the Catholic Church maintained its own schools. The Catholic hierarchy was not satisfied with the outcome, but it was hushed into silence by a papal encyclical of December, 1897, which urged acceptance in the interests of harmony. No concessions were made in law, but they came in practice and were widely accepted. It was soon another fact of life in Manitoba that the Public School Act was as much honored in the breach as it was in the observance. There was occasional thunder from the extremes of both sides, but generally a *modus vivendi* was arrived at which was politically comfortable and which was preferable to open conflict. Local situations were often most permissive. The late Deputy Minister of Education, Dr. Robert Fletcher, was employed as a fledging teacher in a Catholic school district which lacked an available priest. Fletcher, a staunch Protestant, conducted catechism for the last half-hour of the school day, without arousing contrary comment.

Preoccupation with schools had served to hold popular attention and to keep the Liberals in power, but other problems had been piling up since 1890. There was no general brightening of the economic landscape. The long depression continued. There had been some intermittent lifting of the gloom. There was a general remission at the beginning of the 1880's which led to the excesses of the boom and a further and less catastrophic interval in the late 1880's and early 1890's. This hope had been dashed, in turn, by a recession which began in 1893 and which led to a new general low in 1896. All this meant continuing trouble to Manitoba, whose prosperity depended even then on that of the rest of the world. Immigration, the transfusion that had always lent new strength, slowed to a trickle. On his withdrawal from Canadian political life, Edward Blake wrote forlornly to the electors of West Durham in 1890: "The empty West is empty still."

Such immigration as did take place was of the kind with which Manitoba had been familiar since the early days of the province. It came in large part from eastern Canada, mostly from Ontario, with a few Maritimers and a scattering from Quebec. There were minor additions to the Mennonite and Icelandic settlements, both of which were beginning to spread. The Mennonites began to establish satellite villages westward into the Territory of Assiniboia and the Icelanders south and west into more fertile lands. In the main, however, the Icelanders were moving into Winnipeg and Selkirk, adding a welcome leavening to these urban centers. A few hardy souls came in from the United Kingdom, as they had never really ceased doing since the days of Lord Selkirk. Even new sources of immigration were beginning to open up. Americans appeared in search of good free land, which was no longer so easily obtainable in their own country. They were the first drops of what was to become a torrent at the start of the new century. Several parties of Swedes made an appearance during the late 1880's and early 1890's. Some settled to the north of Minnedosa and others in the Stonewall region. The latter has maintained itself as a separate entity over the years, while most of the others of Swedish origin have become absorbed in the general population. There were other harbingers of the great flood of settlement to come. The first organized parties of Russian Jewish immigrants came in 1882, and these were followed by a reasonably steady if minute trickle of Jewish refugees from the pogroms of the Russian Empire and Rumania. Many of these took homesteads and some held to the life of the farm. Others, through lack of agricultural know-how or through the exercise of native intelligence, sought other occupations in the towns.

In 1892, the first forerunners of Ukrainian settlement, arrived at Winnipeg. Their impetus had been provided by stories of the Canadian West told to them by German neighbors who had direct contact with Canada. They came to Winnipeg and to Gretna, where they found employment among the Mennonites, with whom they could communicate. One, Iwan Pilipiwski, returned to Austrian Galicia and organized a larger party. He and two other leaders were imprisoned for sedition, it being illegal to encourage the emigration from Austria-Hungary of good farm workers and potential soldiers. This may have slowed any large movement for a time, but an intrepid few were to be found at Winnipeg and at Gretna when Dr. Joseph Oleskow came in 1895 to make a report on conditions and prospects for his fellows on the western steppes of Europe. Oleskow's report was favorable, even extravagantly so, and his whole-hearted efforts to find a better life for the Ukrainian subjects of the Emperor Francis Joseph coincided neatly with the new dawn of western settlement. Ukrainian settlers began to arrive in numbers before the great period of immigration began and continued to do so, with the interruption of the First World War, late into the 1920's.

By the early 1890's, immigration into Manitoba and the West was assuming the pattern which, writ large, would transform the province beyond all previous dreams. But Manitoba was not preparing for the transformation to come. Land surveying, largely the responsibility of Ottawa, already lagged behind settlement, since so much surveyed land was the preserve of the railways and therefore not open to homesteaders. More railways were built, and by the end of the century they were at least adequate as a basis from which to build further. The Manitoba & North Western, which had been laid from Portage la Prairie to Gladstone in the 1880's, was extended north to Dauphin and thence to Lake Winnipegosis by a new partnership which was to play an increasing part in the railway affairs of Manitoba, of the West, and of Canada.

William MacKenzie and Donald Mann had experience in western rail construction as subcontractors for the CPR and the Winnipeg & Hudson Bay Railway. In 1895, they bought up the moribund Lake Manitoba Railway and Canal Company which had been chartered in 1889 and which could lay claim, upon actual railway construction, to large land and cash subsidies. Mackenzie was a financial wizard and Mann a practical genius at rail construction. They were ably abetted by Zebulon Lash, an expert framer of legal small print, and David Hanna, who, as superintendent, kept the railway operating efficiently. From 1896 on, they quickly bought up existing lines and built new ones, letting the land and cash grants for each mile laid down pay for the next mile of track. Their Canadian Northern Railway was the first CNR and their rails served the north and west of the then-truncated province well in advance of major settlement. Its pioneer efforts marked a return to the early days of enthusiasm for railways in Manitoba. Some of the new settlers, notably the first of the Ukrainians and Poles, pitched in to help build the grade of the new line to Dauphin and beyond in the fashion of a barn-raising "bee." The Canadian Northern responded by providing free seed wheat in the Dauphin area in the spring of 1897. The railway and the settlers needed each other and, in these relatively simple days, found ways to demonstrate their mutual dependence. Mackenzie and Mann were ambitious. They hoped and planned for eastern and southern outlets independent of the CPR and did much to keep alive the hope of a railway to Hudson Bay, still a vision for many a westerner, farmer, and businessman alike.

The life of a homesteader, be it on the open plain or in the so-called aspen parkland, was far from an easy one. These farm pioneers and their families lived in dreary isolation, burdened by an unending drudgery which was almost totally unrelieved by the use of sophisticated machinery. With his oxen – or, more latterly, with horses – the homesteader had to break the thick, resistant prairie sod or clear the land of bush, scrub oak, box elder, and poplar. Many a poplar-pole shanty, dugout, or sod house was called home – often for a number of years, during which time money was scraped together to build a proper house. It was commonly said that for those who lived in sod houses, a three-day rain on the outside meant a five-day rain on the inside. A microcosm of the experience of the Manitoba homesteader has been set down by Iwan Drohomirecki, a pioneer of the Interlake who took up land at Pleasant Home in 1897:

> I built a temporary shack from poplar poles and branches, and the mosquitoes nearly killed our children before the autumn brought relief. I was unable to build a better house because I spent all my money [he had $5.00 when he reached Pleasant Home] and was obliged to go and dig ditches near Selkirk, where I earned $23. I then returned to my children whom I left with my wife in the dug-out in the bush. We built a modest house before the winter set in, and moved in, although it was only half finished, because the frosty nights made it impossible for the children to

> remain in the cold shanty. My wife plastered the walls inside, and I built a large stove with a flat top, which for two years served as a bed for the children during the cold weather. The next summer I again went to dig ditches and I earned $80 which enabled us to buy a cow, and thus with God's help we have been managing.

On the open plains, wood was more often scarce than not, and buffalo chips continued to serve as fuel long after the buffalo itself had vanished from the scene. Water was often a problem – too much in the spring run-off and not enough in the growing season. Wells were dug and dug again, turning out each time to be dry holes. Everywhere on the prairie, especially in the spring, there was the danger of prairie fire. Before fencing could be afforded, stock tended to stray, while chickens and other lesser livestock – as well as the crops themselves – were the likely prey of insect and animal predators. Crops failed through excessive moisture, drought, stem rust, or early or late frosts. If a crop was harvested, the haul to the railhead could be one of fifty miles or more. When the crop was marketed, prices were generally low and the share taken by the railway and the elevator company seemed excessive. All in all, it was a hard life. There were, however, a few bright aspects. The loneliness was sometimes broken by neighborly visits and there was, in general, an openhandedness and mutual help that is frequently found in conditions of adversity.

On the eve of its greatest period of expansion, Manitoba did not appear to be expecting great events. The recession of 1893 was still evident in foreclosed mortgages, bankrupt businesses, and near ghost towns. The West was far too thinly populated to give reality to the promise of the National Policy. The railway had been built, but settlers had not come as hoped. Domestic manufacturing had been encouraged in the central provinces, but this had led to high prices – especially in farm machinery and in essentials like barbed wire and binder twine. Monopolistic combinations proliferated behind the safety of the Canadian tariff barrier, thus leading to even higher prices. The Government of Canada took no effective action. Indeed, no machinery for effective action yet existed. The successors of Sir John A. Macdonald were no more social reformers than was he. They reflected the *laissez-faire* capitalism which had been the wonder and the tragedy of the nineteenth century. Reform movements in the United States, such as the Patrons of Industry and the earlier Grange, had spilled over the border into Ontario and Manitoba, where they made but fleeting impression. In January, 1896, two Patrons had been elected to the Manitoba legislature, while in June, two were returned to the House of Commons from Ontario. The Patrons, as in the case of the Manitoba and North West Farmer's Union, were soon absorbed by the Liberal party. The twentieth century was well under way before agrarian discontent made a major impression on Canadian politics.

11

Fulfilment

NEVER BEFORE OR SINCE has Manitoba experienced such rapid and multifaceted expansion as took place between 1896 and 1911. This period of expansion was as unexpected as it was unprepared for, but when it came it was as the tide "which taken at the flood leads on to fortune." It has been noted that there were both local and far-flung indications that a change was in the air. There was a long-term trend toward higher prices, though it was not evident to the average man. The nature and direction of European migration to America was undergoing change, but nothing as yet indicated what was in store for the Canadian West.

The aged, confused, and beleaguered Conservative Government of Canada fell before Laurier and his Liberals on June 23, 1896, with a strong assist from the repercussions of the Manitoba School Question. The timing could not have been more fortunate for the Liberals. Even before they had settled into the seats of power, the Canadian economic horizon brightened to a dawn of unforeseen magnificence. Capital which had been almost impossible to obtain a year before was now eagerly offered in London, New York, Paris, Montreal, and even Toronto. Interest rates were low enough to give promise of good profits to the businessman and thus encourage him to expand old enterprises and to undertake new ones. The great volume of new immigrants, in the vain hope of which the CPR had been driven across the Dominion, now began to clamor at the gates. The National Policy of Macdonald was at last to come into its own.

The imminent fulfilment of the cherished dreams of Canada and its West was by no means fortuitous. Its beginnings are to be found even farther afield than the market for fur which first caused Europeans to make Manitoba their home; but they are also to be found as close to Manitoba as its southern border. The land hunger of the restless westward-moving American and his European counterpart could no longer find fulfilment in the United States of the late 1890's. Western Canada's hour had struck at last. No longer was the American West able to absorb the land-seekers who had for so long flocked there. These people now turned to the north and west, flowing over the forty-ninth parallel, as oblivious to its existence as had been the buffalo. In the twenty-five years from 1891 to 1916, over one million Americans settled in Canada. This figure includes many, once Canadian, who had moved to the United States and who now returned to the land of their birth.

Almost overnight, Canada had become the land of promise – and not merely to North Americans. During the same period, a million and a half Europeans made Canada their goal. Shipload upon shipload sailed from Hamburg, Antwerp, Liverpool, Glasgow, Cherbourg, Naples, and a dozen other Old World ports heading for Halifax, St. John, Quebec, or Montreal. Of this million and a half, 961,000 were from the United Kingdom and 594,000 from the continent, chiefly from southern and eastern Europe. Among the Britishers, many came to farm; but it was not from highly-industrialized Britain that Manitoba received the mass of her future citizens. The bulk of the more than half a million eastern Europeans – Ukrainians, Poles, Russians, and Germans – came to the western land and became the sinews of present-day Alberta, Saskatchewan, and Manitoba.

To obtain this result, Clifford Sifton, Minister of the Interior, and James A. Smart, his deputy and fellow-Manitoban, embarked on the greatest promotion campaign which Canada, or the world, had ever known. The Government of Canada formed the North Atlantic Trading Company, centered on the German port of Hamburg, with the sole aim of attracting the peasantry of central and eastern Europe to the Canadian West. Bonuses of five dollars per man and two dollars per woman or child were paid to the booking agents for these immigrants, bonuses that were not paid for those originating in Great Britain or the United States. Canada, Manitoba, and the CPR had previously operated immigration offices in the United Kingdom and Europe, had used travelling displays, and had spread the printed word – all in the hope of attracting large numbers of immigrants. These techniques were still employed, but they were now employed on a far grander scale. Most important, the time was now ripe for such efforts.

In 1887, an immense source of gold had been found in South Africa. From the Witwatersrand, the "reef of the white waters" on the high veld of the Transvaal, literally tons of gold found their way into the gold-based monetary systems of the major countries of the world. This was the transfusion of which the anemic world economy had long stood in need. It was a sustained transfusion and it was soon augmented by an equally-rich lode in the Yukon-Alaska region, the fabulous Klondike of the "Trail of 98." It was this gold which made possible the movement of the great mass of people who came to western Canada and which financed the many operations necessary to make the region a productive one. Gold provided capital for new railways, country elevators and terminals, flour and feed mills, roads and bridges, farm machinery – in short, all of the many tools of the modern agricultural state. Between 1896 and 1911, the railway map of western Canada was transformed from the single spine-like span of the CPR with its few tenative branches to a veritable replica of the central nervous system. Numbers of landed immigrants, car loadings, bushels harvested; value of imports and exports, volume of bank deposits, loans made; miles of rail laid, roads built, towns incorporated, and cities chartered – all made a mass of happy figures to boggle the mind of any Board of Trade secretary or Dominion Bureau of Statistics analyst. This bid fair to be, as Laurier had promised, "the century of Canada."

World economic conditions aside, eastern Europe was ripe for the plucking of the flower of its agricultural population. In Austria-Hungary, and no less in Russia and Germany, the land hunger was beyond appeasement. The Ukrainians and Poles especially were reduced to the smallest of peasant holdings or to a virtual agricultural peonage. In addition, they suffered under alien political jurisdiction, no less galling for its age-old existence. They were also discriminated against for their nationality and their language; and, in the case of the Ukrainians at least, for their religion. Morever, all were subject to compulsory military service in the armies of their oppressor.

The trials of the immigrant, however, were by no means over when he left his homeland. Most were woefully short of cash, and even at the extremely low rates then charged for passage, they had little on which to subsist until they were established on the land. The Canadian government offered no form of direct subsidization to the newcomers. Many of them suffered additionally as the prey of unscrupulous or fraudulent travel agents who took advantage of their general lack of knowledge of conditions in Canada, their difficulty with English, and their almost universal illiteracy. Though they travelled in groups, the Ukrainian and Polish immigrants lacked organization. They were not especially convoyed and settled, as had been the Icelanders and Mennonites, under the direct care of the Canadian government. Their choice of land in Manitoba was severely limited, since most of the good empty land was held by the railways and other promoters at prices which, even if modest, were far beyond the limited means of the eastern European. More often than not, the land on which they settled was far from the best. With the exception of those who set down to the north and south of Riding Mountain, the Poles and Ukrainians had, quite literally, a tough row to hoe. In the Interlake, in Stuartburn, or northeast of Winnipeg they needed all of their vaunted powers of endurance and optimism, as well as a sense of humor. Accustomed to small acreages, some were attracted to twenty- and thirty-acre river lots in the Ste. Agathe area – much to their regret. Placed on land which was less than "fairly fit for settlement," the Ukrainians and Poles strove mightily; and more often than could be reasonably expected, they strove successfully.

Other immigrants were attracted to Winnipeg and other centers, where they were a welcome addition to a labor market in which demand always outran supply. It was the eastern European who labored to build most of the new railways: the Canadian Northern, the Grand Trunk Pacific, and their myriad branch lines. His labor also drained much of the bogland of the Interlake, of Springfield, St. Clements, Brokenhead, and elsewhere. Wages were low, but the work was often needed in order to supplement a difficult homestead operation or as a means of getting by while skills were learned, among them the English language. In the matter of language, the Ukrainian and Polish settlers had some difficulty, since their more rapid urbanization made it necessary for them to understand, and be understood by, the omnipresent Anglo-Saxon boss. Their mastery of English was helped by their dealings with Jewish merchants and Mennonite employers, who served as a sort of catalyst in the learning process. The Jewish merchant, shopkeeper, or itinerant pedlar was, more often than not, a good friend to the newly-arrived Slav. Thus, the violence and intensity of Europe's Slavic anti-Semitism found only barren ground in Manitoba. The Mennonite, on the other hand, exacted as long and as hard labor from his hired hands as he did from himself, and little love was lost between him and the newcomers.

The Ukrainian settler had a further disadvantage in the lack of spiritual advisors to whom he could turn with confidence. The Ukrainians were either Greek Orthodox or Greek Catholic and therefore turned from the Roman Catholic clergy as being foreign and no better than the Polish priests whom they had mistrusted at home. Neither of their churches made any effort to accompany them to the New World. Indeed, the clergy, as agents of the Russian or Austro-Hungarian Empires, were opposed to emigration. The Canadian government was, not unnaturally, unwilling to subsidize a Ukrainian priesthood. There was no precedent here and none was created. The Mennonites arrived with a built-in clergy and the Icelanders could claim a spirituality of their own. Until their resources were adequate for the support of a clergy of their own, the Ukrainian had to make do with itinerant Greek Catholic or Greek Orthodox priests from the United States. The devotion of the Ukrainians to their church was a major factor in the maintenance of their ethnic identity, though they began slowly to integrate into Manitoba society. This integration was accomplished more quickly in some areas than in others – in Dauphin, for example, long before Winnipeg. The Ukrainians had no tradition of democratic institutions, but they soon became politically involved. At first, they tended to be the unknowing tools of Anglo-Saxon politicians, but before long they mastered the game themselves.

The number of Poles and Ukrainians who entered Canada grew from a trickle of two or three thousand a year in 1897 and 1898 to tens of thousands a year in 1910 and 1911. In all, over 200,000 Poles and Ukrainians found their way into western Canada, where they joined the even greater numbers of British, Americans, and Canadians. The larger part of this immigration moved through Manitoba into the Northwest Territories, giving that area the population which caused the Government of Canada to erect the provinces of Alberta and Saskatchewan in 1905. Many tarried in Manitoba, where they served to fill the gaps between existing cores of settlement, venturing out, wherever possible, into tracts which had hitherto been vacant. Railway and other reserved lands were taken up by newcomers who had capital – eastern Canadians, Britishers, and Americans, for the most part – and by the expansion of the acreage of older settlers. It had become evident to the government that 160 acres was not sufficient to maintain a family on the plains and the regulations had been altered to make possible the occupation of an additional 160 acres through homesteading.

Manitoba's population soared. From just over 150,000 in 1891, the province reached 554,000 in 1916. The distribution of the population also underwent a drastic change. Whereas in 1891 over seventy percent of the people lived on farms, by 1916 only fifty-six percent did so. The population of the cities and towns rose from 41,000 in 1891 to 241,000 in 1916. This was a manifestation of Manitoba's new role in the Canadian economy. It was, in essence, merely the time-honored role writ large. Manitoba found its first firm population in supplying the fur trade at the beginning of the nineteenth century, and it was now to become the supplier of the great Canadian breadbasket of the twentieth century. As Winnipeg had been the middleman and the processor for the original agricultural settlement in the Province of Manitoba, so the province as a whole now turned to serve the same function for the rest of the prairie West. Manitoba held and even increased its enviable reputation as a grower of grain, but more and more effort was to be directed towards the carrying and processing of all manner of goods moving into and out of the West.

There was no revolutionary change in the nature of Manitoba's economic activity. There was, however, a great intensification of that activity, and refinements and alterations were made for the greater effectiveness of the whole. Lumber and flour mills, coal and fuel yards, farm-machinery dealers, meat-packing houses, printing plants, wholesale grocery and dry-goods establishments – an endless list of enterprises grew, both in number and in volume. Many new activities were entered upon. Suppliers of steam engines and their appurtenances were soon joined by dealers in the new internal-combustion engine and its most change-making manifestation, the automobile. Not long after the turn of the century, automobiles began to appear on the streets of Winnipeg and the doom of the 10-miles-per-hour speed limit was at hand. The horse remained prevalent in the city until after the First World War, and on the farm long after that – but its days were numbered, both on the road and in the fields.

The main purpose of all this activity revolved about the handling of the grain crop, which was increasing by leaps and bounds. The growing and handling of the grain crop was a continuous and expanding operation, expanding indeed throughout the years of the First World War. This rapid growth bears some surface similarities to the marketing of cotton in the southern United States in the period before the Civil War. Cash was plentiful only during harvesting and the fall movement of the crop. For the rest, business was conducted largely by credit, and credit was made easily available by the banks, which were given additional power to circulate bank notes in the fall. Along with prices, population and the cash value of the crop kept climbing steadily.

It was already being noticed that much money tended to flow into few hands. The mansions of the grain and other merchant princes were rising on Wellington Crescent and on corresponding streets in Portage la Prairie, Brandon, Dauphin, Killarney, and elsewhere. There was also, however, much evidence of a new-found farm prosperity – not the least of which was the three-storey brick farm house with its brick outbuildings. In 1905, the western grain crop reached 100,000,000 bushels for the first time and moving facilities were strained over the whole of the winter. While general prosperity prevailed, there were indications that this bed of roses was not without its thorns. The prevailing free-enterprise economy was something of a mixed blessing. Many went under – on the farm and in business alike. There were sharp edges to catch the unwary. Some became wealthy and many became affluent, but this was by no means the case for all.

The railways still strode across the land with a regal lack of concern for lesser beings. The Winnipeg Grain Exchange had become a world market, as important, if not more so, than Chicago in the setting of grain prices. The Grain Exchange, the railways, and the line elevator companies were suspect in the minds of the farmer as garnering far more than a fair share of his labor. The grain growers began to organize in their own interest and were destined to break forth in righteous political wrath when their accumulated frustrations became too much to be contained. In Winnipeg especially, there was a growing labor force. It was largely unskilled and divided by differences of race and language, but it was gaining an increasing leavening of skilled workers, both from within and without. This labor force was also gaining an organization. The Brotherhood of Locomotive Engineers was given a Winnipeg charter in January, 1881, to be followed at the end of the year by the International Typographical Union. The Metal Workers and other railway brotherhoods soon followed, along with other craft unions. A movement in the direction of industrial unionism on the model of the American Knights of Labor came to naught in the 1890's and English-style craft unions prevailed, uniting into the Winnipeg Trades and Labor Council in 1894. Industrial unionism returned during World War I as the One Big Union and played a central role in the strike of 1919. Manitoba's advance into a technical society quickly exposed and irritated the many seemingly inevitable blemishes of such a society.

Manitoba's farmers and workers began to seek the removal or amelioration of such blemishes, but each in his own way and with no display of revolutionary zeal. The pronouncements and predictions of Karl Marx went unheeded, as did the rantings of "Big Bill" Haywood and the "Wobblies," the American-born Industrial Workers of the World. So long as general prosperity prevailed, it was, in truth, "an era of good feeling."

The good feeling, however, did not extend to Manitoba politics. The period of great economic growth was also the greatest period of political agitation between the two major parties. Grave charges were hurled about with wild abandon, and serious matters – such as temperance legislation, school reform, and female suffrage – were all but lost sight of in the welter of real and supposed electoral corruption. As the new era had been heralded at Ottawa by the advent of the fifteen-year Laurier administration, it was followed three years later at Winnipeg by an equally long-lived Roblin Government. The Greenway Government did not long survive either the loss of the School Question as an issue or of Clifford Sifton as a guiding hand. Greenway was well-meaning but irresolute, and his administration had at first been dominated by Joseph Martin and then by Sifton. After Sifton took up the Interior portfolio at Ottawa, there was no one to direct the local administration. The concessions of the Laurier-Greenway Compromise, as moderate as they were, weakened Greenway's hold on the Protestant majority; while that same moderation of concession failed to mollify the Catholics. There were still formidable railway problems regarding branch lines and rate structures. The supposed magic of complementary Liberal administrations at both Ottawa and Winnipeg had led neither to the return of Crown lands, to an extension of boundaries, nor to any increase in federal subsidies. Old age, as inevitable in government as in men, was taking its toll. The Conservatives were now united, and in 1896 Rodmond P. Roblin returned to lead them. He had led the party on his conversion from the Liberals in 1890, but had been gerrymandered out of a seat in 1892. Roblin was the new Manitoba strongman, and he was to direct events until 1915.

Smelling victory from afar, Roblin moved with a political dexterity which belied his physical bulk. It was a dexterity which was to be the despair of the Liberal Party of Manitoba. In 1898, Roblin withdrew from the Conservative leadership in favor of Hugh John Macdonald, the only surviving son of the Father of Confederation and a fixture of the Manitoba Bar since 1882. Macdonald had first moved west with the Wolseley Expedition and had fought in the rebellion of 1885. Not only did he possess the magic of his father's name, but he was also an amiable and courteous gentleman who had already sat in the House of Commons for Winnipeg. Roblin's withdrawal was strategic. The Conservatives hoped to gain by the supposed weakening of Greenway on the School Question, and Roblin, who had led the fight against the Public Schools Act on its introduction in 1890, was hardly the man to point the finger of scorn at Greenway. A provincial election was held in December 1899 and Greenway was routed. The Conservatives returned twenty-three to the Liberals' fifteen.

On January 8, 1900, Macdonald assumed the premiership, Roblin remained outside the Government, though he was undoubtedly the most powerful figure in the councils of the party. The Conservatives had espoused the cause of temperance legislation in its electoral canvass. Temperance – and its inevitable shadow, prohibition – was a matter of growing political concern in Manitoba. As early as 1892, a temperance referendum had registered 12,000 to 7,000 for stricter regulation of the sale of liquor. This sentiment was reinforced by a Dominion-wide referendum on the same question in 1898. Manitoba voted 12,000 to 3,000 to close the saloons. In conformity with this result, and in order to fulfil his election pledge, Macdonald carried through legislation which would effectively close the saloons by forbidding the sale of liquor by the glass. Within weeks of the passage of this act, he retired from the premiership to contest Brandon against Sifton in the general election of November, 1900. Following his defeat in Brandon, Macdonald withdrew from active political life. He became Winnipeg's police magistrate in 1911, a knight bachelor in 1913, and a respected figure in the life of Winnipeg until his death in 1929. It is difficult to escape the conclusion that Hugh John Macdonald was urged into his disastrous attempt to unseat the mighty Sifton only as a means of making way for Roblin. Macdonald's concern for his electoral promises was, at best, embarrassing to a government whose political machinery was based on the city saloons and their rural hotel equivalents.

Roblin became premier on October 29, 1900, and his close associate, Robert Rogers, MPP for Manitou, joined the Government. Together, they were to forge a political machine with which they accomplished much for Manitoba, until the too-great trust of Roblin and the too-easy permissiveness of Rogers combined to bring them down. Roblin referred Macdonald's temperance act to the courts on the grounds of its doubtful constitutionality, though the decision in the Local Prohibition Case of 1896 had placed the control of the sale of liquor squarely in the laps of the provinces. In due course, the Judicial Committee affirmed the legislation, upon which a further referendum was held. The temperance forces urged that it be boycotted as being unnecessary and as an act of bad faith – which in fact, it was. It also was defeated. On the basis of this result, Roblin then decided to drop liquor legislation and to leave control to local option, enforceable by municipal plebiscite.

Roblin took full advantage of the tide of prosperity which was running in favor of Canada. He was a firm believer in free enterprise and in the sanctity of private property. Neither he nor any of his Government were social reformers or believers in the awakening ideas of governmental responsibility for the correction or amelioration of social inequities. His implacable opposition to votes for women is an indication of his attitude, as was his devious behavior on the temperance issue. He reacted readily, however, when essentials were being mishandled or inadequately dealt with in the moving of grain, in the provision of telephone communication, and in the development of hydroelectric power. In these cases, he struck out to preserve the interests of the province with measures of unrepentant socialism which are not a part of the memories of his political heirs. Roblin was as much a "boss" as Manitoba has ever had; but he was never liable to being labelled a "tool of the interests," as the expression then ran.

Thus, Roblin early on paid attention to the inadequacies of the existing rail system and grain-moving facilities in the face of a geometrically-expanding volume of grain. He was no more enamored of the CPR than was his predecessor, John Norquay. The Northern Pacific was passing through one of its regular bankruptcies when Roblin took office, and he took advantage of the event to assume control of the Northern Pacific & Manitoba Railway. He leased its lines on a 999-year basis in January, 1901, and three weeks later transferred the lease to the Canadian Northern Railway. The terms of the lease reflected the continuing suspicion in which the CPR was held. Mackenzie and Mann of the CNR agreed never to unite with, or to pool traffic with, the CPR. The province was to receive an annual rental which would rise to $300,000 per year and the CNR agreed to accept provincial control of its rates. When all of its lines in Manitoba were consolidated in 1903, the CNR cut its rates both on general freight and on grain by fifteen percent. Mackenzie and Mann became recognized overnight as benefactors of Manitoba and Roblin took a full share of the credit. The CNR was well set on the way to its transcontinental destiny – as well as toward eventual bankruptcy. Meanwhile, however, it could do no wrong in Manitoba. No more than could Roblin, who had helped Manitobans to break the iron grip of the CPR. Manitoba stood firmly behind the CNR's plans for further expansion. There was, after all, the hope that the railway to Hudson Bay would finally be built.

Mackenzie and Mann had come a long way since they extended the Manitoba & North Western Railway to Dauphin in 1895. In 1898, they had taken up the charter of the defunct Manitoba South Eastern and had built it from Winnipeg to Sprague on the American border. With the financial help of the Manitoba government, they built through Minnesota south of Lake of the Woods, turning back into Canada at Rainy River, then building and buying their way to Port Arthur. In January, 1902, they could handle grain directly to Lake Superior and began to build two 1,000,000-bushel terminals there to store it for the lake freighters. In 1899 and 1900, the daring but canny Scots had built north from Sifton along the east side of Duck and Porcupine mountains and then thrust west into Saskatchewan, heading for Prince Albert and beyond. Meanwhile, though more slowly, they built west from Dauphin, south of Duck Mountain in the direction of Kamsack. By 1903, the CNR had rail coverage of Manitoba that was second to none.

Rail facilities were now close to being adequate. In fact, in time and through a general excess of enthusiasm, there was to be an excess of rails in some areas. There remained, however, other abuses in the movement of grain which first stirred the farmers themselves to action and which, in due course, produced a reaction from the provincial and federal governments. Freight rates aside, the railways had aroused rural ire through the inadequate supply of grain cars, especially at harvest time, when to be among the first through Winnipeg meant a better price on the market. Not only were there not enough box cars, but there was a well-founded suspicion that the railways exercised a high degree of favoritism in the distribution of such cars as were available. They favored certain country elevator points over others and appeared partial to the line elevator companies over the independents. In 1897, the CPR had decreed that henceforth it would no longer pick up grain from the so-called "flat warehouses" or from loading platforms. This would certainly speed the movement of grain by increasing the turnover of grain cars. As part of the same speed-up, the railways offered a site at a nominal rent and an assurance of box-car service to anyone who would build a standard elevator of 25,000 bushel capacity, powered by a steam or gasoline engine. This did encourage the construction of elevators, but it also tended to deprive the farmer of an alternate buyer and a cheaper if more laborious means of loading his grain. Many of the elevators were suspected of giving short weight and of undergrading so as to sell grain at a higher grade than that for which the farmer had been paid.

Farm protests against these evils were heard at Ottawa, and the Minister of Railways, A. G. Blair, ordered that the CPR provide cars for warehouse and platform loading. These protests also led to the appointment of a royal commission on the grain trade which reported the overwhelming dominance of the elevator business by the line companies and the flour millers. There followed the Manitoba Grain Act of 1900, which gave federal guarantees to warehouse loading of grain equally with elevator loading and set down clear rules as to grading, weighing, and dockage. A bumper crop in 1901 produced a serious dislocation of grain movement, properly characterized as the "grain blockade." As a direct result, a farm organization for the redress of this and other grievances was formed at Indian Head in the District of Saskatchewan on December 18, 1901. The farmers of the Indian Head region took advantage of a sheduled debate between Rodmond Roblin and F. W. Haultain on the subject of possible westward extension of Manitoba to fit in a protest meeting on the preceding afternoon. Here was formed the Territorial Grain Growers' Association, which gained wide membership during 1902. As a result of the efforts of Peter Dayman and W. R. Motherwell, the Territorial Grain Growers' Association secured amendments to the Manitoba Grain Act which provided a "first come, first served" basis for the distribution of grain cars. In the fall of 1902, the Territorial Association took action against the CPR agent at Sintaluta for failure to observe this fair distribution. The association won its case, and the CPR was obliged to put more grain cars into service. The shortage of cars is explained by the fact that the railways were reluctant to invest large sums in grain cars, since these cars were used for only three or four months of the year. In due course, a system of leasing was developed by the Canadian and American railways in which the rolling stock of each line was pooled and followed the harvest from Texas in the early months of the year to the Canadian West in the late fall.

Their first small success in the Sintaluta trial encouraged the farmers and on March 3, 1903, a Manitoba Grain Growers' Association was formed at Brandon, with Roderick McKenzie as secretary. McKenzie was a perennial moving spirit in the struggle to improve the lot of the farmer through gaining for him a fairer share of the product of his toil. In April, 1906, at the Leland Hotel in Winnipeg, farmers from Sintaluta, together with others of the Manitoba Grain Growers' Association, formed the Grain Growers' Grain Company. The Grain Company was a co-operative designed to handle the grain of its shareholders through the market and to pay dividends on the basis of the amount of grain marketed by the individual shareholder. In the late summer of 1906, the new company, chartered under the laws of the Province of Manitoba, purchased a seat on the Winnipeg Grain Exchange. The dividend-paying policy of the company was interpreted by the council of the grain exchange as commission-splitting and the company was expelled from the exchange in November, 1906. The Grain Growers' Company appealed to Rodmond Roblin. The premier, ever alert to the needs of his electorate, enacted legislation in 1908 which permitted the company to operate on the exchange. The company had to eliminate its patronage dividend clause, but this was a small price to pay for a place among those who controlled the flow of grain to market.

The line elevator companies handled grain from the farmer's wagon into their bins, thence to box car and, via railway, to whatever terminal the grain was destined for. With something like one million acres per year being added to the land under cultivation during the decade of 1901-11, and with widespread construction of branch railways to serve this land, elevator construction boomed. Elevators were built in large numbers, but the operation of the various line companies remained largely uncompetitive and their charges high. The organized farmers began to put pressure on the governments of the three prairie provinces to operate elevators as a public utility. The concept of government ownership and government regulation of public utilities was widely accepted in Manitoba. Government aid to and support of the railways was regarded as being in the nature of things, and regulation of rail rates was considered as natural as the presence of a police force. Public ownership of telephones got underway as early as 1906, and the provincial government viewed with benevolent eyes the embarcation of the City of Winnipeg on the business of generating and distributing hydroelectric power. Since a grain elevator was certainly a public utility, Roblin was open to persuasion.

In February, 1909, the Manitoba Grain Growers' Association presented the Roblin Government with a petition bearing 10,000 signatures and asking for a government-owned and government-operated line elevator system. During the summer of 1909, the directors of the Manitoba Grain Growers' Association repeated the appeal. A by-election in Birtle saw the election of a Grain Grower candidate over the Government's man in a campaign in which the winner had supported public ownership of grain elevators. Thus, in December, 1909, the Government announced that it would establish a line of elevators in the province as a public utility. The directors of the Grain Growers' Association, together with Thomas A. Crerar, president of the Grain Growers' Grain Company, offered a plan to Roblin for the implementation of his promise. This plan would have left complete control of the public elevators in the hands of the Grain Growers. Roblin was not prepared to go this far, no matter how high-minded the motives of the Grain Growers. The legislative session of 1910 saw the passage of a bill setting up an Elevator Commission under the Department of Public Works. The commission was to be appointed by the lieutenant-governor-in-council and was empowered to buy, lease, or build elevators in response to the petition of sixty percent of the farmers in the area to be served. In the case of the purchase of an existing elevator, any dispute as to price would be settled by arbitration through a third party appointed by agreement between the government and the seller.

The experiment was a failure. It profited no one, except some with elevators to sell and others to whom the government felt indebted. The going price for elevators rose over fifty percent in the course of one year. As many as three elevators were acquired at a single point, and in some cases, elevators which were purchased were never used. The first year's operations resulted in a $84,000 deficit and less than fifty-five percent of the commission's costs were recovered. In all, 174 government-operated elevators were established at 100 shipping points. After the first year, the Government was ready to get out of the elevator business, blaming its lack of success on the failure of the farmers to use the system. The Grain Growers, however, attributed the lack of success to political interference, patronage, and needless duplication. Roblin cut his losses. On July 20, 1912, the publicly-operated elevator system was leased to the Grain Growers' Grain Company for two years at an annual rent of six percent on a capitalized value of $1,160,000, the government to pay the cost of maintenance of the elevators. The experiment served to extend greatly the activities of the farmers' company. In the same year, they contracted for terminal space for two million bushels at the Lakehead, and in 1913 they began building country elevators on their own. In 1913 also, the company leased a flour mill at Rapid City and began the co-operative sale of farm supplies. In 1916, it entered the export market, establishing an office in New York; and in 1917, it joined with the Alberta Co-operative Farmers' Elevator Company to form the United Grain Growers, Limited, based at Winnipeg. In just over a decade, the prairie farmers had built a marketing and supply agency which stood tall among the others of the grain trade.

The failure of the experiment in the operation of grain elevators as a public utility did not disillusion Manitoba as to the value of public ownership. The Roblin Government financed the successful stockyards, abbattoir, and cold storage operation at St. Boniface as a sort of public utility, and the people had always before them the example of the successful telephone system. The telephone had come to Manitoba in the late 1880's and had rapidly caught on as a valuable means of personal communication. It was operated by the Bell Telephone Company as a private enterprise and by its very nature became a monopoly. With the increase in population, the demand for telephone service increased – as did its value in such vital matters as the dissemination from Winnipeg of grain prices. The Bell Telephone Company's service proved inadequate and expensive. The company, moreover, did not feel obligated to extend lines except where they could be expected to yield a profit. Thus, its long distance lines did not reach into many rural areas, and these areas strongly felt the lack. In the mood of the times, the Government was looked to for an improvement in telephone service and was quick to respond.

In 1906, the legislature approved the Manitoba Telephone and Telegraph Act. This act empowered the government to establish a Telephone Commission which was to acquire the Bell properties in the cities and its long distance facilities within Manitoba. The act also enabled municipal councils to expropriate local privately-owned systems with financial help from the province. Public approval was sought through municipal referendums and was gained in the fall of 1906 with over sixty percent of the municipalities approving public ownership. On January 15, 1908, the province took over telephone service as the Manitoba Government Telephones. Long distance coverage was increased and rural tolls reduced. After a somewhat shaky financial beginning, the system was reorganized under a single telephone commissioner and rates were raised in order to put the system on a paying basis. With commendable speed, practically all of the settled parts of the province were connected by means of telephone lines, and the public and privately-owned municipal systems were absorbed into the Manitoba Telephone System, as it later came to be called. This large-scale public venture into the telephone business was the first of its kind in North America. As such, it is a tribute to the pioneering spirit of the province; but it is also an indication of the already chronic addiction of Manitobans to the use of the telephone as a social amenity.

In the same year that the Province of Manitoba ventured into the field of communications, the City of Winnipeg undertook to generate and distribute hydroelectric power. Up to 1906, electric power had been steam-generated at the rate of twenty cents per kilowatt hour. The Winnipeg Electric Company was the first to develop part of the huge potential of the Winnipeg River, and on June 16, 1906, power from Pinawa was made available for ten cents per kilowatt hour. The previous rate of twenty cents had inspired leading citizens such as Sanford Evans, Thomas Cockburn, and R. D. Waugh to investigate the possibilities of public ownership under the auspices of the City of Winnipeg. Their plan for a generating station at Point du Bois was approved by an overwhelming vote of the ratepayers on June 28, 1906. The Roblin Government interposed no objection, nor did the Government of Canada, and in October, 1911, the Winnipeg City Hydro began to deliver power in Winnipeg introducing an era in which the city's rate of three cents per kilowatt hour was long the lowest on the continent. Hydroelectric power brought the Winnipeg River once more into the mainstream of the province's economy. This water highway, pioneered by La Vérendrye almost two centuries before, now assumed a permanent and valued role – albeit, at the cost of much of its natural beauty. The success of City Hydro inspired the city fathers to create the Greater Winnipeg Water District and to construct an aqueduct from Indian Bay in Shoal Lake, the westernmost part of Lake of the Woods. Thus, from its formal opening in 1919, the Winnipeg area was assured of an ample supply of good water, in spite of the subsequent increase in the city's population.

As the years of expansion of the first decade of the twentieth century advanced, so too did the political fortunes of Rodmond Roblin. In 1903, 1907, and 1910, his party won easy victories at the polls. The Conservative success was in the nature of things, as governments will gain credit for good times – as well as blame for the bad. Through all of this period, Roblin was aided by division and lack of leadership in the Liberal Party of Manitoba, which also failed to benefit from the presence of a Liberal administration at Ottawa. This is almost an axiom of Canadian politics; a provincial government tends to be suspect of subservience to Ottawa when it is of the same political stripe as the national government, and few provincial governments have ever suffered at the hands of their electorate for taking a strong stand against the aggression, real or imagined, of federal power. Roblin's Government took full credit for holding the line against Ottawa's blandishments on separate schools and was vociferous in its demands for control of Crown lands (now being more generally referred to as "natural resources"), as well as for boundary extension.

Thomas Greenway now withdrew from provincial politics; he was elected MP for Lisgar in 1904 and was appointed to the Board of Railway Commissioners just prior to his death in 1908. After some confusion, Edward Brown of Portage la Prairie emerged as Liberal leader in 1906, but he was hampered by a party platform which suffered too much of "me too," as well as by a cold and uncongenial public personality. He failed of election in 1907 and leadership devolved upon Tobias Crawford Norris, MPP for Lansdowne since 1899, who held together a small group in the legislature, including such able men as Thomas Johnson and Valentine Winkler. These men were fully occupied in sniping at the growing political and financial corruption of the administration. Both parties had much to answer for on these scores, the one provincially and the other federally. Direct bribery of voters, plural voting, mass enfranchisement of newly-arrived immigrants, ballot-box stuffing – all were the order of the day. Favoritism in employment, public-works construction, railway building, mail-delivery contracts, liquor-license granting and withholding – all were employed as a matter of course. Charges of electoral fraud were so common that it became a routine practice for party leaders to meet in order to cancel out each other's lists of protested elections following a provincial or federal vote.

This situation was by no means restricted to Manitoba. It was the accepted way of doing things on both sides of the border, in all the provinces and states. It was more spectacular in the United States only because there was more there to steal. Remedies brought forward in the United States – especially in the adjacent states: the

Dakotas, Minnesota, and Wisconsin – were picked up in Manitoba by the organs of agrarian discontent and were accepted warily, if at all, by the political parties. Schemes of direct legislation through initiation and referendum had been adopted to the south and were mooted in Manitoba, here to be given grudging acceptance by the local Liberals on the eve of World War I. The principle of recalling legislators who failed to act as their constituents expected was also imported from the United States, but it was regarded here as being alien to the principles of a constitutional monarchy. Votes for women became a popular cause among women, but it remained anathema to Rodmond Roblin, in spite of its acceptance by the Grain Growers' Association and the Winnipeg Trades and Labor Council. Roblin's distaste was perhaps due to the fact that the cause was eventually taken up by the Liberals under Norris. The agitation for effective temperance legislation increased, along with the women's suffrage movement. In fact, the two seem inextricably interrelated and were achieved almost simultaneously in 1916.

Premier Roblin continued to resist any proposed legislation which was aimed at providing compulsory schooling or at correcting the increasingly multilingual nature of the province's public schools. His reason for doing so was that such legislation would reopen the old wounds of the School Question controversy. In truth, it would have; but it would also have alienated many of the Government's stalwart supporters. To some, a child served better, and was better served, by working on the land; while to others, no school at all was preferable to what they considered the "Godless" public school system. In 1906, Roblin decreed that all public schools, in order to qualify for provincial grants, must fly the Union Jack. For this, he was created a Knight Commander of the Order of St. Michael and St. George in 1912, thus joining the increasing number of local "colonially made gentlemen." At the time, it was cynically rumored that the knighthood was doubly-earned by the part which Sir Rodmond played in the defeat of the Laurier Government in 1911 and by making schoolhouse ensigns more visible to the young by not requiring that they be inside the school where the flag could not so easily be seen.

The federal election of 1911 marked the high point of Rodmond Roblin's political power. The issue in the West –reciprocity with the United States – was a consummation devoutly wished for by the farmer who had for so long borne the main burden of the National Policy and who had, for an equal length of time, envied the lower costs of his American counterpart. The organized farmers, aided by the powerful voice of John Dafoe, editor of the *Free Press,* worked mightily for the success of the reciprocity agreement at the polls. Its Liberal proponents, however, had been long in office; Laurier, in fact, had been prime minister uninterruptedly for fifteen years – a unique phenomenon. What is more, he and his party were tarnished in the eyes of many for the lavish and often corrupt building of rails to the east. The peak of immigration had passed, and people were now beginning to doubt that this was actually "the century of Canada." Natural resources were still held by Ottawa, and the northern boundary stopped woefully short of those of Alberta and Saskatchewan. The Canadian Northern had built to The Pas, but the Hudson Bay railway was still only a promise – a promise, indeed, which had by now lost its enchantment.

Sir Clifford Sifton, long estranged from Laurier, was as active in his opposition to reciprocity as John Dafoe was in support of it. The weight of a still-strong attachment to Britain and the fear of annexation by the United States were powerful factors, as was the lavishly-spread wealth of the Canadian Manufacturers' Association and the CPR. Sir William Van Horne feared a loss of east-west traffic and was out "to beat the damned thing." The issue of reciprocity as "veiled treason" toward the United Kingdom and as the dread forerunner of annexation were made much of in Ontario and thus in Manitoba, which was, as in the past, a good reflector of Ontario's thought. In Quebec, the Liberals stood accused of strengthening the bonds of Empire through the Laurier-inspired Canadian navy, which gave rise to a belief in the possibility of involving Canada in Britain's wars.

When the votes were counted, Ontario had rejected Laurier by the wide margin of 73 seats to 13. In Quebec, 27 out of 65 went "Nationalist" and these worthies suffered an overnight change into Conservatives in what has since been characterized in Quebec as "the great betrayal." The Maritimes split fairly evenly: 19 Liberals to 16 Conservatives. The three prairie provinces returned 17 Liberals to 10 Conservatives. Alberta and Saskatchewan went all-out for reciprocity, returning only one Conservative each. In Manitoba, the afterglow of Ontario influence, blown to white heat by the bellows of Roblin, had reversed the trend to free trade with the United States. Robert Cruise of Dauphin and J. P. Molloy of Provencher were the only Liberals returned. Eight of the 10 seats went Conservative. Roblin was rewarded with his knighthood in 1912, and his principal political lieutenant, Robert Rogers, was advanced to the

Department of the Interior at Ottawa. It was a promotion which placed him in the seat, if not in the tradition, of Sifton. Rogers left behind a legacy which was to destroy Sir Rodmond Roblin politically and which was to cast the Conservative Party of Manitoba into outer darkeness for a generation.

Manitoba itself did not go unrewarded for its support of Robert Borden and the federal Conservative Party. Boundary extension had been one of Manitoba's chronic complaints since its premature birth in 1870. A considerable extension had been achieved in 1881, consolidated disappointingly on the east by the Judicial Committee decision of 1884. This extension did not long satisfy and with the advent of the great era of settlement at the end of the 1890's, the demand for an extension of the boundaries increased – both in volume and in degree of importunity. The hope for a Hudson Bay railway made many look primarily to a northern extension which would include the shore of the bay. This idea was not welcome in Toronto, where a future northern maritime greatness for Ontario was a comforting dream. Until the creation of Alberta and Saskatchewan in 1905, however, Manitoba's ambitions were more to the west than to the north. Rodmond Roblin was no more a "collector of deserts" than was the later Italian dictator, Benito Mussolini, and the then District of Keewatin appeared less hopeful of development than any desert. The Canadian Shield was still more a cross to be borne than a treasure house of minerals to be exploited. As early as 1901, Roblin had sought westward extension into what were then the Districts of Assiniboia and Saskatchewan on the grounds that the West was Manitoba's hinterland and the province needed space and people for the proper undertaking of its responsibilities. He was supported in this by the Liberal leader, Greenway, and by Sifton's brother-in-law, A. T. Burrows; but he received no encouragement at Ottawa. His invasion of the Northwest Territories to advance the claims of Manitoba were not well received. The people of the Territories were no more anxious to be ruled from Winnipeg than Manitoba was to be ruled from Toronto.

Early in 1905, Robert Rogers and the attorney-general, Colin H. Campbell, were sent to Ottawa to plead Manitoba's case for westward expansion and for a northward extension as a second choice. The westward ambition went forever into discard with the passage of the Autonomy Bills of 1905, which firmly divided the prairie West on a north-south basis for purposes of local government. The new provinces were projected northward to 60° north latitude, far outstripping Manitoba's northern limits of 52°50′ N. Like Manitoba, the new provinces were denied control of their natural resources, but they were given subsidies on a scale much higher than those accorded Manitoba. Thus, Manitoba was able for some years to exercise to the full a complaint about unfair treatment. However, it failed to respond to broad hints from Ottawa that a Liberal provincial administration might be heard more clearly. Progress was made. In 1908, Laurier introduced a boundary-extension bill which would extend Manitoba's western boundary to 60° north latitude and its eastern boundary to the point at which 89° west longitude cuts the shore of Hudson Bay. This proposition, which did in fact become the final settlement, was accepted by the House of Commons in July, 1908. Roblin objected on the grounds that such a solution gave too much of the shore of Hudson Bay to Ontario. His real hope, however, was for control of natural resources or for better financial terms. By April, 1911, agreement had been reached whereby Manitoba would accept a large grant of swamplands in lieu of full control of natural resources. At this point, the election of 1911 intervened.

The new Government of Robert Borden quickly took up the question of Manitoba's boundaries where Laurier had left off. No substantial change was made. On November 21, 1911, Roblin announced that final agreement had been reached and that the question of subsidies in lieu of natural resources would be arbitrated on the basis of equality with Alberta and Saskatchewan. On April 1, 1912, the Legislature of Manitoba passed an "Act to provide for the further Extension of the Province of Manitoba," and the new territory was officially added to the province on April 6. This last expansion of its boundaries added 179,020 square miles to the province's area and 6,000 to its population. The average of thirty square miles per person was not a cause for disappointment. The significant fact was that Manitoba now had a frontier to challenge its people for generations to come. No less remarkable was the fact that the now mightily-transformed appendage of the northern fur trade had returned in its greatness to lay claim to the shore of the inland sea that had given it birth.

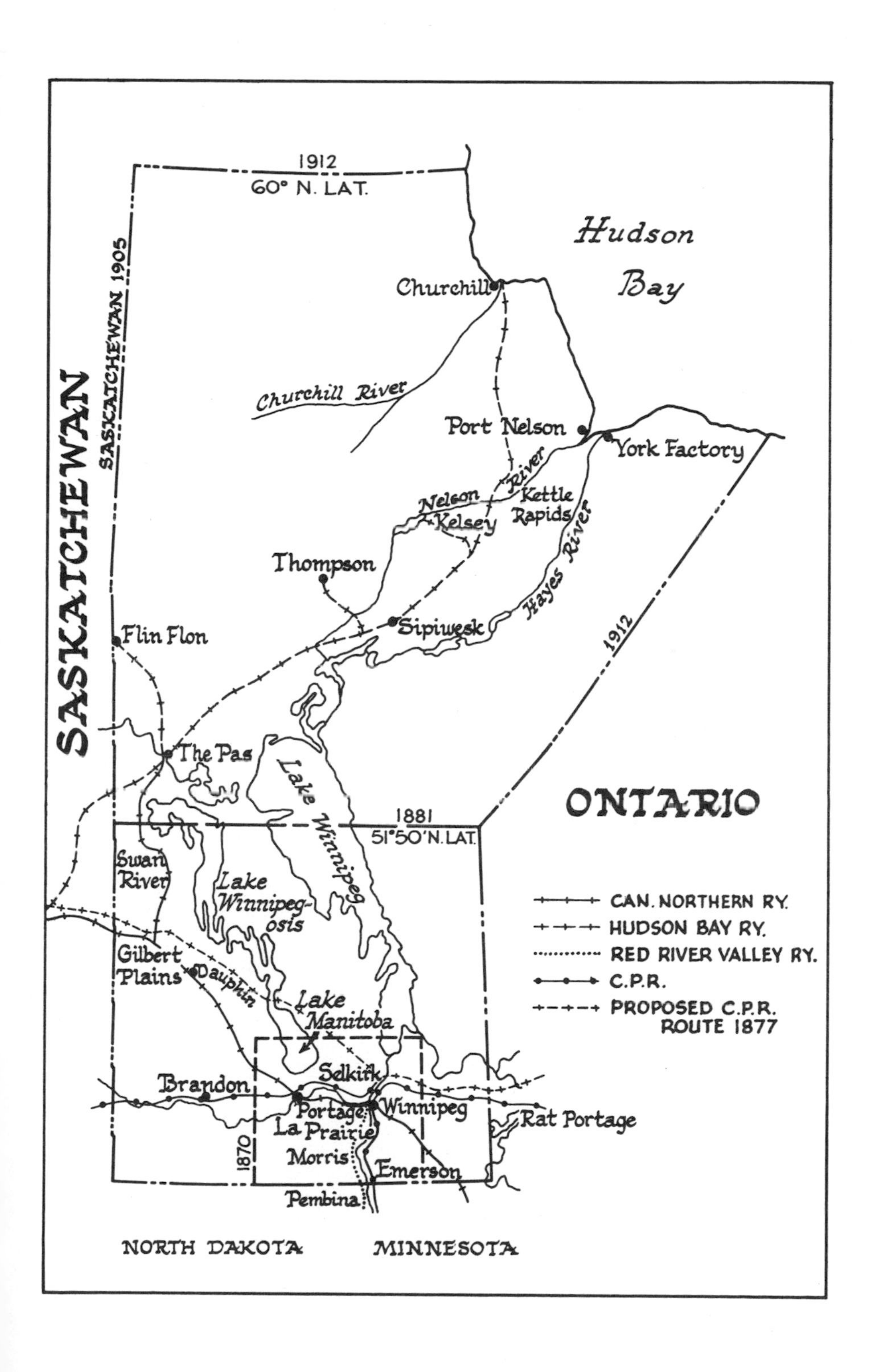

1912
60° N. LAT.
Hudson
Bay
Churchill
Churchill River
Port Nelson
York Factory
Nelson River
Kettle Rapids
Kelsey
Hayes River
Thompson
Sipiwesk
Flin Flon
SASKATCHEWAN
SASKATCHEWAN 1905
The Pas
Lake Winnipeg
1912
ONTARIO
1881
51°50'N. LAT.
Swan River
Lake Winnipegosis
CAN. NORTHERN RY.
HUDSON BAY RY.
RED RIVER VALLEY RY.
C.P.R.
PROPOSED C.P.R. ROUTE 1877
Gilbert Plains
Dauphin
Lake Manitoba
Selkirk
Brandon
Portage La Prairie
Winnipeg
Rat Portage
1870
Morris
Emerson
Pembina
NORTH DAKOTA
MINNESOTA

12

Politics and War

ON THE EVE OF WORLD WAR I, Manitoba felt assured of its place in the sun – though clouds had appeared intermittently since 1912. Its good agricultural lands were fully settled, and the fruits of cultivation poured bounteously from plain and valley, transported via its railways through the great markets at Winnipeg and thence east and south to the markets of the world. The population of half a million was in excess of all sober hopes held at the beginning of the century. This population was by no means a homogeneous group, and much had still to be done in order to reconcile the many differences of language, race, and religion and to set people to working and living easily together. But none despaired. Time and new Manitoba-born generations would take care of the stresses and strains that had been imported from the Old World and from the older portions of the New. The province was still the crossroads of the West, still the great supplier, catering to the needs of a vast wheat economy and turning more and more to the task of processing goods both coming out of and going into the West and the North.

The panic of 1907 on the New York and London stock exchanges had not gone unnoticed in Manitoba. There had been a brief slackening of the economic upsurge, but there had been no darkening of the still-bright horizon. In 1912, the surge of expansion ceased and the economy began to recede. Rising rates of interest, higher rail rates, and increased land prices had been no problem so long as capital and immigrants continued to pour into the West. But by 1912, this double flow was drying up. European capital was now turning to the greater profit which was to be made from the preparation for war. As the scale of armament rose, the flow of men and money into western Canada declined. Grain prices fell; foreclosures and business failures multiplied as marginal operators were swept away. Unemployment became a serious problem in Manitoba for the first time in the new century. The Grand Trunk Pacific, the Canadian Northern, and the National Transcontinental continued to lay rails through the resistant and unproductive Canadian Shield. But the rate of rail construction slowed – then stopped altogether. Many branch lines, built in an excess of enthusiasm and the hope of a quick profit, were left to rust or were torn up.

The Hudson Bay railway remained the unfulfilled promise of both political parties and its future was now doubly uncertain. In February, 1910, the Canadian Northern had opened a line from Hudson Bay Junction in Saskatchewan to The Pas; and in 1913 it had built a bridge there over the Saskatchewan River. In the federal election campaign of 1911, Robert Borden had promised to build to the mouth of the Nelson "by the people, for the people." World War I slowed construction to a walk, and then brought it to a complete standstill. The main reason for the lack of progress on the Hudson Bay railway was to be found far to the south. In 1914, the United States opened the Panama Canal, a triumph both of engineering and of "dollar diplomacy." Now, grain from the western prairies could find its way via Vancouver at water carriage rates, which were always much lower than rail rates. Vancouver thus became the escape hatch for western grain which Manitoba had hoped would be found on Hudson Bay. The long-range and permanent effect of the Panama Canal on Manitoba's development extended much beyond its effect on the prospects of the Hudson Bay railway. It posed the first real threat in over a century to the province's position as the entrepôt of the Canadian West.

With the cutting of the Isthmus of Panama, Manitoba was separated from much of its former hinterland. The effect, though, was not immediately felt. The general dislocation of World War I and the uncertain years immediately thereafter cast confusion on the whole picture. When the haze finally cleared in the 1920's, Winnipeg found itself bereft of its central position in the western Canadian market. In 1914, however, this ill fortune was yet to be revealed. Winnipeg was still the third city of Canada, and far and away the first in the West. Portage and Main was a world-famous crossroads – or at least Winnipeggers liked to believe it was. The city was by no means a second Chicago in either numbers or wealth, but it was certainly Chicago's counterpart as a grain and cattle market, rail center, banker, and wholesale distributor. Winnipeg's skyline was proudly etched against the endless westward-flowing plain, and it was to remain almost unaltered until very recently – proof, in its immutability, that grain, like all other goods, seeks the cheapest route to market.

In 1914, Winnipeg was the market place of the West, but it was far from being a mere market place. Its streets were well paved and better lit than were the streets of most North American cities. Trees, carefully planted and tended, were beginning to provide refreshing shade and color in the city's newer sections. Winnipeg's system of parks had been initiated by referendum in 1892 and was generously supported by its people. Public libraries were introduced in 1905 through the largesse of Andrew Carnegie, the Scottish-American steel magnate whose rails bore much of the city's commerce. Somewhat earlier, in 1901, the University of Manitoba, active as an examining and degree-granting body for the church colleges since 1877, set up off Broadway as a teaching institution. A Baptist academy which had been established at Rapid City in 1884 moved to Brandon in 1890 as Brandon College, a training center for Baptist clergy. From 1898 to 1910, it was affiliated with the University of Manitoba and then for a generation with McMaster University at Toronto and later Hamilton. As Brandon University, it remains Manitoba's only center of higher learning outside of greater Winnipeg. After an uncertain start in Tuxedo, an agricultural college was rising south of the city on a great bend of the Red. The city boasted two new technical high schools and had plans for more. Music also had a place. There were bands (a tradition reaching back to the arrival of Wolseley in 1870), string quartets, and both men's and women's choral societies. There were literary circles and the nucleus of a school of art. The financial renaissance, however, did not produce a comparable literary establishment – or even much beyond a meager beginning. In fact, the literary history of Manitoba, with some noteworthy exceptions, is still largely a void.

In matters of sport, Winnipeg and Manitoba stood well to the fore in Canada. The Winnipeg Bonspiel was already a curling classic of venerable status, the first having been held in 1876. Manitoba could boast more curling clubs than all of Scotland, and Manitoba's curlers yielded to none. Nor did the province's hockey players, lacrosse teams, scullers, paddlers, or snowshoers. The Stanley Cup had only in 1910 become a trophy for professional competition and had already been won twice by the Winnipeg Victorias. Skiing was still an aberration of the Norse and football more a matter of kicking than of carrying or throwing. The name "Grey" was associated with the respected governor-general, deputy of the new King George v, rather than with the cup which today inspires the annual early winter madness of football fans. The hunting of game birds and animals, as well as fishing, took on more and more the guise of sport, as opposed to livelihood. A hunting lodge at Netley or in the Delta marshes was a status symbol for the social elite. More and more Winnipegers were establishing summer homes on Lake of the Woods or even at Detroit Lake in adjacent Minnesota, while the burghers of Portage la Prairie encamped at Delta Beach and those of Brandon at Clear or Rock lakes. The more modestly situated Winnipeggers made do with jaunts by rail to the new resorts along the eastern and western shores of the southern basin of Lake Winnipeg, or went by trolley to Lockport, Selkirk Park, or Stonewall.

The lesser cities, Brandon, Portage la Prairie, and St. Boniface – plus a host of large towns and villages, both old and new – also flourished. In economic function, they were essentially offshoots of Winnipeg, but each had a distinct atmosphere of its own. They were marked by the backgrounds of those who had built them, but all were part of the West, spreading out from or sheltering beneath the grain elevators. Socially, as well as economically, the towns tended to emulate the city, with some ethnic and cultural variations. Social life generally revolved about the church or the rural school. Chautauqua and perambulating evangelists brought in external influences, and townsmen ventured forth to neighboring communities as members of baseball and hockey clubs. There was still much isolation, however, and both distance and climate tended to impede the integration of new Canadians. The steady flow of people from the land to urban areas continued – and was to increase. The lure of the city was constant, even though opportunities for employment were no longer so great. The Icelanders increasingly enriched the life of Winnipeg and were joined by many newer immigrants, many of whom had made no intermediate pause on the farm. The first cracks were becoming evident in the firm façade of Mennonite Manitoba. The drift to worldliness, the avoidance of which had driven their fathers from the Russian steppes, was luring the sons from the prairie communities. An increasingly technical society was to speed up the process by fostering an always uneasy compromise between the call of faith and a natural ambition to advance and excel.

As the recipient of most of those who sought life in the city, Winnipeg was becoming more and more balkanized into ethnic communities. These communities viewed one another with greater or lesser suspicion based on natural caution or Old World antagonisms. At best, they endured an uneasy relationship. The Jews, Poles, and Ukrainians tended to live north of the CPR main line, in the North End; the Icelanders spread themselves north and south in the area between Central and Sargent parks; while the Anglo-Saxons had begun their long migration south of the Assiniboine. St. Boniface was still largely French and Belgian. A few Dutch, new Scots, and others found their way among the descendants of the Selkirk settlers in the Kildonans, and a miniscule Italian community was to be found immediately west of Winnipeg's General Hospital in the near West End. The roster is a long one, but its history is as unmarked by open clashes as it is by warm comradeship. The people were absorbed in making a living in their new surroundings and tended to keep to themselves, remaining in uneasy accord with their neighbors.

There was also the other side of the coin. The slum blight was clearly visible in the north central part of Winnipeg. There was a recognized though illegal "red light" district. The saloons abounded in the downtown area and came equipped with swinging doors and sawdust-covered floors. There were no seats in these all-male preserves. The patron stood to the bar, or stood not at all. Prices were moderate: beer was five cents, whiskey ten cents, three for a quarter being the general scale. North Main Street had already taken on some of the attributes of a skid row, and not all of the grimier side was by any means a matter of choice. Not all had shared in the bounty of the fat years. In 1914, the lean years had already begun. The Salvation Army was established in its Citadel on Rupert Avenue and fared forth to battle for the bodies as well as the souls of the unfortunate. They received help, but not much as yet, from the government. The Indian, in the meantime, fared no better on the reserve or in the city than he had at the beginning of the century.

The Government of Manitoba faced increasing opposition as it moved into the electoral campaign of 1914. It was under heavy attack for its disregard of the temperance and women's suffrage movements. The inadequacies of school legislation plus the workings of machine politics made education a scandal of low standards and linguistic chaos. The farmers, organized and otherwise, blamed their troubles on the Government and little remembered what Sir Rodmond had done or tried to do for them. The electorate is not necessarily grateful for past achievements, as Roblin's grandson was to discover in 1968. There were noisome rumors that all was not well with the construction of the new Legislative Building and that there had been much to be desired in the contracts for the building of the new agricultural college and for the law courts. The usual charges of electoral maladministration and direct corruption were rehearsed in the *Free Press* and ridiculed in the *Telegram.* This time, the former was even more direct in its accusations and adduced ample proof of plural voting and other crimes. Robert Rogers, the master manipulator, had been translated to Ottawa and perhaps his surer hand was missed. Sir Rodmond was himself above reproach, but too many of his political allies were beneath contempt. Roblin's position had become the classic one. His enemies he could handle, and handle well. His disparagement of a British critic as a "jelly bag of an Englishman" and of the Liberal naval policy as "Laurier's tin pot Navy" have found honored places in the lexicon of Canadian politics. Roblin had become the victim of his friends, and his party equally so.

The Liberals benefited much by the obvious indications of the Government's faltering. Their leader, Tobias C. Norris, along with a coterie of able followers, made much of the Government's acts of omission; the Liberals became the stout champions of temperance, votes for women, and direct initiation of legislation by referendum. Norris, Tom Johnson, E. A. McPherson, A. B. Hudson, and Valentine Winkler were formidable campaigners, hitting at older grievances such as control of natural resources and compulsory education, and making a promise to guard the constitutional rights of Catholics in education. This was a vague promise, but it at least provided a thin ray of hope to the Catholics without serving as a warning beacon to the Orange element. Balloting took place on July 10, 1914, with the vote delayed in three new northern ridings. The initial result gave the Conservatives twenty-five seats and the Liberals twenty-one, including one French-speaking constituency. The combined Liberal and independent vote exceeded that of the Government by 7,000. To no one's surprise, however, the three northern ridings returned Conservatives and Roblin appeared safe for another four years at least.

So much for appearances. While Roblin and Norris exchanged oratorical salvos across the breadth of Manitoba, more deadly salvos were being prepared in Europe. On June 28, 1914, the Archduke

Franz Ferdinand, of Austria-Hungary, was murdered by Bosnian separatists in Sarajevo. On July 28, Austria-Hungary declared war on Serbia. The military juggernauts began to roll, and none could stop them. At midnight, August 4, England's ultimatum to Germany expired and the British Empire was at war. The first of the two great bloodbaths of the first half of the century was under way. Canada was part of it, and Manitoba would not have it otherwise. In Manitoba, as in practically all areas on both sides in the struggle, the outbreak of World War I was greeted with wild enthusiasm. It was all "Canada at Britain's side," with little or no attention paid to the reasons for the war, not at least at the outset.

With first-generation Anglo-Saxons leading the way, Manitobans flocked to the colors. There was a general submergence of racial, religious, and language differences in the greater common cause. But as the war advanced, these lesser considerations tended to return, now geared to a determination to win a total victory. To many of the Ukrainians and Poles, the war began to symbolize the realization of national self-determination for their homelands. This consideration assumed a deeper import after the collapse of the Russian autocracy early in 1917. Even before this, the war had taken on the guise of a struggle for universal freedom from oppression and a struggle against militarism itself. It was "the war for democracy" and the "war to end war." Manitoba responded with men, money, and food, all on a generous scale. The war became a central point, around which all other things revolved. The rising death toll and the endless casualty lists posted in every city, town, and village brought desolation to many – but never defeatism. There was the inevitable chauvinistic reaction against anything German. Goethe disappeared from library shelves and Beethoven's music was neglected; but Manitoba's Altona remained, while Ontario's Berlin became Kitchener. Others who had been, or still were, nationals of any of the Central Powers now became suspect to their neighbors and even objects of attention for the already ubiquitous Royal North West Mounted Police. Espionage and sabotage, however, were nonexistent. Manitoba remained unsophisticated in a world of power politics.

This lack of sophistication, however, did not extend into matters of local politics. The war provided only a brief respite from internecine party strife. This strife soon reached a crisis which shook the province to its foundations, destroyed Sir Rodmon Roblin's Government, and introduced fundamental changes – many of which were long overdue. On September 15, 1914, the Legislature was called into special session. The proceedings were brief and were confined almost solely to the implementation of legislation needed by the Government of Canada to better co-ordinate the war effort. A moratorium on mortgage payments was enacted and the Manitoba Patriotic Fund was established. In addition, gifts of flour (50,0000 bags) and $5,000 were made to Belgian War Relief. All of this was done in a nonpartisan, highly-patriotic manner. Before the session was prorogued, however, the Minister of Education, Dr. W. H. Montague, introduced supplementary estimates for the building of the new Legislative Building. He explained that according to engineering and architectural advice, caissons should be substituted for pilings in the foundation of the building and steel for reinforced concrete in its construction. This change would increase the total cost from under $3,000,000 to $4,500,000. The advice was sound and the added cost to be expected, but the new estimates served to trigger the suspicions of the Liberals, and especially of Tom Johnson. During the recess between sessions, Johnson asked for copies of all vouchers and correspondence which had been tabled in the Legislature on the subject of the new Legislative Building. Johnson's curiosity may have been merely a routine part of the customary sniping at the Government, but the session of 1915 soon revealed that the Government was in serious trouble.

The existing Legislative Building had been built with federal subsidies back in the early 1880's, together with a Law Courts Building and Government House. The Law Courts and the Legislative Building had long been inadequate and the Government, inspired by the expansionist spirit of the times, decided to replace them with structures which would be more in keeping with the province's greater status and its even greater expectations. A new Law Courts had been built in 1912 by Thomas Kelly & Sons, a firm which had a close association with the Conservative Party. In 1911, a competition was held for plans for a new Legislative Building to be built on the Fort Osborne site. Out of sixty-five entries, a bipartisan committee of the Legislature chose those of F. W. Simon of Liverpool. In 1912, the final estimates were submitted to the Legislature and the contract was awarded to Thomas Kelly & Sons, who began work in 1913.

The use of building contracts to reward a government's friends is as old as the institution of government itself, and it was a policy generally practised at all levels of government. The sin lay in being found out. The amount of "boodle" involved in railway construction in Canada, for example, cannot even be estimated. Sir John A. Macdonald was found out in 1873, thus bringing on the "Pacific Scandal" – but it put him into only temporary eclipse. The miracles of accounting achieved by the builders of the Canadian Northern and Grand Trunk Pacific railways have never been equalled, and much of the burden still rests on the shoulders of Canadian taxpayers. The Manitoba Government of 1900-15 was merely following a well-trodden path and one which is by no means obliterated even now. Their fault lay in overconfidence, and as a result they were found out. Rumors of unjustifiably high prices for land and materials, of padded payrolls, of goods paid for but not delivered, of kickbacks – all were as common in Manitoba as crocuses in spring.

In the early spring of 1915, however, rumor began to give way to shrill accusation and to revelations that even the most determined sweeping could no longer keep under the rug. In March, 1915, the Liberals succeeded in forcing an inquiry into the Legislative Building contracts by the Public Accounts Committee of the House. The committee's Conservative majority endorsed a report which completely exonerated the Government of any wrong-doing. The Liberals, however, had smelled blood and were not to be deterred. They forced a lengthy debate on the report when it was moved for adoption. A. B. Hudson moved an amendment which charged "gross and culpable negligence" and which specified that Thomas Kelly & Sons had been overpaid by some $800,000. The Government was further accused of withholding evidence, conniving at the unavailability of witnesses, and mutilating documents. Hudson demanded a royal commission of inquiry to consist of three judges of the Court of King's Bench. The debate raged from the afternoon of March 30 to 1:00 A.M. on April 1, at which time the House adjourned. Sir Rodmond had been quite explicit during the debate in stating that he would not grant a royal commission. Thus, on the evening of March 31, T. C. Norris presented the lieutenant-governor, Sir Douglas Cameron, with a petition signed by all twenty-one members of the opposition. The petition outlined the Liberal charges and called on Sir Douglas not to prorogue the House until the judicial committee of inquiry had been established.

The petition of Norris and his fellow Liberals had the desired result. Sir Rodmond informed the House on the afternoon of April 1 that a royal commission would be appointed, and this was reiterated by Sir Douglas Cameron in his speech in prorogation later the same afternoon. The commission was not appointed until April 20, and in the interim there was much manoeuvring among the interested parties and an unusual though fully justifiable display of independence on the part of the lieutenant-governor. It may be that Sir Douglas threatened Sir Rodmond with dismissal were the proposal of a royal commission not accepted by the Government. In any event, the lieutenant-governor certainly exercised his own judgment about the composition of the commission in rejecting Roblin's nominees, one of whom he characterized as "a mere creature of the Tories." Pressure was definitely brought to bear on Cameron to appoint commissioners who were friendly to Roblin. The lieutenant-governor was threatened with dismissal for exceeding his powers and was then offered a second term of office if he would let the issue drop. Both Bob Rogers and Sir J. A. M. Aikins, MP for Brandon, came from Ottawa to help put out the fire. Rogers sought pliable appointees to the commission and Aikins strongly suggested to Cameron that he had a constitutional duty to accept the advice of his ministers, whatever his personal opinion might be.

On April 17, Roblin presented Cameron with a draft order-in-council which provided for a limited inquiry and which named Chief Justice T. G. Mathers of the Court of King's Bench. Mr. Justice Mathers was a former law partner of Joseph Martin and a Liberal appointee to the bench. Alexander Haggart had been MP for Winnipeg and had stepped down to provide a seat for Robert Rogers. David Walker was no longer a young man, having served in the cabinet of John Norquay. Cameron refused to sign the order-in-council, demanding a widening of the inquiry and the right to name the commissioners. He had previously suggested Chief Justice Mathers and Judges A. C. Galt and D. A. Macdonald of the Court of King's Bench, but he now agreed to accept Sir Hugh John Macdonald rather than either Galt or D. A. Macdonald. Roblin accepted Cameron's wishes with regard to the wording of the order and chose Sir Hugh John in place of Galt. This choice confounds any belief in the general political bias of the bench, since Galt, who was dropped, was a Conservative appointee, while D. A. Macdonald had been elevated to the bench by Sir Wilfrid Laurier. No one ever questioned the impartiality of Sir Hugh John Macdonald. The Royal Commission on the Parliament Buildings was appointed on April 20, 1915.

The commission, consisting of Chief Justice Mathers, Judge D. A. Macdonald, and Police Magistrate Sir Hugh John Macdonald met on April 21 and indicated its independence by rejecting the counsel appointed for the commission by Roblin. They reported on August 24 to the effect that Sir Rodmond Roblin, J. H. Howden, G. R. Coldwell, Dr. W. H. Montague, all members of the Government, Dr. R. M. Simpson, president of the Manitoba Conservative Association and custodian of party funds, and Thomas Kelly, the contractor, were all culpable of conspiracy to defraud the province. Sir Rodmond, in the meantime, had not waited on events. On May 12, 1915, he had resigned on behalf of himself and his Government, asking Sir Douglas Cameron to call on T. C. Norris to form a government. This was no case of the Liberal St. George slaying the Tory dragon; it was simply the result of prior agreement among party leaders. Sir Rodmond agreed to step down and to admit culpability in the matter of the Legislative Building contract in return for a cessation of the investigation by the Mathers Commission and the substitution of a civil action suit against Thomas Kelly for return of the overpayments.

The change of government was made, but public pressure made it impossible for Norris to carry out his end of the bargain – it having become common gossip that such a deal had been made. Excuses were made by A. B. Hudson that Roblin had not sufficiently abased himself in his letter of resignation, as he had promised to do. In revenge, the Conservatives charged before the Mathers Commission that Norris had received $50,000 for Liberal Party funds as a fee for the Liberals' dropping election petitions against various Conservative MP's. On investigating these charges, however, the committee declared them unfounded. The new Government approached Mathers to drop the inquiry, but he refused to do so unless so instructed by the Government. This Norris dared not do in the face of aroused public opinion. What had originally been planned as a "gentlemen's agreement" had since gotten badly out of hand. The investigation by the Mathers Commission continued, and others were instituted into the construction of the law courts and the agricultural college, as well as into the building of roads. The various investigations piled Pelion on Ossa and cast the lot upon Olympus. In addition to laying charges against the former ministers and the others, the Mathers Commission assessed that Kelly had been overpaid something in excess of $700,000. Other investigations later revealed heavy overpayments for land for the agricultural college and in the building of the law courts, as well as a veritable thieves paradise in the building and maintenance of roads.

Indictments for conspiracy were laid against those charged by the

Mathers Commission and there followed a long, involved series of legal manoeuvres involving postponements, jury disagreements, questions of competence of jurisdiction, absentee witnesses, and procedural disputes which almost led to courtroom brawls among learned counsel. Dr. Montague died suddenly before the case was brought into court. The trials of the others were postponed for ill-health and for other reasons, and finally were never proceeded. Sir Rodmond withdrew from public life and returned to private business to repair his shattered fortunes. Thomas Kelly was extradited from the United States, convicted of obtaining money under false pretences, and sentenced to two and a half years in the penitentiary. This judgment was upheld on appeal, but Kelly served less than the minimum sentence – and that in the relative comfort of the warden's house at Stony Mountain. He carried on a successful contracting career in the United States and died in retirement in California in 1941. The court had ordered him to repay $1,207,000 to the province. This was carried on the province's books until Kelly's death and then was reduced to the nominal sum of $25,000 – which is still owing. In all, $30,000 was recovered from the Kelly concern.

All of this was still far in the future when Tobias Crawford Norris assumed the premiership on May 12, 1915. He was concerned with placing his administration firmly in power. It had been part of the agreement under which the Roblin Government had resigned that Sir Rodmond and his ministers would quit their seats and open them to acclamations for Liberal candidates. When public disclosure soured the deal, Norris was still in a good position. The enemy were prostrated before him, and he, in the political spirit of the day, was the last to give them time to recover. Work on the Legislative Building was temporarily stopped and the Kelly contract was cancelled. A general cleaning-out of the more obvious Conservatives hangers-on in the public service was put in hand. The Legislature was dissolved and an election was called for August 6, 1915. The Conservatives were in complete disarray. Only one of the former ministers presented himself for election. A rush convention of the Conservative Party made a mighty and successful effort to free the party from its machine, but it was far too late. Sir J. A. M. Aikins resigned his seat in the House of Commons and ably fought the elections as Conservative leader on a platform of reform. To the electorate, however, it smacked of deathbed repentance.

The Liberals were content to use their 1914 platform of compulsory education, votes for women, direct legislation, and now, prohibition of alcohol, rather than mere temperance. The war emergency had given a great impetus to the temperance movement, and the movement had cast aside this cloak in favor of all-out prohibition. The result was foreordained. Forty-two Liberals were elected as against five Conservatives, four of the five Conservatives being from French-speaking constituencies. Two Labor candidates were returned in Winnipeg. These men, Fred Dixon and R. A. Riggs were in the growing tradition of Winnipeg nonconformity and were symbolic of the large and restless proletariat of the city. The Liberal landslide was not due to any general belief in the greater virtue of that party. It was the only alternative to a thoroughly-discredited administration. In January, 1916, Norris met the new Legislature with as sweeping a legislative program as the province had ever seen. Manitoba was to be in the van of political and education change and was to pioneer the concept of the social service state in Canada.

On January 27, 1916, third reading was given the legislation which gave women the vote in Manitoba on an equal basis with men. Manitoba was the first of the provinces to do so. The fight for women's suffrage had been a long one throughout the English-speaking world and one which was not unmarred by fanaticism, especially in the United Kingdom. Women had not been completely excluded from the exercise of political functions. In Manitoba, women owning property could vote in municipal elections in the 1880's and, starting in 1890, could vote and stand for election as school trustees. Increasingly, women pressured for the correction of this obvious injustice. Female suffrage bills failed miserably in the Legislature in 1892, and again in 1893. At the turn of the century, the movement was joined by the equally increasing popular strength of the temperance movement and in due course became the irresistible force confronted by the immovable body of Sir Rodmond Roblin. Mrs. M. J. Benedictson of Selkirk, E. Cora Hind (the *Free Press* crop reporter), Mrs. Lillian Thomas, Mrs. Margaret McWilliams, and the highly-vocal Nellie McClung were all potent forces both for votes for women and for temperance legislation. The achievement of women's suffrage was rapidly followed by prohibition of the sale of alcohol, though not as immediate cause and effect.

In the election of 1914, the obtuseness of the Roblin Government on the liquor question had done as much to improve the political fortunes of the Liberals as had votes for women. Legislation against the saloon was largely obviated by the proliferation of so-called private clubs, whereby any excuse for a social organization served to secure a licence to sell liquor by the glass, providing it was politically acceptable. Many areas were dried up by local option, but Winnipeg and the *Canadien* and Slavic areas were regarded as so many strayed lambs by the prohibitionists. It was fondly hoped that prohibition would help in the assimilation of the "foreigner."

The session of 1916 passed the Manitoba Temperance Act, which had been drafted by the temperance organizations at the request of Premier Norris. He was quite willing to let any blame for the shortcomings of the legislation rest on those who demanded it. On March 13, 1916, the legislation was voted on by the people in a referendum and was approved two to one. This measure of social progress was approved everywhere except in St. Boniface and in North Winnipeg. Norris did not permit the newly-enfranchised women to vote on this occasion lest he be accused of setting things up for a prohibitionist victory. The absence of a considerable number of the men of drinking age on military service may have added to the lopsided character of the victory. There can be no doubt that the move was generally accepted and that there was a real if vain hope for better, drier days ahead. Thus, Norris proclaimed the Temperance Act to take effect on June 1, 1916. Henceforth, liquor could only be legally purchased in the province by a doctor's prescription through a registered pharmacist. These prescriptions were by no means hard to come by and the province's druggists prospered mightily. An inspection of the prescription files of any pharmacy of the period indicates a remarkable number of complaints – from back aches to eyestrain – for which twenty-six ounces of rye whisky was the specific remedy.

Liquor could still be brought in by express or parcel post from Quebec, where its sale was still legal; but this gap in the dyke was closed by federal enabling legislation in 1917. Manitoba was to remain completely dry, except for its pharmaceutical oases, until 1923. The hopes of a better day were not long in being dispelled. In the first six months after the implementation of the Temperance Act, there was a marked reduction in the number of charges of drunkenness and associated crimes. But it was only temporary. Soon, the bootlegger was a common fixture, his wares easily if not cheaply come by, though they were usually of an inferior and often a dangerous quality. The crime rate rose, and the incidence of drinking increased at all age levels. The experiment proved no more successful in Manitoba than it did in the United States. However, it did bring an earlier realization in Manitoba that one cannot change human nature by acts of the legislature. Prohibition served to train some Manitobans in the skills of the illicit maker and marketer of liquor, which proved very profitable to them in serving the immense thirst of the Americans during their longer struggle with prohibition. In fact, some who served their apprenticeship in bootlegging in Manitoba were to rise to heights of affluence, eminence, and respectability which made their fame known all over America and throughout the world. In 1923, the province began a long and uphill struggle to achieve a reasonable system for controlling the sale of liquor. The prohibition forces fought hard against each concession and only grudgingly came to see virtue in genuine temperance.

The reforms in voting and in liquor control were merely a beginning in the first session of T. C. Norris' Legislature. It was as if the dam had broken and a long pent-up series of changes were poured forth to the almost unanimous approval of the representatives of the people. There had long been a demand for compulsory education. The language clause of the Laurier-Greenway Compromise of 1896 had unwittingly turned Manitoba's school system into a latter-day Tower of Babel. The performance of many of the financially-crippled parochial schools left much to be desired. In rural areas where a school's population was largely Protestant or Catholic, there had been little friction; but in Winnipeg, the gap was frighteningly wide between public and parochial schools. In 1912, therefore, amendments had been introduced into the Public Schools Act by Hon. G. R. Coldwell which would have had the effect of giving public aid to the existing parochial schools. This was not done to give justice to the Catholics. The move was one of conciliation toward Quebec in order that that province might not make difficulties, based on historic claims, to Manitoba's extension to Hudson Bay. The move may have helped in the extension of the boundary, but it was of no help to Winnipeg's Catholics in their problem of "double taxation." The Government neglected, though not by accident, to repeal that clause of the School Act which provided heavy penalties for school trustees who permitted the segregation of pupils by religion during the school day. Winnipeg's trustees were unwilling to risk jail for a cause in which they did not believe. The Coldwell amendments, therefore, served merely as an irritant to both sides.

The changes introduced by Dr. R. S. Thornton, the new Minister of Education, were aimed at these many abuses. There was to be compulsory schooling for all children between the ages of seven and fourteen in either public or private schools inspected by the Department of Education. This measure, considered revolutionary twenty years before, was accepted with little protest throughout the province and with no protest at all in the Legislature. No change was made in the provision for religious instruction on petition of the parents of the requisite number of children. A second new departure was that henceforth English was to be the sole language of instruction at all levels and in all schools. All protests were ignored, even those of the *Canadiens*. German-speaking citizens had little to say, since the war had put their language into the category of the unpatriotic. Dr. Thornton did not demand instant confirmation to the English-only decree. The change came gradually, but it did come; and with it came a complete reorientation of teacher training and certification, to the extent that the teachers were at least conversant with the English language. The whole purpose was, in Dr. Thornton's words, "one common school, teaching the things which are common to all." There was fierce resistance from *Canadien* members of the House on the grounds of the dual language nature of the country; but the *Canadiens* were forty years too early to be heard. It was considered essential that English be learned, and the historic claims of the French were ignored for the common good. The Coldwell amendments were rescinded and private and parochial schools were forced to pay their own way, as they had since 1890.

In 1916, Norris also implemented the promise of the 1914 Liberal platform to introduce direct legislation. This policy was taken bodily from the farm protest movement of the United States. It was a device intended to ensure that an elected legislature fulfilled its pre-election promises. A measure could be initiated by the petition of ten percent of the voters and submitted by referendum to the whole electorate. If approved, its passage became mandatory on the legislature. Its attempted adoption in Manitoba was another reflection on the public image of the political parties. Norris' legislation, the Initiative and Referendum Act, provided for this facility in Manitoba. The measure was rejected by the courts as unconstitutional, being irreconcilable to the position of the lieutenant-governor as part of the legislature in the same way that the King was part of Parliament. With a similar view to the policing of political parties, an Elections Act was introduced in 1916 and finally approved in 1917. It provided for closer checks on the conduct of elections and did much to eliminate the old evils of rigged election lists, plural voting, and ballot-box stuffing. Henceforth, the names on voters lists at least represented living human beings. In 1918, a Civil Service Commission was appointed to fill jobs in the public service by competitive examination and on the basis of merit.

A small beginning was made in farm legislation, including measures for the control of noxious weeds and the provision of loans to farmers for the building of dairy herds, especially in the Interlake. In 1917, there followed a Farm Loans Act, which provided provincially-backed, long-term, low-interest mortgages, and Rural Credits Act, which encouraged, by means of provincial funds, the establishment of rural credit societies. Similarly, there were substantial amendments to the Workmen's Compensation Act and other statutes designed to bring them into line with the needs and demands of labor. All in all, a considerable amount of tidying up – but no radical change. The new Government was feeling its way, and all farm governments are essentially conservative in their approach. The concept of the state caring for its people in distress was still new but had not been entirely neglected by the previous regime. The province had provided land and money for a tuberculosis sanatorium and for hospitals, and it had supported privately-administered charities. The Norris Government took its first tentative step in the direction of the social service state with the Mother's Allowance Act of 1916, which provided payments to the widowed mothers of infants.

While Norris cleaned the Augean Stables and struck out in new directions, World War I continued to exact a fearsome toll in lives and treasure. Manitoba's enlistments continued to be high and the demands of war industry for labor continued to increase. Winnipeg became a large producer of artillery shells and of uniforms. The double drain of the army and of war industry soon made it difficult, if not impossible, to obtain farm help. The new School Attendance Act was left largely in abeyance as the children lent a hand. The price of grain rose spectacularly with war demand, but so did the farmer's costs. There had been the greatest of all crops in 1915, but that of 1916 was badly hit by rust and those of 1917 and 1918 by drought. In 1917, the Government of Canada instituted a system of orderly marketing. A Board of Grain Supervisors was set up to market the crop, largely in the interest of preventing wild fluctuations in price. Government marketing was quite agreeable to the producers, if not to the Grain Exchange, and its cessation after the war helped to drive the farmers into politics.

National politics began to loom large on the Manitoba scene in 1917. As early as 1915, Norris had called for a national government on a non-party basis for the better conduct of the war. The United Kingdom formed a union government in 1916 and the example was held up for admiration by Manitoba's Liberals and Conservatives. Early in 1917, the matter became one for practical consideration when Sir Robert Borden realized that voluntary enlistments could no longer fill the gaps in the battered ranks of the Canadian forces in Europe. Practically all political leaders outside of Quebec were in favor of conscription. In Quebec, there was no objection to voluntary service, but many *Canadiens* would not be forced to fight in a war which they firmly believed to be directed to the greater glory of the British Empire. Sir Wilfrid Laurier would not go against the wishes of his people and would therefore not enter into a coalition. In Manitoba, the Liberals had been routed federally in 1911, and of its two MP's, only J. P. Molloy of Provencher remained loyal to his leader. The Conservatives in Manitoba, both the federal and the provincial remnant, were enthusiastic for a union government.

The federal election of 1917 was fought in Manitoba, as in the rest of the country, on the issue of the completeness of Canada's commitment to the war. The issue was a contrived one in which support for a union government became identified with loyalty and patriotism. The newspapers hailed the unionists as harbingers of victory and reviled the Laurier Liberals as defeatist, at best, and traitors, at worst. The election was held on December 17, 1917, and conscription duly followed – with little or no effect on the outcome of the war, but with a considerable effect on Manitoba's politics.

The war ended on November 11, 1918, and its end was greeted in Manitoba with far more enthusiasm than had been its beginning. There was deep thankfulness that the carnage had ceased at last. The accumulated suffering was to persist for a generation. The shattered villages, blasted forests, and mutilated plains were far away in France and Flanders, but each community in Manitoba bore invisible scars. Each had its monument and each its memories. All swore that it must never be permitted to happen again.

Life goes on, and it went on briskly at the political level. The 1917 election had shattered the Liberal Party both federally and provincially, so that it bid fair to be as spent a force as was the Manitoba Conservative Party. The Union Government moved to return, with all haste, to normalcy. It was announced that orderly marketing would be dropped in favor of the free market. Except for a reasonably fair scheme for settling returned soldiers on the land, there was little done to provide for the future of the returning heroes. T. A. Crerar of the United Grain Growers, formerly Manitoba's representative in the Union Government as Minister of Agriculture, left the Government on its resolve to adhere to a high protective tariff. The National Policy was beginning to pinch the West again, and at a time when it had a multitude of other ills to trouble it. Not the least of these was the railway situation. Two of the three transcontinental systems lay in ruins, bankrupt as a result of their own greed. The Hudson Bay Railway stood in a state of abeyance once again. The great Laurier died suddenly on February 17, 1919, and left a shattered Liberal Party to try and piece itself together. Manitoba had tried both parties locally and federally and had found them both wanting. The price of grain plummeted in the post-war slump, but there was no parallel drop in costs. The war had left more than death and destruction; it had left Manitobans wondering, as it had all Canadians, if it had all been in vain.

The Canadian farmer was upset, disappointed, and angry. He was ready to seek change, not outside the political arena, but with his own rules and his own men. The farmer, in his wrath, began to think of political action. When political action came, however, it came first in Ontario. In Manitoba, it was the organized force of labor which first stirred the already choppy waters into an angry storm. Labor in Manitoba had had central direction since the formation of the Winnipeg Trades and Labor Council in 1894, and the growth of industry had meant an equal growth of the trade union movement. As the greater number of Manitoba's artisans were of British origin, they brought with them the English tradition of the union of skilled craftsmen. Each union was confined to the members of a particular trade who achieved the status of journeymen after a long apprenticeship. In eastern Canada, where unions were far older than the tradition of the individual, unions of skilled craftsmen had firmly set. In the West, however, the number of workers involved was much smaller and the craft union tradition was not as firmly fixed. There was also a greater influence, from the newer departures in English trade unionism, toward the close association of all trade unions for greater strength and a drift toward political action. Western Canadian labor was also affected by American influences promoting industrial unionism. This movement for the organization of all workers, skilled and unskilled alike, in a class war against the owners of capital reached its greatest strength in the Industrial Workers of the World, led by "Big Bill" Haywood. Its greatest strength was among the lumber workers of the west coast, and its influence in Canada was in the labor movement of British Columbia. Ideas of industrial unionism moved eastward into labor circles on the prairies, though its more violent aspects were left behind in the American Northwest.

These wider concerns aside, Manitoba's trade unions were generally concerned with the usual questions of wages, hours of work, and working conditions. They also placed considerable emphasis on the virtues of education, conducting classes on all manner of subjects in the interest of self-improvement. They also reflected a considerable interest in political action, generally outside the existing two-party system. In this, labor was far ahead of the farmers, both in thought and in deed. The Independent Labor Party was formed in Winnipeg in 1895, supporting reforms such as the eight-hour day, an end to piecework, abolition of overtime, nationalization of railways, and the municipal ownership of water works, electric power, and street railways. They also strongly supported compulsory schooling, votes for women, and temperance legislation – but not prohibition. In 1900, the ILP succeeded in electing A. W. Puttee as MP for Winnipeg, due largely to a wide split in the ranks of the local Liberals. More radical branches of labor politics appeared in 1904 with the Socialist Party of Canada and the Social Democratic Party, which sought quick and decisive alterations in the social structure, though still by constitutional means.

Change set in quickly after 1914. The war-induced labor shortage increased the bargaining power of the unions and they took full advantage of this power to gain greater union recognition, as well as a greater share of the wealth which they helped to produce. The common belief was that the two major parties were looters of the public treasury and connivers at the legal escape of the guilty within their own ranks. Labor took the highroad to political action. They chose the weapon of the strike to gain their ends. There was no lack of eloquent and able leaders to point out the differences between the "haves" and the "have nots," and to wonder aloud if the gulf between Wellington Crescent and Annabella Street was not indicative of some fundamental flaw in the nature of things. These men were almost exclusively of British origin. Indeed, only one of the prominent figures on the labor scene in the period after 1914 was of Canadian birth. The rest, to a man, were of English, Scottish, or Welsh birth. The principal figures of the Jewish faith, Sam Blumenberg, A. A. Heaps, and Jack Blumberg, were all born in England. Their leaders, however, were by no means of one mind. There was a radical wing which was imbued with Marxism and which was caught up enthusiastically in Lenin's takeover in Russia. They already saw the dawn of a new day for the proletariat. Among the radicals were R. B. Russell, George Armstrong, William Pritchard, and R. J. Johns. There were also those who leaned to the gradualist approach to socialism – men such as A. A. Heaps, W. J. Ivens, and John Queen. Many were moderates whose interests did not extend beyond the advancement of the trade union movement. These included F. G. Tipping, Ernest Robinson, James Winning, and H. Veitch.

This labor ferment first boiled over in the summer of 1918. There were wage and hour disputes between the City of Winnipeg and many of its organized employees, as well as serious difficulties in the negotiations between the Metal Trades Council and various employers. The dispute with the civic workers was settled after they had threatened to strike and the City Council had questioned that right. However, the metal trades, consisting largely of machinists and led by Johns and Russell, did strike – and the strike dragged on for many weeks. The main issue was whether or not wage increases which had been granted to railway metal workers should also be accorded by the lesser employers. Rather than see their fellows beaten, the Winnipeg Trades and Labor Council considered the calling of a general strike. A vote was taken among the members of the various unions and it came out seven to one in favor. The metal trades dispute was settled without further difficulty, but the weapon of the general strike had been flourished and it was but a matter of time and events before it was actually put to use.

In 1918, appeals to the patriotism of the workers had not gone unheeded. They were not to be accused of impeding the victory of Allied forces in Europe. By the early summer of 1919, however, considerations of patriotism no longer carried much weight. An opportunity afforded itself for a major exercise of the power of labor coincidentally with the first display of the political power of the organized farmer. In that year, the United Farmers of Ontario, the political arm of that province's agriculture, captured the government of the province – much to everyone's surprise, including their own. The motives of the Ontario farmers, as were later those of the farmers of Manitoba, were much different from those of labor – both as to method and as to aim. They did have some points in common. There was a continuing belief in the essential incapacity, as well as the deceit and duplicity, of the regular political parties. Each group felt that it received less than an equitable share of the fruits of its labor.

Winnipeg's labor movement had a recognized issue – one, in fact, which is now generally accepted and legally sanctioned. Collective bargaining was the point in question. The right to unionize and to be recognized as the bargaining agent within a shop or factory had been the law of Canada since 1872. With the growth of industrialization, bargaining by individual shops began to give way to the demand for labor contracts which covered all the operators of an entire industry. This was anathema to many employers – both the marginal ones, who could not compete for labor on a craft-wide basis, and the major entrepreneurs, who would brook no interference with their freedom of action. Besides the issue of collective bargaining, there was also that of the industrial union. The benefits of unionism had not reached the unskilled and their numbers were growing as industry became more mechanized. The English had experimented briefly with industrial unionism in the nineteenth century, and the current American experiment, the IWW, was somewhat hampered by the imprisonment of its leaders as wartime subversives.

It was in this atmosphere of war-born suspicion that the western Canadian industrial union first appeared. In Calgary, in March, 1919, the One Big Union was established through the combined efforts of the various western trades and labor councils. The OBU was to be an all-encompassing labor union, designed to gain for the laborer the fruits of his toil by means of political action. Since most men were workers rather than bosses, all that was needed was to organize them and, with their votes, to invade the citadels of power in a constitutional manner. Significantly, in the light of the "Red scare" aspects of the later Winnipeg trouble, a resolution of this convention demanded that a western general strike be called if Canadian troops were not withdrawn from Vladivostok by June 1, 1919. Organization of the OBU would take time and a great deal of persuasion, especially of the highly sensitive unions of skilled workers, such as those of the railway running trades. To men like Dick Johns, Bill Ivens, and Bob Russell, this delay was intolerable. They felt that Winnipeg was ripe for a strike and that time would work against any major achievement. Much of the world was already in revolutionary flames. Russia had formed a soviet state; and a satellite, or rather a meteor, had appeared under Bela Kun in Hungary. Germany was in a ferment with the Communist-led Spartacist movement. In the United States, a "Red scare" was in full voice, with the American way of life in dread danger according to Attorney-General A. Mitchell Palmer. With this as a background, many of the OBU leaders and organizers spoke of red flags, soviets, blood-sucking capitalists, and the coming dictatorship of the proletariat. At the time, they may even have believed it. One thing is certain: they spoke for themselves and their immediate following alone. There was no conspiracy directed from Moscow, no "pluto-Bolshevik-Jew" plot to take over the earth.

All this talk of bloody revolution fell on receptive ears. Not the ears of potential revolutionaries, but the ears of those who lived in a state of almost pathological fear of a Bolshevik-style revolution. From the safe remove of fifty years, the concern manifested by responsible people like J. W. Dafoe, the Hon. Arthur Meighen, Isaac Pitblado, A. J. Andrews, and a host of others appears almost ludicrous. So, indeed, do the revolutionary pronouncements of John Queen and Bob Russell, both of whom were humanitarian socialists and no more Communists than was General H. D. B. Ketchen, the commander of Military District No. 10 at Winnipeg. Indeed, General Ketchen proved to be one of the most level-headed men in the whole business. When Dick Johns spoke of arming the people against their oppressors, and when Isaac Pitblado burned up the wires to Ottawa with dire predictions of blood flowing in the streets, Ketchen calmly went about maintaining order and refusing to be stampeded. There was hysteria in the air. All three levels of government, and certainly the Royal North West Mounted Police, believed that there was a conspiracy afoot which had its roots in Moscow. The only roots of trouble, however, lay in the disturbed and dissatisfied condition of labor. There was not even agreement among the strike leaders as to what should be done or how it should be accomplished.

The Winnipeg General Strike began, as had the labor troubles of 1918, in wage disputes. In this case, the disputes were between the building trades and metal trades and their employers over wages and hours. The essential issue was the right of collective bargaining, which the employers stoutly resisted. The TLC, imbued with the concept of the all-embracing OBU, determined on a trial of strength. It was not merely a show of strength, but also a determined effort to obtain a fundamental bargaining right for labor. Labor was faced with falling employment and high prices. The labor market was disturbed by the cutbacks in war contracts and by the thousands of ex-servicemen who were returning to Canada to seek employment. Without bargaining rights, the worker – especially the unskilled worker – was at the mercy of the employer in a glutted labor market. It was believed that a general work stoppage of a few days would suffice.

The building and metal trades went out on May 1, and the two unions appealed to the TLC for support. A ballot was taken of all the members of all the unions and it went 11,112 to 524 in favor of a general strike. Premier Norris and Mayor Charles F. Gray of Winnipeg belatedly tried for a settlement of the wage dispute and failed. On Thursday, May 15, 1919, at 11:00 A.M., the general strike began. Essential services, such as light and water were maintained after a fashion; but otherwise, most of the life of the city and its suburbs ground to a halt. Street cars returned to the barns. Rail workers poured cheerfully from the Weston and Transcona shops. Postal workers, telegraphers, and telephone girls went out. Railway stations were bereft of express, freight or baggage service, though trains continued to run; the railway brotherhoods had been forbidden to strike by their Canadian headquarters. Bread and milk deliveries ceased temporarily, and newspapers ceased publication. Winnipeg took on its Sunday image of a well-lighted graveyard and this image persisted, day after day. The police had voted to go out, but stayed on, by request of the Strike Committee, to protect property. There was no danger to life and limb. The firemen went out and were replaced by volunteers.

The need for bread and milk deliveries was immediately recognized by the Strike Committee, as were other essential services such as the telegraph, gasoline, and coal-oil supplies. Theaters and movie houses were permitted to operate so as to provide a pastime for the idle. These activities were marked as being conducted by the permission of the Strike Committee and gave the impression, true enough, that it was acting as a government. This fact began to arouse public opinion against the strike; and, as the strike continued to drag on, this negative opinion became a greater force. The Strike Committee and its OBU thinkers never accepted the fact that there was such a thing as the public. All they could visualize was workers and bosses. The fact that all were members of the public and that all suffered was to bring them down in the end. A citizen's Committee of One Thousand was formed to carry on essential services, which it did with some success. However, each day that the strike continued increased its unpopularity – and there was to be no quick victory.

The strike was marked by a minimum of violence and a complete absence of parades and demonstrations in the streets. The Strike Committee urged the strikers to avoid trouble, to take it easy, and to wait it out – which, to a remarkable degree, they did. There were many mass meetings in parks and theaters, where the public listened to the ready oratory of the strike leaders. This was especially the case in Victoria Park, the closest open area to the Labor Temple. Fortunately, it was an early summer, so that fuel shortages or waiting in the cold were not problems. Indeed, it was such a warm June that the heat frazzled tempers on all sides. Messages and emissaries passed to and fro between the seats of government in Winnipeg and those in Ottawa, with much wringing of hands by officials, but with little action. The fears of Bolshevik revolution remained and were by no means quieted by the plaintive wails of the doom-cryers. There was a general suspicion that the whole thing was the fault of "foreign agitators," and the RNWMP never lost hope of somehow rooting them out. A general anti-foreign atmosphere prevailed – even among many of the strikers, who feared that aliens would be used as strikebreakers – while the authorities looked in vain for the aliens who had caused the whole thing. Of Winnipeg's population of 180,000, only 60,000 were non-British, and, of these, the Scandinavian element was hardly suspect. There was still some anti-German feeling, as evinced by the mob of discharged soldiers who refused to permit the holding of a memorial service in Market Square for the murdered Spartacist leaders, Karl Liebnicht and Rosa Luxemburg, on the grounds that they had been German.

The veterans and the soldiers who were awaiting discharge were in a difficult position. As soldiers, they might be expected to be amenable to orders from authority; but as veterans of heavy fighting, they were more likely to be fully fed up with doing what they were told to do. Many had labor backgrounds, and almost all were faced with the necessity of finding a job. Generally, the soldiers shared the public's increasing impatience with the strike. Neither Ottawa nor the Norris Government had any sympathy for the strike. Early in June, despair began to grip the strikers. They began to parade in protest at the lack of settlement. On June 16, the first move toward an agreement between the aggrieved metal workers and their employers was made. At the same time, the Government of Canada decided on drastic action. On June 17, the major strike leaders were arrested on charges of seditious conspiracy and seditious libel and were lodged at the Stony Mountain Penitentiary. The leaders were soon released on bail and a mass meeting was planned for Market Square on Saturday, June 21. Mayor Gray forbade the demonstration. It took place, however, and the mayor read the Riot Act. The RNWMP, armed with clubs, rushed the strikers twice. On the second occasion, they used their pistols against the unarmed crowd. (They later claimed to have been fired on first.) One member of the crowd was killed and another mortally wounded. Troops from Fort Osborne arrived in trucks after it was all over. The strike was broken and on June 25, the TLC declared it over.

In the clean-up that followed, other arrests were made, including those of Fred Dixon, MPP, and J. S. Woodsworth, who had been editing the *Western Labor News*. Four aliens of Slavic origin, without the slightest connection with either the origin or conduct of the strike, were rounded up and quickly deported. Dixon was acquitted of seditious libel after conducting his own brilliant defence, and the charges against Rev. J. S. Woodsworth were dropped when it was disclosed that his main offence consisted in printing extracts from the Bible. A. A. Heaps was acquitted. R. B. Russell was sentenced to two years for seditious conspiracy while Queen, Johns, Pritchard, and Armstrong were given one year each. They served the minimum time on the prison farm at Stony Mountain and were well treated, spending their weekends greeting their families and friends. Collective bargaining was recognized in due course. The Winnipeg General Strike did not accomplish this of itself, but the right was granted lest there be a repetition. The strike split Manitoba's labor movement badly and crippled its power for years to come. It gave Winnipeg a further reputation for radicalism, as well as serving as confirmation of the city's general eccentricity. The Communist Party of Canada rose from the strike, feeding on the support of the irreconcilable. The Communist Party has continued to claim the General Strike as its heritage, with as much validity as the Communist Party of the United States claims Abraham Lincoln as its own. The leaders, especially those who were jailed, became heroes of labor; and those who chose to do so, enjoyed long and active political careers. John Queen was elected mayor of Winnipeg seven times and sat long in the legislature. Woodsworth and Heaps were elected to Parliament, and Woodsworth became the founding leader of the CCF, continuing in Parliament until his death in 1942. As the city settled down, however, storm warnings were up on the farms.

13

The Progressive Achievement

GENERAL DISSATISFACTION HAD BEEN MANIFEST among Canadian farmers for many years. This discontent, however, was most vocal west of the Ottawa River. Here, farmers had organized the various provincial Grain Grower's Associations at the beginning of the century in order to put pressure on railways, grain handlers, and governments, and thus to strike a better balance in the distribution of the rewards of grain production. The various provincial organizations had combined, for united action, into the Canadian Council of Agriculture. In 1916, the CCA published its aim in "The Farmers' Platform," which called for public ownership of railways and utilities generally, as well as a proportionate tax on income. Its principal plank demanded a "for revenue only" tariff, a complete abandonment of the protective principal. Free trade was the farmers' highest hope of economic emancipation. For a variety of reasons, the CCA had avoided political action, as had the various provincial groups. There were cases where farmer candidates presented themselves for election to a legislature or to the House of Commons, but not many did so outside of the existing political parties. The farmers had good memories and could recall the signal lack of success of other farm movements in the political field – movements such as the Grange, the Manitoba and North West Farmers' Union, and the Patrons of Industry. They had achieved some results by pressure-group tactics, including marches on Ottawa and the various provincial capitals. They were generally suspicious of politicians and political activity and avoided these if they could. The exposure of both political parties on the local and national levels as being incompetent, corrupt, and imprisoned by eastern interests completed the alienation of the farmer from the exercise of politics. Though urged by his press, especially the *Grain Growers Guide,* to take political action, the farmer was reluctant to do so. With the coming of the war, it became a patriotic duty – and one which was cheerfully assumed – to put political questions aside until the war was won.

Both the *Grain Growers Guide* and the CCA were strong advocates of a nonpartisan coalition to win the war, and the outstanding farm leader T. A. Crerar, president of the United Grain Growers, entered the Union Government as Minister of Agriculture. The resounding victory of the Non-Partisan League in the 1916 state election in North Dakota provided an encouraging example and it was played up in the *Guide.* The war provided further fuel for the fires of farm grievances. The drain of men into the army and the imposition of conscription left the farmers without essential labor, though they had been promised liberal agricultural exemptions. High prices and shortages, high rail rates and the bankruptcy of both the Grand Trunk and the Canadian Northern, the retreating wraith of the line to Hudson Bay, the announced demise, at the war's end, of the system of orderly marketing – all drove the farmer to seek his own salvation. Labor had tried, in vain, to find a solution in the general strike. The farmers turned to direct political action with great immediate success and with no little long-range effect on the development of Manitoba. Outside of the provincial sphere, their aim was not to take over the reins of power, since they had not the requisite strength of numbers. It was, rather, to show what strength they did have, and, as a pressure group, to bring the other parties to realize the error of their ways. There had been some early indications of a trend toward direct political action in the election of 1917. Three candidates of the Non-Partisan League had made the attempt in Saskatchewan and J. A. Maharg had been elected as an independent supporting the Union Government.

With the war out of the way, the farmers moved quickly. Their entry into politics was a matter of incidence of elections, rather than a matter of the bold stepping first into the arena. In 1919, farmers' candidates won by-elections in both Alberta and Saskatchewan. In the same year, the opportunity came in Ontario when the United Farmers of Ontario entered candidates in the October 20 general election and emerged with forty-four seats to the Hearst Government's twenty-six. Ernest C. Drury was chosen leader and headed the Government of Ontario until 1923. Also in 1919, the CCA revised the farmers' platform as the "New National Policy," which again demanded low tariff and insisted on both reciprocity with the United States and free trade with the United Kingdom. Since neither of the major parties took up the New National Policy nor showed any particular interest in placating the farmer, he moved into the national field. In 1920, meeting at Winnipeg, the CCA created the Progressive Party with the New National Policy as its platform and T. A. Crerar as its leader. Meanwhile, the Union Government had broken up. The uneasily reunited Liberals had chosen W. L. Mackenzie King to succeed Laurier and in so doing gave the party thirty-six years of only briefly interrupted power. Sir Robert Borden retired and was succeeded by Arthur Meighen of Portage la Prairie. The prairie was already on fire. The United Farmers of Alberta took over the government of the province, and in Saskatchewan the farmers were taking over the Liberal Party.

In Manitoba, an election was called for June 9, 1920, and Norris found himself deeply embroiled. Farmers' candidates were put forward in many constituencies as representing the United Farmers of Manitoba, which, however, had no provincial political organization and certainly no common platform. Many farmer candidates represented the rejection of political parties as such, while others based their appeal for votes on their opposition to the School Act amendments of 1916. In the latter cases, some represented a belief that the amendments had gone too far in the direction of anglicization and others that the amendments had not gone far enough in putting the "foreigner" in his place. One or two ran on a platform of trust in God, without paying due attention to the caution about keeping their powder dry. In Winnipeg, labor and socialist candidates appeared in force. There were also labor candidates in Brandon and farmer-labor in Dauphin. The result put Norris in a minority position with 21 seats. The Conservatives went up to 7; Labor took 11; the UF of M 13; and there were 4 Independents. The election was not only remarkable for its revelation of the disturbed state of the province's politics, but also for the fact that some of the Labor members-elect were still in prison. It marked the first election of a woman to the legislature – Mrs. Edith Rogers of Winnipeg, who fittingly enough, was a great granddaughter of the "little emperor," Sir George Simpson. The general result put an end to party government for a generation. It was replaced by a sort of multiparty yet nonparty arrangement, whereby members held to local allegiances, exercised different prejudices, and still managed to remain united as a government. Putting it more strongly, the Government tended to view the legislature as a sort of glorified municipal council. For better or worse, this attitude prevailed until the fall of the Campbell Government in 1958, and traces of it can still be discerned.

The new Legislature was the first to take up the magnificent quarters in the new Legislative Building, which was now finally completed, though far from paid for. Its appearance and appointments went far to justify the travail of its construction. Above its dome, shone the gilded statue of a youth, torch of progress in hand and sheaf of wheat under his left arm; he faced northward, where, hopefully, a bright future lay. The Golden Boy had already survived the war as ballast in a freighter; and through years of winter's smoke, he was to tarnish to the point where the wheat he carried was judged to grade at Number 6 Smutty. Today, he stands in illuminated glory under a coat of gold leaf. Two magnificent buffalo guard the grand staircase and serve as reminders to all who pass of the beginnings of this present greatness. In the session of 1921, the UF of M set a precedent which was to be followed nationally by the Progressive Party. They refused to become the official opposition. Rather, they would represent their constituents, guard the interests of the farm, and support any proposal that they felt was right. They did not, then or later, regard themselves as forming a party as such and they had difficulty in operating under the time-honored concepts of a responsible government in a constitutional monarchy. A. E. Smith, Labor MLA for Brandon, attempted to gain approval for a proposal of "group government." His motion, that the executive be composed of members of each party on the basis of its numbers in the Legislature, was defeated by the casting vote of Mr. Speaker J. B. Baird.

In the interim between the sessions of 1921 and 1922, a severe economic recession took place, a slightly-belated effect of the war. The marketing of grain by the Government of Canada through a Wheat Board ended in 1921. Coincidentally, world wheat prices collapsed. Number 1 Hard had been at $2.85 a bushel on the Winnipeg Exchange in September 1921; by November, it had dropped to $1.78, falling still further in November, 1922, to $1.02. Farm costs remained high. Many farmers had expanded their operations in the days of high wartime demand, and they were now encumbered with mortgages which lay as heavily as the word implies. Foreclosures and business failures muddied the economic waters. The financial trouble culminated in 1923 with the failure of the Home

25 Portage Avenue, looking east from Hargrave, c. 1908 (Winnipeg Grain Exchange in the background)

26 Model T snowmobile, operating between The Pas and Flin Flon, 1928

27 Motor Country Club outing, setting off from the Leland Hotel, Main and William, 1915

26

27

28 Handcar on the Canadian Northern Railway, between Hudson Bay Junction and The Pas, 1909

29 *Legislative Building under construction (Photographed from the southeast corner of the grounds, 1915)*

30 The Political Equality League with its petition for female suffrage, 1915

31 *Volunteers leaving from Union Station, Winnipeg,* c. *1915*

32 Great War Veterans Association demonstrating against the Winnipeg General Strike, June 4, 1919

33 The mounties disperse the mob, June 21 (Photograph taken looking north from William and Main)

34

35 *Drought, 1930's*

35

36 Flooding at St. Boniface Hospital, 1916

37 Flooding of "the flats" north of the Assiniboine at Brandon, 1922

36

37

38 *Winnipeg Flood, 1950 (St. Mary's Academy, Wellington Crescent and Academy Road)*

39 Western Canada Airways, flight leaving for the gold fields, 1927

40 Original shafthouse and mine, Flin Flon, 1927

39

40

41 *Hudson Bay Mining & Smelting plant, Flin Flon, 1956*

42 The Duke of Edinburgh opens the Pan-American Games at Winnipeg, 1967 Prime Minister L. B. Pearson and Premier Duff Roblin on his right, Mayor Steve Juba on his left

Bank, which was heavily involved in farm mortgages. The economic distress produced political quicksand in which T. C. Norris was quickly mired. In 1921, the Legislature had adopted a motion calling for the abolition of the Public Utilities Commission. Norris did not act on the recommendation and in 1922 he was called to task for this omission by P. A. Talbot, the Liberal member for La Vérendrye. Talbot had a personal grievance against the Public Utility Commission and was also strongly opposed to the Government's unilingual school policy. His defection was costly to Norris, who chose to regard Talbot's motion as one of no confidence. Conservatives and Labor supported the motion, as did most of the UF of M members. To the farmers' members, Norris' disregard of the wishes of the House was but another example of the arrogance of the oldline parties. The motion carried and Norris offered his resignation and that of his Government. Lieutenant-Governor Sir James Aikins refused to accept the resignations, insisting that the business of the session, especially the voting of supply, be completed. When this was done, the House was dissolved and an election called for July 18, 1922.

The issue was never in doubt. The old parties were in eclipse and whatever emerged would be a purely-Manitoba phenomenon. The UF of M had no leader, but it did have a province-wide organization which entered candidates in 40 of the 44 constituencies. Winnipeg now returned 10 members at large from a city-wide riding by proportional representation. In the federal election of 1921, the Progressives had taken all 12 Manitoba seats outside of Winnipeg. The three Winnipeg seats returned a mixed bag. A. B. Hudson was nominally a Liberal but was blood brother to the Progressives. J. S. Woodsworth in Winnipeg Center represented Labor and E. J. McMurray in Winnipeg North was a straight Liberal who was to serve as solicitor general in the Government of Mackenzie King. All in all, the prospect was not pleasing to Norris. He also suffered from recurring criticism at the hands of the Winnipeg Board of Trade, then voice of the Winnipeg "establishment," which hoped for an economy-minded farm government. Their hope was fulfilled, even more than they had wished. The UF of M carried 28 seats and thus the right to form a government. Their caucus began at once to search for a leader. Of the seven Liberals returned, only Norris and his attorney-general, Robert Jacob of Winnipeg, were survivors of the cabinet. The Conservatives took six, including Portage la Prairie, which was won by their new leader, Colonel Fawcett G. Taylor. Six Labor members and eight Independents rounded out the total.

Norris resigned on August 8, 1922, and was succeeded by John Bracken, the unanimous choice of the UF of M caucus. Bracken's name had been mentioned during the campaign, but he had not been tempted to seek a seat. As president of the Manitoba Agricultural College and a renowned expert in the techniques of dry farming, the Ontario-born Bracken felt fully and usefully employed. A political career held no charm for him. George Chipman, editor of the *Country Guide,* had been mentioned as a potential leader, but he failed of election in Winnipeg. Colin Burnell, president of the Manitoba Grain Growers' Association, another prospect, had even failed of nomination. The UF of M caucus discussed names which included – not surprisingly, in this nonparty period – Norris and his minister of agriculture, George H. Malcolm. Approaches were made to T. A. Crerar and to R. A. Hoey, Progressive MP for Springfield. Both declined with thanks. Bracken had been asked if he would accept the position were it offered him. He had firmly declined, but he was now recalled by the caucus and was made a direct offer of the leadership and the office of premier. Again, he put the offer firmly aside. The impression he made on the MLA's-elect was so great that they sent a delegation to Bracken's home on the agricultural college campus and there pleaded again, this time with the reluctant leader's wife present. Alice Bruce Bracken interposed no veto, and on this third occasion, Bracken took up the crown. It was no passing fancy. John Bracken remained premier of Manitoba until January 8, 1943.

The Government of the United Farmers of Manitoba set to with a will to give competent and careful administration to the province. At no time could it be accused of extravagance or of an excess of imagination. The immediate budgetary difficulties were handled by the slashing of expenses. Salaries and even widow's allowances were cut. The number of civil servants was reduced. Strict economy became, and remained, the watchword. To repair the deficits of the Norris years, resort was had to a provincial income tax – minute by present-day standards, though still a tax which made the name Bracken anathema in the City of Winnipeg. Nevertheless, some of Bracken's ablest colleagues, men such as R. W. Craig and W. J. Major, were able to gain election in the city. Under Bracken, the division between rural and urban Manitoba reached its greatest extent. The metropolis lost what sympathetic contact it had with its hinterland and took the view that the city was being milked for the benefit of the country. At the same time, Winnipeg never gave up the concept that the whole West was being milked for the benefit of Toronto and Montreal. In truth, the greater resources of the city were tapped – directly and indirectly, as they had been before – to provide necessary services in the way of schools, hospitals, telephones, electric power, and roads throughout Manitoba. The issue of roads especially was an object of urban suspicion, at least until the late 1950's. There was always a flurry of road-building and road-planning going on, but the general state of the highways was long medieval.

Bracken's Government early made a move which combined a gesture to Winnipeg and a flow of cash into the provincial coffers. It was made at the cost of prohibitionist support, though only the most irreconcilable of these remained. In 1923, in response to a favorable plebiscite of 108,000 to 69,000 the Legislature passed the Government Liquor Control Act, which established a Liquor Control Commission that was empowered to import, buy, and sell liquor. Sales were to be from state-operated outlets located throughout the province. Quantities sold were to be limited and made only by mail order to permit-holders. Permits were to be sold only to persons who were over twenty-one and who were not interdicted by previous alcohol offences. It was a beginning to a more reasonable approach to temperance which was extended in 1928 by a new Liquor Control Act which repealed the Manitoba Temperance Act of 1916.

The new act provided for direct retail sales from liquor stores operated by the government to permit-holders in limited quantities. It also made provision for breweries to operate stores on their premises under government supervision and to make home deliveries. Hotels could be licensed for the retail sale of malt beverages to men only. The new system was neither prohibition nor temperance. It permitted highly-restricted public drinking, but under conditions which made such drinking hardly respectable by surrounding it with countless niggling regulations. The liquor stores had all the attraction of a tax office and performed much the same function. Manitobans managed to put up with it or to circumvent the system as they had in the past. The druggist went back to his pills and put in a soda fountain, but the bootlegger survived because of the high prices charged by the government and the restricted hours of sale. All in all, the government found the liquor business a profitable addition to provincial revenues.

In the same year that liquor reform began, the farmers' government gave a clear indication of its concept of how the people's business should be conducted. In response to Progressive pressure, the King Government enacted a continuation of orderly marketing through the Wheat Board, contingent upon enabling legislation by the prairie provinces. It was approved at Edmonton and Regina, but at Winnipeg there was some farm objection since Manitoba farmers, being closer, often benefited by higher prices on the early fall wheat market. The Winnipeg "establishment," of course, was also opposed to the bill. Bracken had a division in his cabinet on the question, with the majority in favor. No cabinet solidarity was expected and no party discipline imposed. Bracken called for a free vote. With unconscious irony, he called on the members to vote as their consciences dictated. The measure was defeated with three of the cabinet opposing, and the Wheat Board disappeared. The method of free voting and the tendency of MLA's to regard themselves as delegates from their ridings, rather than as representatives of the whole province, was characteristic of the period from John Bracken through Stuart Garson to Douglas Campbell. Its persistence affected all groups and made possible future coalitions, first with the Liberals and then with Social Credit. Finally, in 1940, a grand coalition was achieved of all parties – including, for a time, the CCF.

The end of government-controlled orderly marketing opened the way for the co-operative marketing of grain through the so-called "pools." Grain would be marketed in such a way that each producer would obtain the average price over the crop year for his harvest by assigning it to the pool which would handle the marketing after making an initial payment. The final payment, which was made when the crop was all marketed, was based on the amount delivered, its grade, and the average price for that grade obtained by the pool operators. A similar arrangement had been successful in the marketing of eggs, butter, and raisins in the United States. An American pool expert, Aaron Sapiro, preached the word throughout the West to an enthusiastic audience. He was able to recruit the help of most farm organizations, including the United Grain Growers Limited. In 1924, forty percent of Manitoba's farmers signed up with the Manitoba Cooperative Wheat Producers Limited, and for some years the pools of the West, united as the Canadian Co-Operative Wheat Producers Limited, prospered as the result of farmer support and steadily-rising grain prices. Though a free market operated through the Winnipeg Grain Exchange, that body had not regained the confidence of the prairie farmer.

The election of P. A. Talbot as speaker and the addition to the cabinet of Albert Prefontaine did much to ease the *Canadien* outcry against the 1916 School Act amendments. The issue of separate schools was by no means settled, but the permissiveness which had held the peace under Greenway and Roblin returned to make the system tolerable. The Mennonites of the Old Church, who could not reconcile themselves either to compulsory or to English-only education, decamped for Mexico or South America. This loss, together with a new if lesser influx of Mennonite refugees from the Bolshevik Revolution, led to a more rapid integration of the Mennonite community. The principal question in education, however, did not concern the nature of what was to be taught. The question, rather, was whether or not anything was to be taught at all. The reliance on small school districts for the provision of schools and for the payment of teachers placed a heavy burden on the many districts which had little in the way of taxable resources. It also provided an easy out for those regions which saw little value in education and which therefore provided an absolute minimum of funds, severely limiting the chances of the local children to obtain an adequate schooling and effectively barring them from higher education. In 1924, the Murray Royal Commission on Education reported that ten percent of all public schools were closed for lack of funds and that an even greater proportion were closed for part of the school year at least. The University of Manitoba remained on the brink of financial disaster and its plans for settling in Tuxedo or even Fort Garry on the campus of the agricultural college were in abeyance for lack both of money and of any inclination on the part of the Government to strike out boldly. The province already had a heavy dead-weight debt and the Government's reluctance to increase it lead to an almost pathological fear of debt that was greatly intensified in the bitter years of the 1930's. The university received as little financial help as did the elementary and secondary schools. Attempts to remedy the situation through adjusted grants and equalized assessments ran onto the rock of local autonomy and roused the wrath of the relatively affluent City of Winnipeg. In the field of education, little was accomplished in the whole of the Progressive period.

The so-called Progressive period can be said to extend from the formation of the Bracken Government in 1922 to the defeat of that of D. L. Campbell in 1958. The period was never progressive in the broad sense of the word. The Progressive Party underwent several changes of name and two of leader; but it never was, nor did it ever pretend to be, anything more than a careful and cautious custodian of the public purse. It was concerned always with economy and efficiency in its approach to public problems. Manitoba always did its share in programs which were advanced by Ottawa in the development of the social service state or which were required of the province alone to that same end. The contributions of Manitoba tended to be minimal and were so hedged about to protect the public treasury as to deprive them of any shred of understanding or humanitarianism. The Government's hard-headedness exposed it to charges of hard-heartedness. This suited its farm constituency and retained its confidence beyond all statistical expectation.

The federal election of 1921 had put Mackenzie King and the Liberals into power, but their tenure rested on the forebearance of the Progressive Party. Mr. King was quite willing to make an arrangement with the western insurgents; but his conservative support, led by Sir Lomer Gouin, felt that political rebellion should not be rewarded. The Progressives themselves were of two minds. Many, especially those of Alberta, wished no truck with the unreliable eastern power blocs. Others, including those of Manitoba and their leader, T. A. Crerar, were unwilling to split the country politically on a sectional basis. They would welcome an alliance based on the achievement of at least some of the aims of the New National Policy. Mr. King's natural inclination to conciliation was thus restrained by those of his party whom he had not yet had time to master. The Progressives did achieve the restoration by statute of the Crow's Nest Pass rates on the rail shipment of flour and grain, a right still zealously guarded in the West. And were it not for the defection of Manitoba, they would have accomplished the restoration of orderly marketing. There were some tariff concessions, especially with regard to farm machinery, but no direct assault on the principal of protection.

These concessions by Mr. King held the votes of most of the Progressives, though a small group of Alberta's MP's, called the "Ginger Group," remained simon-pure in their rejection of party politics. The Progressives were driven to the edge of open revolt against the Liberal Government by its failure to proceed with all due speed toward the completion of the Hudson Bay Railway. The line had been laid to Kettle Rapids in 1917, but there all construction had halted – despite the fact that millions had already been spent in building port facilities at the mouth of the Nelson. In 1924, there was formed at Winnipeg a vigorous organization called the "On to the Bay Association." Made up of farm and business leaders from the prairie provinces and adjacent states, the association began to prod Ottawa with all of the pent-up exasperation of some forty years. Mr. King promised action on the line as a first priority; but in the session of 1924, the Government voted $15,000,000 for the Welland Canal and nothing for the Hudson Bay Railway. The Progressive and "On to the Bay" protests forced a recantation during the election campaign of 1925. In this campaign, Manitoba, now at its maximum of 17 seats, returned 7 Progressives, 7 Conservatives, 2 Labor members, and only one Liberal. The Progressive strength in the House of Commons was reduced to 24, but Mr. King had only 99 Liberals to Arthur Meighen's 116 Conservatives. Mr. King chose to stay in power on the assumption that the Progressives were more likely to vote for his measures than they were for those of the Conservatives. To justify this assumption, he made a substantial gesture to the West. The Throne Speech of 1926 announced that the Hudson Bay Railway would be put in hand forthwith. It was, as Mr. Meighen characterized it, "a naked, shameless bribe."

Charles Dunning, who had been premier of Saskatchewan, became Minister of Railways and Canals, accepting the office only on the condition that the Hudson Bay line be finished. Studies had indicated beyond a doubt that Churchill afforded a good harbor, while Port Nelson was no port at all – in spite of the sums that had been spent to create one there. The new location required an additional seventy-five miles of railway, but the savings in port facilities and in time were well worth the investment. At mile 356, the railway turned north. On April 3, 1929, the last spike was driven at Cape Merry at the mouth of the Churchill River. From the end of steel, Fort Prince of Wales was clearly visible across the harbor. Manitoba's past and its hoped-for future had now come together. In the fall of 1929, a token shipment of one ton of Number 1 Hard was embarked for Europe on the HBC ship, *Nascopie* – a fitting choice, neatly symbolic of the great changes which had been wrought over two hundred years.

By August, 1931, the terminal elevator dock and other port facilities were in operation. In that first season, two shiploads of grain were sent to England. Navigational aids were installed on the route to Churchill through Hudson Strait at heavy expense. The supposed danger to shipping along the route caused marine insurance rates to be so high as to obviate any savings in freight charges. The sanguine hopes which had for so long been held in the West were not to be realized. In 1956, its best year, Churchill handled only five percent of Canada's grain exports; and incoming cargo never matched the volume of outgoing grain. The Panama Canal had long since robbed the Hudson Bay line of its greatest opportunities, and the competition of the St. Lawrence Seaway struck another mortal blow. As for Churchill, it is still, as Captain James Knight complained back in 1717, a most "misserable place." The port, however, may yet come into its own. The use of Churchill as a staging point for aircraft during World War II and as a fueling base during the subsequent cold war were of great benefit to the site. The railway to the bay cuts through the heart of the Canadian Shield in Manitoba and branch lines serve both the great nickle complex at Thompson and the power site at Kelsey. Similar branches have long served The Pas, Flin Flon, and, more latterly, Lynn Lake. Churchill lives on its hopes.

The Hudson Bay Railway was completed just as the world was about to undergo the trauma of the Wall Street crash and the great depression of the 1930's. Before this dread decade, however, Manitoba, along with the rest of North America, enjoyed a brief period of economic growth and expansion. For most Manitobans, it was a period of gentle prosperity untroubled by the fever of speculation, which, left unchecked, was to lead to disaster for all. Grain prices began to rise in 1923 and continued to do so until 1929. Other manifestations of recovery from the economic consequences of the First World War also became evident. There was another wave of immigration – albeit, a ripple as compared to the influx at the beginning of the century. Some tens of thousands came in during the decade 1921-31; some were British, but most were eastern Europeans who had been dispossessed by the upheavals of the war, the Russian Revolution, and the subsequent civil war. They joined their precursors on the farms, in the towns, and especially in the cities. They became a part of Manitoba society without incident, guided by the knowledge and experience of those who had come before them. The newer Ukrainians brought with them an intense nationalism which was unfamiliar to the earlier arrivals and which, for a time, bid fair to instil Old World animosities such as those which had troubled the politics of Manitoba in earlier days.

It was an age of increased technological advance. New strains of wheat and of other grains appeared, and agriculture became fully diversified. There was more attention paid to the raising of cattle, sheep, and hogs. Dairy farming, eggs and poultry, market gardening, honey – all played a more prominent role. The diversification in grain was clearly seen in the bumper crop of 1928 in which Manitoba produced over fifty million bushels each of wheat, oats, and barley. The steam threshing machine gave way to the gasoline-driven variety, and it, in turn, began to be replaced by the combine. The tractor became an even more serious threat to the horse than it had been before, but it did not finally triumph until after World War II. The automobile all but completely displaced the horse in Winnipeg, and it became necessary to introduce the first of the eventual maze of traffic lights and directional signs. The highways remained quagmires or, alternately, dust bowls. In spite of this drawback, the summer trek to resort areas continued to increase and substantial cottage towns surrounded the beaches on Lake Winnipeg and Lake Manitoba. Riding Mountain National Park became a summer mecca and Manitoba's own Whiteshell was opening up. The prosperity of city and farm could be seen in the proliferation of homes in the French chateau and Spanish mission styles. In Winnipeg, the socially elect began to desert Wellington Crescent and the area around River Heights for the more select surroundings of Tuxedo.

The province was as sports-minded as ever. The blood sports eagerly welcomed a new generation of Nimrods and the followers of Izaak Walton were legion. The reporting of team sports gave the press a welcome relief from the blasting of political evils, real or imagined, though it did little for the correct use of English. Lacrosse exceeded baseball as a summer favorite, both in popularity and in blood-letting. The province's junior and senior hockey teams maintained an enviable record, making Winnipeg a regular home for the Allen and Memorial cups. Football was serving the apprenticeship which was to lead to national glory after 1935, while soccer teams continued to abound. A reluctant Legislature authorized pari-mutuel betting on horse races and the rather scratch track at River Park in Winnipeg gave way to the sophisticated establishments at Whittier Park in St. Boniface and at Polo Park in west Winnipeg. Curling more than held its own and continued to encourage the young to enter into its mysteries. Snowshoe clubs enjoyed a blazing sunset before falling into neglect and being replaced by skiing as the number-one outdoor winter sport. It was the dawning of the age of radio. Ruben Spinach, Ebony and White, and others convulsed city and farm listeners from Whitemouth to Virden and from Emerson to Norway House. The radio gave new and greater strength to music. Choral groups were still the province's pride and the annual Manitoba Schools Musical Festival became far-famed. The twenties were a gentle period in Manitoba's social history. The distressed and poverty-stricken remained, but not in numbers sufficient to distract or discomfit the public mind.

It was in the midst of this general euphoria that John Bracken first put his Government to the test of an election. In 1927, his legislative mandate was about to be exhausted by the passage of time. It is perhaps indicative of the Government's lack of concern for political manoeuvring that both in 1927 and in 1932 it held elections only when mandatory, rather than taking advantage of a favorable political moment in which to do so. In any event, Bracken had the advantage of a rising economy and the enthusiasm which was generated in the general celebration of Canada's Diamond Jubilee, the sixtieth anniversary of Confederation. The United Farmers' platform called for the continuing and complementary development of agriculture, of mining resources, and of secondary industry. Educational and social service facilities were to be reorganized, though not necessarily expanded. There was also a promise to settle the Natural Resources Question, a promise which the public regarded as the least likely to be fulfilled. The provincial Liberals remained in a state of disorganization, and labor suffered politically through the decline in urban unrest, which varied inversely with the rise of prosperity. The Conservatives alone, under the able and affable Colonel Taylor, showed signs of recovery. In the election, the UF of M Government gained 29 of the 55 seats; the Conservatives took 15; the Liberals 7; Labor 3; and the Independents one.

The revival of the Conservative Party coincided with new charges of political corruption and of wrong-doing in high places. In 1925, it had become evident that more hydroelectric power would soon be needed. Winnipeg City Hydro reached the maximum output from Pointe du Bois in 1926 and secured the rights for Slave Falls. The next great power development would come at Seven Sisters Falls and in 1925 both the Manitoba Power Commission and private interests approached Ottawa for permission to develop. The Natural Resources Question was now so near to settlement that the Department of the Interior referred the decision to the Government of Manitoba. In turn, Manitoba sought the advice of T. A. Hogg of the Ontario Hydro Electric Power Commission. Hogg reported in 1928 that public development would be too costly and that the site should be privately developed. The advice was sound and especially appealing to a government which was burdened by debt not of its own making and which was unwilling to add to that debt, even if it were self-liquidating. Thus, in March, 1928, the Seven Sisters site was leased to the Winnipeg Electric Company and the North Western Power Company, which contracted to supply the Manitoba Power Commission with 30,000 horse power per year at $13.80 per horsepower over a 30-year period.

The contract was not submitted to the Legislature, which is understandable, since in strict legality it was a matter for the Government of Canada to determine. It was, however, an impolitic ommission. Winnipeg City Hydro had wished to bid for the Seven Sisters site, but had been blocked by the City Council, most of whose members were opposed to further public ownership. In July, 1928, Colonel Taylor charged bribery in the Seven Sisters lease. He claimed that the terms were too favorable to the private companies and that the UF of M had been paid $50,000 by the Winnipeg Electric Company for campaign purposes. The Conservative leader described the Seven Sisters lease as "the worst political bargain ever made in this province." It was to be 1915 all over again, only this time with the shoe on the other foot – or so the public was led to believe. Premier Bracken insisted on a royal commission of investigation, and one was set up under Chief Justice D. A. Macdonald, who had served his apprenticeship in such matters on the Royal Commission on the New Parliament Buildings.

The Macdonald Commission probed into the matter, though not deeply enough for some observers. For one thing, it did not insist on examining the financial records of the Winnipeg Electric Company, whose president, Edward Anderson, remained in ill-health in California. He was visited there by the commission, but the commission returned home none the wiser. It was revealed that one minister of the Crown had purchased Winnipeg Electric stock after the lease had been made but before it had been announced. So had the wife of another minister and the law firm of a third, as well as the Speaker of the House. Hon. W. R. Clubb and Hon. W. J. Major resigned from the cabinet. They and the others were exonerated by the royal commission, which found no evidence of wrongdoing. It was a period of general stock market speculation, and Winnipeg Electric stock was a favorite among those who were taking a flyer in the market. The royal commission did find that the Winnipeg Electric Company had given $3,500 to the Conservatives, $3,000 to the UF of M, and $500 to the Liberals for campaign purposes. But these were by no means large sums and were fully in keeping with the usual policy of remaining on good terms with each party in rough proportion to its political prospects. A minority report by Judge A. K. Dysart complained that the matter of political contributions had not been fully explored. In due course, both Clubb and Major returned to the cabinet and the matter was generally forgotten – though not perhaps in the City of Winnipeg, where Bracken could do no right.

In 1928 also, the UF of M went out of politics. The Bracken Government took on the name "Progressive" and began to move ever closer to the provincial Liberals, as the more moderate of the federal Progressives had already done. The Manitoba Liberal and Progressive parties soon had greater reason to forget their differences. Manitoba was about to gain control of its natural resources, after having striven to do so since 1870. The year 1928 also marked a significant change in the attitude of Manitoba to the Dominion of Canada. In the 1920's, there was much talk of the need for some measure of re-confederation – a readjustment, particularly in financial matters, in order that the various provinces would have the funds with which to handle their growing responsibilities. John W. Dafoe and the *Free Press* were in the van of this movement and it increasingly attracted the attention of John Bracken. Manitoba was a "have not" province; both its population and its taxable resources fell far below those of the central provinces. From Manitoba's point of view, the whole tax structure left much to be desired. Profits which were made in Manitoba, in the West generally, and in the Maritimes became taxable only in Ontario and Quebec, which served as the home of the head offices of the majority of Canadian corporations. Manitoba, following the lead of the great Canadian, Dafoe, did not seek to strengthen its hand by weakening that of Ottawa. Instead, it sought to strengthen Ottawa's hand and thereby to make possible a truly Canadian nation.

John Bracken began to emerge as a nationalist, a "Canada first" rather than a "Manitoba first" political leader. As he saw it, the strengthening of Ottawa would tend to strengthen Manitoba. He did not view Canada as a compact between equals and certainly not as the creation and creature of Ontario and Quebec. Canada was a federation in which the Ottawa government stood above those of the provinces – not just "first among equals," but first in fact and first in power. To Bracken, there was no advantage to be gained by voicing jealousy of Ontario and Quebec. Rather, he would prefer to see Ottawa assume its rightful dominance and make the central provinces share and share alike. That such an eventuality would restrict the power of the Government of Manitoba he was quite willing to accept, as were most Manitobans. Only one obstacle stood in the way of full co-operation with the federal authority in the matter of financial equality. This was the Natural Resources Question, and by the late 1920's it was all but resolved.

In 1918, T. C. Norris and the premiers of Alberta and Saskatchewan had achieved an understanding with Sir Robert Borden by which natural resources would be placed in the hands of the prairie provinces. The eastern provinces then demanded that if the western provinces were to be indemnified for lands which had been alienated by Ottawa since 1870, they too should receive equivalent compensation. Here, indeed, was a harkening back to the days of Canadian colonialism. In those days, easterners claimed that they had bought the West and that it was theirs to exploit. Apparently, they had not been disabused of this concept. The full-throated western disavowal of any deal on those grounds had an effect. At a federal-provincial conference on the occasion of the sixtieth anniversary of Confederation, the eastern provinces withdrew their claim for compensation. The way was now open for a final settlement. In 1929, a federal royal commission reported in favor of the transfer and of compensation to the prairie provinces alone. The commission concluded that since railways had been built and the land settled, the "purposes of the Dominion" had been fulfilled. Manitoba's share of the compensation was to be just over $4,500,000. The transfer of natural resources and the payment of compensation took place at Winnipeg on July 15, 1930, sixty years to the day after the Province of Manitoba had been proclaimed. The long struggle for the control of Crown lands was finally resolved and Manitobans could now turn wholeheartedly to the task of being good Canadians – though with a few reservations regarding trade policy.

The transfer was not immediately followed by a massive assault on the riches that were locked in the Canadian Shield. Indeed, such efforts as had already been started were now coming to a stop. The great depression was underway. In the years following World War I, a fair start had been made in taking advantage of little-exploited resources and in probing into the unknown. In 1926, a paper mill and a model town were erected on the Winnipeg River at Pine Falls. In 1927, its flow of paper began and the *Free Press* became the first local journal to make use of it. The stunted forests of the shield were an endless supply of wood for pulping and, in time, for a multitude of wood-based synthetics. The beautiful and easily-worked limestone of Tyndall and Garson had long been used locally for building purposes. Both St. Andrew's Church and Lower Fort Garry stand witness to its durability, and its use in the new Legislative Building had made it known far beyond Manitoba. Tyndall stone graced buildings in Montreal and was used in the interior finishing of the new Parliament Buildings at Ottawa. Since the war, the limestone and clay necessary to the making of cement had been brought together at Fort Whyte, giving the place a function undreamed of in the days of the railway dispute.

The extraction of mineral wealth from the Canadian Shield had long been under way in the eastern provinces. In Manitoba, such exploitation had to wait on transportation and technical advances in mining and metallurgy. Valuable metal deposits were long known to exist, but the problem lay in getting at the deposits and then extracting the metals from the imprisoning granite. Progress was made in the twenties and continued thereafter – until brought to almost a dead stop in the general stagnation of the thirties. In 1925, gold was being produced by Central Manitoba Mines Limited at Rice Lake, and later at Long Lake. The town of Bissett began to flourish on gold mining in the 1930's. Copper and zinc were known to exist in economic quantities north of The Pas in the Cold Lake region. In 1926, the Government of Manitoba underwrote the cost of rails from The Pas to Flin Flon and in the following year Sherritt-Gordon Limited began mining copper ore and building the necessary processing plants. Additional copper and zinc properties were staked out further to the north at Sherridon and south of Flin Flon at Schist Lake. Production at Flin Flon was short-lived. Operations there slowed down in 1932 due to depressed metal prices, and full production was not resumed until the eve of World War II.

These brief exercises in mining development were by no means in vain. They provided training in the entirely new techniques of finding and extracting metal in a grim and almost trackless environment. Aircraft became the useful tool of the prospector, irreplaceable as a means of annihilating endless distances over a barren landscape. Intrepid bush pilots played an essential role in the early phases of northern development, and their activities were by no means confined to mining exploration. By 1926, regular commercial flights were being made to the remotest parts of the province from Winnipeg, The Pas, Lac du Bonnet, and other strategic jumping-off points. The roar of aircraft engines echoed even more resoundingly from the rock-girt lakes than did that of the bull moose, and was equally familiar.

Though base-metal mining practically ceased in the thirties, exploration and prospecting went on apace. Cargo-carrying aircraft made their appearance on the innumerable northern lakes and the tractor train was developed to handle even bulkier loads. Tractor and airplane greatly reduced the traveller's dependence on railway and canoe, though they could never replace them entirely. The former predominance of the fur trade was clearly gone, but the trade in fur remained. Conservation efforts were restoring the beaver, which had been reduced to near-extinction as the result of over-trapping. Muskrat, fox, marten, and other furs continued to be taken by Indian, Métis, and halfbreed trappers. The Hudson's Bay Company store still flourished in the wilderness, and its employees still served as local arbiters, as had the company's officers in the past. Scientific methods of conservation led to the more efficient taking of fur – particularly muskrat – by the allotment of what amounted to fur farms at Netley, Delta, The Pas, and elsewhere. Furs emanating from these farms were marketed in the trappers interest by the government of the province. One new departure in the fur trade of the twenties was the proliferation of fox farming. Red and silver fox – and later, mink – were raised through selective breeding for the provision of more and higher-quality fur. Winnipeg remained a center for the distribution of quality fur, especially for the American market.

By the end of the 1920's, Manitoba had recovered from its economic and political troubles of the war and of the immediate post-war years. The diversification of agriculture, the extension of secondary industry, and the promising ventures into both metallic and non-metallic mining made the future look bright. The heterogeneous population was becoming more noted for its unity than for its division into racial and religious factions – though time and events were to show that the divisions remained. Even as Manitobans gathered on the grounds of the Legislative Building to celebrate the transfer of natural resources and the gaining of full equality with the rest of the country, the worm was in the bud. The greatest economic crisis ever was shaking the foundations of ordered society everywhere. The first tremors had already been felt in the financial citadels on Main Street and Lombard Avenue. The outlook was bleak, and the reality would be bleaker still.

14

The Great Depression and Its Aftermath

THE ECONOMIC BLIGHT WHICH SETTLED upon the world after 1929 did so with universal devastation. It was an economic ice age from which none could escape. By comparison, all previous economic catastrophes were insignificant. In retrospect, it is possible to see the storm warnings – though at the time, they had flown largely in vain. The few who heeded the warnings were themselves unheeded. It is true that the world grain market was glutted, that steel production had been cut back, that inventories were high, and that unemployment was statistically out of line. But these and other indicators of imminent collapse were no more obvious in the summer of 1929 than were the indicators which had presaged Manitoba's ascent from darkness at the end of the nineteenth century. The 1929 disintegration of stock prices on the New York stock exchange was reflected simultaneously in London, Montreal, Toronto, and Winnipeg.

In Manitoba, the direct effect of the market crash was not great. The province's wealth, even on paper, was not such that any appreciable number of individuals was directly involved. Nor was the stock market convulsion regarded as anything more than just that. Things would straighten out; the market merely needed settling. Calm was the order of the day. There was no doom-crying in the press or from those deemed knowledgeable. Worldly-wise John Dafoe of the *Free Press* was confident that all would be well by spring. Manitoba was an essential part of a wheat economy which could not be divorced from a worldwide market. Manitoba's view was not parochial – the province kept an eye on the affairs of the world. This time, however, it was blind.

As though man had not created difficulties enough for himself, nature intervened to add to the West's misfortunes. In the fall of 1929, a long period of drought began. Moisture was baked out of the ground and a long winter of low temperatures and little snow was followed by a long, hot summer with dry, heavy winds. The top soil, dried out and loosened, began to blow away. South-central Saskatchewan became a dust bowl which spread eastward into the Souris and Portage plains. As dry summer and drier fall were succeeded by another almost snowless winter, the contagion spread through the plains and into the parklands. Crops were planted; but before it could sprout, the seed was blown away with the surrounding soil. The hardy Russian thistle throve, polluting such crops as could be persuaded to grow. Grasshoppers came in numbers that had not been seen since the days of the Selkirk settlement. They devoured what little wind-dried, sun-shrivelled vegetation remained. Soil drifted against buildings in banks which rivalled the usual snows of winter. It lay deep in the ditches and among the hedges of wild rose, hawthorn, and willow. Too late, the warnings of Palliser were remembered – it was dangerous to strip the prairie of its protective shield of buffalo grass. Land which should never have felt the plow was blown, in choking dust clouds that often obscured the sun, into Hudson Bay or added to the desolation of the Canadian Shield.

In 1931, Manitoba produced 28 million bushels of wheat and 15 million of barley; in the bumper year of 1928, it had produced more than 50 million bushels of each. The short crop was not altogether unfortunate, since there was no one to buy it in any case. Canada produced forty percent of the world's wheat supply, and when the market all but disappeared, so did the local price. In 1932, Number 1 Hard could be had on the Winnipeg Exchange for thirty-four cents a bushel, with few takers. Cash all but ceased to be seen in rural areas and was almost equally scarce in the city. The diversification of agriculture, hailed as ensuring a permanently high standard of living, served instead to give some variety to a subsistence level of living. Cattle were slaughtered for lack of feed and poultry pecked aimlessly in parched farmyards, deserted even by the grasshoppers. Machinery rusted in soil drifts; gas-starved automobiles stood abandoned, their deflated tires rotting and their upholstered seats splitting at the seams. Farm families did not starve; in fact, they ate better than their urban peers. This, though, was little enough solace. They spent the long, dust-filled summer days and even longer winter nights sustained only by the western aphorism that "there are only two years, this year and next year." Hoping for next year, they gathered round the battery-operated radio to be cheered by Amos n' Andy or Edgar Bergen and Charlie McCarthy. Earlier in the day, they shared vicariously in the troubles of Ma Perkins or Pepper Young's Family.

In the city, they also listened to the radio. Here, they had the advantage of electric light, though little other advantage – unless it was the closeness of neighbors in misery. Unemployment in Winnipeg in the winter of 1929-30 exceeded that of 1920-21. As the thirties advanced, so too did the number of unemployed. At one time or another during the decade of 1929-39, virtually half of the families in Winnipeg were receiving some form of direct public assistance. Relief, as it was called, was not generous – nor was it cheerfully given. Its custodians were always desperately trying to stretch their funds to meet the widespread need, but never quite succeeded. A tattered appearance and hunger-pinched face were so common as to go virtually unremarked. Charities worked wonders, but only miracles would suffice – and the age of miracles had long since passed. Soup kitchens, clothing depots, wood lots, "man a block" schemes, winter works in national and provincial parks, drainage ditches, road building and major public works – all were the proverbial "drop in the bucket." Canada, like much of the civilized world, found itself in the abyss.

The best efforts of all levels of government were powerless to do anything more than ameliorate slightly the effects of what was an almost complete breakdown in the functioning of society. It was the dislocation of the general strike of 1919 a million times over. Since no one had ever experienced such a complete and far-ranging log jam, there were no plans either to clear it or to hold back the disastrous fall. Not only were there no plans, but no one even proposed plans of the Herculean proportions needed. The actions of the national government were about as effective as a band-aid on the stump of a severed arm. The world was truly out of joint. The accustomed three-way trade – whereby Canada's perpetually-unfavorable trade balance with the United States was balanced by a favorable one with the United Kingdom – no longer worked, nor was it ever again to be fully operative. Economic nationalism had first infected the Americans and then the English. Canada pursued the same policy, but with disastrous results. The Government of Manitoba felt, as did the various national governments, that the whole thing would pass easily. President Hoover had said that prosperity was just around the corner, and Richard

Bennett was soon promising that he had the answer. They were both wrong.

Under the terms of the British North America Act, the provinces were responsible for public welfare. They, in turn, had passed on this responsibility to municipal corporations. Relief costs were soon beyond the capacities of most municipal governments. The City of Winnipeg had the heaviest load and continued to carry it, though the province's credit neared exhaustion in the effort to keep lesser agencies afloat. Rumor had it that many rural municipalities would pay a family's fare to Winnipeg and then sustain the family until it had qualified by residence to be taken onto the city's relief rolls. The city's resentment against its hinterland and against the rigidity of the Bracken administration rose still further.

The depression soon wrought political change. Mackenzie King, after weighing conditions and consulting his spirit advisors, called a general election for July 28, 1930. His advice from the spirit world had confirmed his own judgment. An election now would see him safe in office until the worst had blown over. He felt secure. The National Progressives, with the exception of a few recalcitrants, had been lured into the Liberal fold. T. A. Crerar had joined the Government. The budget was balanced and the sales tax was reduced from two to one percent. The election was one of King's few political mistakes. Another was his reply in the House of Commons to demands from the hard-pressed provinces for unemployment relief: "I would not give them a five-cent piece." The Conservatives had a strong new leader in R. B. Bennett of Calgary, who replaced the astringent Meighen in 1927. Bennett bellowed defiance at the world's economic ills and received the temporary attention of an electorate to whom any change looked like an improvement. The Conservatives took 137 of 245 seats, and the Liberals were reduced to 91. In Manitoba, 11 Conservatives were elected to 4 Liberals and 2 Labor.

Within Manitoba, the Progressive Government had reacted to the depression in a nonpartisan manner. Bracken proposed a general coalition of all parties to face the economic storm. Both Labor and Conservatives spurned the offer. Labor was approaching an understanding with the remaining radical farm leaders and wished no involvment with a stand-pat regime. The Conservatives had been much encouraged by their recovery at the polls in 1927 and especially by their heavy federal victory in 1930. They declined also. The Liberals proved more amenable. Early in 1932, they merged with the Progressives into what was called the Liberal-Progressive Party and were given three posts in the cabinet. Thus reinforced, Bracken called an election for June 16, 1932. His platform was, as usual, unimaginative. It offered more of the same careful housekeeping and emphasized the nonpolitical nature of his Government. The election results, however, seemed to justify his approach. The Liberal-Progressives took 38 seats to the Conservatives' 11; Labor went up to 5; and 3 Independents were returned. The Conservatives may have suffered from the voters' disillusionment with the performance of the Bennett Government or from the general farm nonpartisanship, which had been strengthened by the Liberal's union with the Progressives. Labor's increase of two seats tended to confirm the increased urban discontent which had been indicated earlier by job-seeking marches from Market Square to the Legislative Building.

The election did nothing to improve things in Manitoba. Together with the premiers of Alberta and Saskatchewan, Bracken reached an agreement with Ottawa for the sharing of relief costs. This meant submitting to federal overlords in financial matters, but pride gave way to grim necessity. Along with the continuing and growing burden of relief costs, Manitoba had been obliged to underwrite $3,500,000 in bank advances to the wheat pools, which had become badly managed and overextended. The pool was reorganized and carried on as the Manitoba Pool Elevators Limited. With federal help, a program of major public works was undertaken from 1932 onward. Winnipeg gained a sewage disposal system – inadequate even at the time of its construction – and a civic auditorium. There was considerable work done in the provincial parks, and drainage projects were undertaken. Some roads were built and others were improved, including parts of the Manitoba link in the Trans-Canada Highway. These things helped to sustain the life of the province, but only to sustain it – and at a cost in human dignity which cannot be measured. The slim purses of the citizens were not spared. To ensure federal aid, the provincial treasurer, Ewan McPherson, had to achieve a near balance in Manitoba's budget, and in order to do so, a two-percent wage tax was placed on all incomes of over forty dollars a month. This tax was applicable almost solely in greater Winnipeg, where it was regarded as yet another rurally-inspired burden. In its political weakness, the city could do nothing but appeal for the status of a "free" city – an appeal which fell on deaf ears.

There was little else to do but bear it – to grin as well as bear it was too much to ask. The times were hard but by no means dull. The local scene was brightened by continuing political agitation. This was most evident on the left, but there were also traces of strong right-wing thought – even of anti-Semitism. As in all times of distress, there was a revival of interest in religion, especially in the revealed religions and pentecostal sects. There was also much to be observed south of the border. It was the era of John Dillinger, of Bonnie and Clyde, and of Huey Long, the Louisiana "Kingfish." The election of Franklin Roosevelt as president was viewed with interest. From his hopeful words to his people – "We have nothing to fear but fear itself" – Manitoba took hope also. Hope was a necessary trait for survival, for there was to be no lightening of the economic gloom until 1937.

The people of Manitoba were by now becoming accustomed to revelations of scandal in high places, but they were not above taking a lively interest in such matters. After the election of 1932, it was announced that the University of Manitoba was in serious financial difficulties. This, of itself, was nothing new; but this time, it appeared that what little the university had in the way of endowment had largely disappeared. Defalcations which had begun as far back as 1903 were now made public. The bursar was held responsible for the loss of just under $1,000,000 of the university's money, $800,000 of that of the Church of England, and numerous other sums. The offenders were jailed, but the money was never recovered. It had gone into the Wall Street maelstrom. Since the days of Sir Rodmond Roblin, successive provincial governments had permitted a situation to exist whereby one official of the university held positions which would normally have served as a check on one another. The accounts of the university had not been properly audited since World War I, and had not been audited at all since 1925. The Government's ultimate responsibility was clear, and the case later hurt it electorally – though the hurt was by no means fatal. Now further crippled financially, the university had to accept more salary and staff cuts and to say farewell to plans for expansion. The Machray Scandal prompted the Government to finally settle the whole university on the site of the agricultural college in Fort Garry. A toe hold in Winnipeg was retained until well after World War II in the "temporary" buildings on Broadway.

The universal extent of the debacle in the economy began to penetrate the consciousness of governments and to call forth extreme efforts. Franklin D. Roosevelt, elected to balance the budget and to practise economy, turned his attention to the control of financial speculation and to the launching of vast programs of government spending. The pump-priming economic theories of John M. Keynes were put into operation and by the end of 1933 the rot in the United States had at least ceased to spread. There was no miraculous recovery, but complete social disintegration was avoided. Roosevelt's advanced ideas achieved a belated convert in R. B. Bennett. In January, 1935, Bennett announced a Canadian New Deal. His own minister of trade and commerce, H. H. Stevens, had exposed ugly conditions of starvation wages and high profits in textile and other manufacturing enterprises. The West's worst suspicions of the necessity of tariff protection for infant industries were at last confirmed. Industrialization behind a tariff barrier had meant misery to the eastern factory hand, as well as cripplingly high costs to the western farmer. There was no advantage to the people of Canada as a whole. Stevens quit the cabinet and tried to form a party of his own. Bennett's real sense of shock, his experience with the depression, and the example of the patrician Roosevelt worked a transformation in the Canadian prime minister. It may have been genuine conversion, or it may only have been death-bed repentance; but whichever the case, Bennett tried to legislate a social revolution. He failed, however, because of the rigidities of the constitution and because of the disenchantment of the electorate.

Bennett let the Parliament of 1930 run full term. The ensuing election took place on October 14, 1935. The heralded New Deal had worked no wonders, the depression ground remorselessly on, and Mackenzie King had but to wait upon the counting of the votes. King did promise that a study would be made of the financial situation between the provinces and the dominion. John Bracken had long been in favor of such a move. The result of the voting was never in doubt. The Liberals returned 173; the Conservatives, forty. In Manitoba, only one Conservative survived. Fourteen Liberals were elected and the two seats in north Winnipeg returned the same two Labor members, now under the banner of the Co-operative Commonwealth Federation. There were almost 6,000 votes cast for six Social Credit candidates and over 9,000 votes for two Communists. The Communist vote was remarkable only in being the highest yet recorded: three percent of the popular vote.

The Communist vote was an indication of the public's feeling of desperation. The Social Credit and CCF votes were indicative of new trends, in opposite directions though toward the same end. Even before the depression, farm and labor radicals had talked union and the thought produced action in the climate of the 1930's. In 1932, they came together at Calgary to found the Co-operative Common-

Wealth Federation, which, having fended off the deadly embrace of the Communist Party, issued the "Regina Manifesto" in 1933. The manifesto promised an end to capitalism through the nationalization of all means of production and distribution through gradual and peaceful means. The new party's natural leader was the unnatural politician, James S. Woodsworth, a humanitarian who was revered by many and respected by all. The new party organized provincially at Portage la Prairie in 1933. It was to prove a durable third party which had more success in wooing labor votes than it did those of the farmers. Social Credit was entirely different. It represented protest at the intolerable state of affairs and focused on control of the money supply as the key to economic salvation. Other than having an over-fondness for inflationary policies, most Social Crediters were conservative – even reactionary and bigoted – in their views. Social Credit found its prophet in William Aberhart, the Calgary school principal *cum* revivalist preacher. Aberhart used the forum of his weekly Bible broadcasts to urge listeners to support the Social Credit theories of Major Douglas, which, being anathema to bankers, had a certain appeal to the laity. Alberta had long rejected the old parties, but had found little comfort in a United Farmers of Alberta Government. In August, 1935, Social Credit swept the field in an Alberta election and formed a government under Aberhart's leadership. In the federal voting which followed, Social Credit carried ten of Alberta's seventeen seats.

It was in this unsettled political scene that Bracken sought a further mandate on July 27, 1936. The Government's unpopular wage tax had been compounded by an extra five-dollar licence fee on all Winnipeg automobiles. The extra money would be spent in Winnipeg, but this was cold comfort to an already heavily-taxed populace. The new parties entered the electoral field in force. The restored Liberal Government at Ottawa had provided no cures, and the provincial party suffered by association, no matter how remote. Bracken himself offered no more than the mixture which he had previously offered. This was not good enough for the voter. The Liberal-Progressives were reduced to a minority, gaining 23 seats against a badly-split opposition which totalled 32. There were 16 Conservatives, 7 CCF, 5 Social Credit, 1 Communist, and 3 Independents. The defeat, however, did not make the Government think of resigning. There was no possibility that the opposition would consolidate against it. An arrangement was made with the Social Credit MLA's whereby they would support the Government without joining the cabinet. The capacity of the province to implement any monetary change was non-existent and, outside of that, the Social Crediters had no quarrel with the Progressive administration. The Progressive Government continued on its relatively unprogressive way.

A slight lightening of the gloom after 1936 gave hope of an eventual dawn. Grain prices inched upward; unemployment ceased to increase and even began to decline. These cheering events cannot be credited to any locally-adopted palliative. The world was moving toward another cataclysm, one that was more directly of man's making. An aggressive Germany with a paranoic *feuhrer,* a bombastic "sawdust Caesar" in Italy, and a Japan imprisoned by its militarists were actively looking for trouble. All this took money, and even inadequate preparation against the threat took money also. Despite the threatened imminent disaster, Manitobans began to breathe more easily. The massive pump-priming efforts of the Government of the United States penetrated north of the border. The "good neighbor" policy of Franklin Delano Roosevelt coincided with the thinking of Canadians, who were by now disillusioned with economic nationalism. In 1937, a comprehensive trade agreement was made with the United States. It was an agreement which, with modifications and extensions, was to bring the two countries closer to reciprocity than at any time since the treaty of 1854.

Within Manitoba, there was a return of hope and a start on recovery. Relief rolls were high and remained so until World War II. Relief camps for single men remained until 1939. The province made some efforts at recovery within the narrow limits of its administrative thinking and within the even narrower limits of its available resources. The provincial debt was high and its presence inhibited the Government's inititiative. In fact, governmental aversion to debt was so great and remained so firmly fixed that it severely limited the progress of Manitoba for more than a decade after World War II. (This aversion is understandable when it is realized that roughly one third of the province's spending between 1935 and 1940 was devoted to paying interest charges.) Positive action beyond relief measures was undertaken. The Manitoba Telephone System extended its lines into the mining areas of Flin Flon and Sherridon. Perhaps the most important steady progress was made in the field of rural electrification. The Manitoba Power Commission worked slowly and steadily to provide electricity to the farms during the late depression and early war years. Under the direction of Douglas L. Campbell, who became minister of agriculture in 1936, the work went ahead. After 1944, it was greatly accelerated and was extended to cover the whole province.

The immense burden which had been placed on Manitoba by the depression made it imperative that the long-standing imbalance between the provinces' resources and their responsibilities be corrected. Premier Bracken had raised the question at a federal-provincial conference in December, 1935. Alberta had been forced to default on debt payments and had perhaps done so with no real qualms on the part of its Social Credit Government. Manitoba did not default, though the danger was clearly present. Even more than from debt itself, the provincial government shrank from the obloquy of failing to honor its obligations. At the instruction of Mackenzie King, the Bank of Canada investigated the finances of the prairie governments and in 1936 reported a serious situation. Manitoba was given high credit for the efficiency with which it had maintained its solvency, but this condition could not be expected to continue. A complete overhaul of financial arrangements was long overdue. In 1937, King appointed the Royal Commission on Dominion-Provincial Relations, which became known as the Rowell-Sirois Commission after the two gentlemen who served successively as chairman. This commission of five was representative of the country as a whole and the man chosen to speak for the prairie provinces was John W. Dafoe. No man was better qualified than he to speak for the West. Dafoe had no illusions about the task which he had undertaken to share, and he referred to it as being asked "to find foundations for a bridge in a bottomless bog."

The appointment of the Rowell-Sirois Commission and the breadth of its terms of reference were heartily welcomed in Manitoba. With the transfer of its natural resources in 1930, Manitoba had solved its last serious difference with Ottawa. The province had long been an advocate of the realistic reassessment of Confederation. John Bracken was already recognized as a leader of "centralist" thought in Canada. His position was that the lot of the whole country could be improved through strengthening the hand of its central government. His adherence to this cause and the clarity of his advocacy were to make him a national figure. The Government of Manitoba set to work preparing its submission to the commission. The ranks of the government's own civil servants were augmented by a group of experts – lawyers, accountants, and economists. A total of nine volumes of material dealing with various aspects of Manitoba's position in Confederation were published for the edification of the commissioners. It was the most extensive study that had ever been made of the province's government, population, finances, resources, municipal organization, and the effects of Confederation on each of these aspects. Manitoba's brief was introduced when the royal commission sat at Winnipeg in November, 1937, the first stop in its long study of the nature of the Canadian state.

Manitoba's position was simply stated, though amply buttressed with statistics and other documentation. The distressed state of the province's finances had not been caused by the depression; the depression had merely made that state painfully evident. There were defects built into the British North America Act which had become evident with the development of the country and through the interpretation put on the constitution by the Judicial Committee of the Privy Council at London. With regard to the tariff, the West was obliged to sell its products in a free market where the price was set by supply and demand and, at the same time, to buy what it needed in a protected market at high prices. With regard to taxation, Manitoba's chief complaint was that by the nature of corporate organization in Canada, only the central provinces could properly collect corporation taxes on money which was earned in all nine of the provinces. The solution offered by Bracken was that the deleterious effects of the National Policy be offset by a system of equalization payments from Ottawa to the "have not" provinces. As to social services, the country would best be served if full responsibility were assumed by Ottawa. Manitoba was quite willing to shed power if, at the same time, it could shed the concomitant responsibility.

This attitude was generally shared in the Atlantic provinces and in Saskatchewan. British Columbia's attitude was somewhat remote and detached, as was the province itself in relation to the rest of the country. Ontario, through its swashbuckling premier, Mitchell F. Hepburn, arrogantly dismissed the whole concept of the commission. Hepburn was Ontario at its worst. His province could not be called on to bail out the rest of the country. Confederation was everlastingly binding; and as a creation, in large part, of Ontario, it should be conducted to the profit of that province. Quebec, under *le chef,* Maurice Duplessis, was even more hostile than Ontario. Quebec denied the right of the federal government to conduct such an inquiry and refused to make any submission. Alberta's Aberhart could see no virtue in dealing with obvious agents of the chartered banks when those banks had conspired to disallow his banking legislation. The Alberta brief was a call to the people of Canada to see the light and to embrace the faith of Social Credit. Through it all, only the voices of

John Bracken and Angus L. Macdonald of Nova Scotia emerged as being those of Canadians. The Rowell-Sirois Commission heard reports from any number of interested groups, in all nine provinces and in the Capital. Hearings continued for over a year, after which time the commission retired to study the submissions and to formulate a report. This took time. The country had never been so thoroughly poked at or pried into before, and its entire future hung on the findings of the commission. The commission's report was submitted to the prime minister on May 3, 1940.

Up until the outbreak of war, affairs in Manitoba continued at a faltering pace. The crop of 1937 was almost a complete failure due to drought. That of 1938 was good, but prices slipped again – chiefly as a result of the unsettled political condition of Europe and the shutting-off of markets by states who were retreating into economic nationalism. The reconstituted Wheat Board was of great help in stabilizing prices, such as they were. The Farmers' Creditors Arrangements Act offered the farmer firm protection against foreclosure. The general condition of rural Manitoba was better – even if only comparatively. There was now more hope than there had been before, and confidence in the future was manifested in the renewed sales of farm machinery and a revived interest in the improvement of breeding stock. Perhaps most significant was a venture in a new direction in both agricultural diversification and processing. In 1938, a start was made, with provincial assistance, on a sugar refinery in Fort Garry. Beet sugar had been refined in Alberta since the mid-1920's, but this was a new departure in Manitoba. It was a logical move, however, since sugar beets had been grown for many years in the valley of the Red in North Dakota and Minnesota. By 1940, the Manitoba Sugar Company's plant was in operation and was soon capable of processing two thousand tons of beets a day. The volume of copper and zinc refined at Flin Flon picked up greatly as the demand for metals responded to the growing apprehension of war. Bush pilots were busy dropping off and picking up prospectors. In the city, the level of unemployment remained high, but by no means as high as it had been in the early 1930's. There was considerable expansion in the needle-trade industries. Production of a wide variety of garments continued and manufacturers even began to become conscious of style. Generally, business revived; but it still had a long way to go when recovery was suddenly accelerated by the stimulus of war.

After Germany's bloodless seizure of Czechoslovakia in the spring of 1939, the inevitability of war was generally accepted in Manitoba.

There had been high hopes that concessions to Germany would maintain peace, but the march into Prague shattered all illusions. As early as the fall of 1938, at the time of the Munich crisis, the astute Dafoe, champion of collective security, had brought his readers up short with an editorial headed: "What's the Cheering For?" Simply by virtue of Manitoba's position as a world grain center, the people of the province were keenly aware of the deterioration of the European situation. But the extent of the horror at work within the Third Reich and the imminence of its spread throughout Europe were not conceived of by Manitobans – not even in their wildest dreams. On May 24, 1939, King George VI and his Queen visited Winnipeg. During the course of their Canadian tour, they twice crossed the province by rail. It was the first visit by a reigning monarch and was an occasion of great public rejoicing, of ostentatious display, and of squabbling for social precedence. It was mainly, however, an occasion for the pouring forth of real affection for the royal couple and, as such, a fair indication of the strength of Canada's ties with the United Kingdom. It there had been any doubts in this regard prior to the royal visit, there were none afterwards. When war came, Canada would be at Britain's side, of her own volition and by her own act.

In due course, Hitler attacked Poland, whose integrity had been guaranteed by England and France. On September 3, 1939, the United Kingdom declared war on Germany. As Mackenzie King had promised, the Canadian Parliament was called into session and, on September 10, declared a state of war to exist between Canada and Germany. The declaration did not indicate simply that Canada would go along with the English. The nation's reasons went deeper than the call of blood and of historical association. A conviction had been growing that this conflict was to be no mere struggle for aggrandizement by Germany. It was not just that the German dictator and his Italian facsimile were elbowing their way into a "place in the sun." Everything held dear by Western civilization was now at stake; the concepts of liberal democracy, of self-government, and of human dignity were in the balance. They stood to be destroyed by as brutal and as mindless a tyranny as had ever come to pass. Thus, the war came to Manitoba as a dread but inescapable duty. There was no cheering. There was resigned acceptance and even relief that the issue had at last been joined.

As in 1914, there was a quick response to the call for volunteers. Manitoba units which had made a name as far back as the 1885 rebellion were summoned into active service along with those of more recent creation. The cavalry units of the Boer War and World War I retained their traditions but were outfitted with tanks in place of horses. Artillery, the Army Service Corps, and other units which had formerly been dependent on the horse went through the entire war without seeing one – other than as an article of food. It was a new kind of war in which such glamor as existed tended to focus on the Royal Canadian Air Force and, to a lesser degree, on the Royal Canadian Navy. The navy seemed to exercise a strange fascination for young men from the prairies, most of whom had never smelled salt water. Manitoba became a hive of military activity. Shilo, pioneered in the First World War, was rapidly transformed into a vast complex for the training of infantry, artillery, and armored troops. It was but one of many such centers. The established armories at Winnipeg – Minto and McGregor, and Fort Osborne in Tuxedo – spawned satellites in such unlikely places as the Central Immigration Hall and Jerry Robinson's Department Store building. The RCAF established a manning pool for western Canada at the Brandon Arena, and soon schools for the training of airmen were to be found all over the province. Towns such as Carberry, Dauphin, Gimli, Portage la Prairie, and Souris echoed with varieties of English which had not been heard before, even during the great immigration at the turn of the century. This was due largely to the Commonwealth Air Training Plan, whereby Canada became the main training site for the Commonwealth's airforces when British skies became too dangerous for fledgeling pilots. The Princess Patricia's Canadian Light Infantry went overseas at the end of 1939 with the First Division, and the Winnipeg Grenadiers saw service as a relieving force in Jamaica before being sent on the tragic mission to Hong Kong. Manitobans enlisted in all branches of the services and served in all theaters of war in which Canada participated. The provincial contribution is best summed up by the motto of the Royal Canadian Artillery – *Ubique,* "everywhere."

The economy of Manitoba went quickly into high gear and its productive capacity increased greatly. In the field of military equipment alone, the record is outstanding. Uniforms, boots, and other military equipment poured from rapidly-expanded facilities. The various ironworks returned to the manufacture of shells, this time of different caliber and in far greater numbers than those of the First World War. The infant aircraft-parts operation at Winnipeg expanded to include the production of air frames and undercarriages, as well as the wholesale repair and maintenance of training planes. The packing houses turned out veritable mountains of meat, both for military consumption and for the people of allied countries. The switch to a wartime economy was much swifter and more extensive than it had been in 1914. There was more equipment and experience with which to begin, and the depression had provided a readily-available work force.

Agriculture became increasingly diversified, spurred by scientific know-how and by governmental directives. The state decreed which crops should be planted and where. Production in all fields of agriculture increased in the face of steady demand. Prices remained relatively constant due to the work of the considerably-strengthened Wheat Board. Storage facilities at country points were augmented by annexes which were built alongside elevators, thus altering the profile of innumerable hamlets. The exigencies of war put a ban on any appreciable increase in the amount or variety of farm machinery purchased. The farmer was again faced with a serious shortage of labor, though this problem was somewhat eased by service exemptions to essential farm workers and a liberal policy of agricultural leave. Towards the end of the war, additional farm help was made available in the form of prisoners of war. These prisoners had been brought to Canada for safekeeping and many were put to work in the fields at going rates of pay. Compulsory military service within Canada was introduced in 1940 on a short-term basis and was then extended for the duration of the war. Conscription did not prove so politically troublesome as it had in 1917 and did not become the issue of an election. When war had been but a remote possibility, the King Government promised that there would be no conscription for overseas service. In 1942, in view of the dangerous military situation, the Government secured a release from this promise in a national referendum. The referendum was supported by eighty percent of Manitobans.

Along with the rest of Canada, Manitoba accepted, more or less gracefully, an elaborate system of federal controls. These controls began with national registration in 1940 and extended to the rationing of gasoline, tires, sugar, clothing, meats, liquor, and a multitude of other goods. There were price controls which were rigidly enforced and therefore generally obeyed. Taxes rose to what seemed astronomical heights as the Government pursued a policy of paying at least one half of the costs of the war out of current revenue, rather than shoving three quarters of the cost ahead, as it had done in the First World War. There were a series of war loans, in which Manitobans oversubscribed their quota. The needs of the Government of Canada for the war were so all-pervasive that the Government of Manitoba ceased to be a factor of itself. The local administration served willingly and well to speed the national effort.

To better perform this function, the Bracken Government offered coalition to all groups in the Legislature. The move was the natural culmination of the political thinking of the Progressives. They saw no real need of political parties at the provincial level. There were other reasons, however, which made the prospect palatable to the opposition parties. The report of the Rowell-Sirois Commission had been published in February, 1940, and to a large extent it supported Manitoba's position on the redistribution both of taxing power and of responsibility for social services. A fully-united province could help achieve implementation of the report by presenting a united front. It could give solid backing to Ottawa and thus help to offset the expected hostile reception of the central provinces and the confused opposition of British Columbia and Alberta. Also, the war was going badly. After Poland, Hitler paused; but in April, 1940, he overran Denmark and Norway; and in May he moved against France. Here, even the combined forces of France and England could not prevail, and by mid-June, the English were forced to evacuate the continent and the French to seek an armistice. In September, 1940, the *Luftwaffe* launched its attempt to drive the RAF from the skies and thus to open England to invasion. Mackenzie King's political acumen and his spirit-world advisors were in good form. Taking advantage of a denunciation of the adequacy of the Canadian war effort by Hepburn and Drew of Ontario, he called an election in March, 1940, before disaster struck the Allied armies. King swept all before him. The Liberals took 181 seats to the Conservatives' (now National Government) forty. In Manitoba, the Liberals took fifteen seats, leaving one each for the National Government and the CCF. Observing the example of the strong mandate given King, Manitoba's political leaders had no alternative but to present an equally-united front. This feeling was by no means defeatist. Even at this darkest hour, no one thought of the possibility of defeat.

In November, 1940, the Liberal-Progressive Government entered another phase. It was more a form of "group government" than a coalition, very close to the group government which had been so narrowly defeated in 1921. Each of the parties retained its identity and each was represented in the cabinet on the basis of its relative strength in the Standing Committees of the House. The coalition appealed to the electorate on April 22, 1941, with spectacular success. There were sixteen acclamations and, out of fifty-five seats, only four of the members returned opposed the coalition.

Events at Ottawa were moving in the direction of at least partial implementation of the Rowell-Sirois report. In 1940, Parliament had carried a constitutional amendment by which Ottawa assumed financial and administrative responsibility for unemployment insurance. This greatly reduced the welfare costs of Manitoba and the other "have not" provinces. There was, however, a setback of sorts in January, 1941. At this time, a dominion-provincial conference was held to consider the practicality of the Rowell-Sirois recommendations. Any faint hopes that the "centralists" may have held were dashed by the intransigence of Mitch Hepburn. The Ontario fire-eater was doubly anxious to forestall any major surgery on the constitution or the tax structure. He feared that Ontario would be pillaged by its improvident and ungrateful associate provinces. He also smarted under the failure of his attempt to unseat Mackenzie King. He was, if possible, even less gracious in his rejection than he had been before the royal commission itself. In spite of this, agreement was reached among all the provinces that they would surrender income and corporation taxes for the duration of the war and a year beyond in return for equalization payments and the assumption by Ottawa of the provincial relief debts. This was by no means what Manitoba had hoped for, but it was a start in the right direction.

As a direct result of his speaking out in favor of a centralization of power, Bracken had become known and admired throughout much of the country. He was regarded as speaking for the underprivileged everywhere. He was not involved in federal politics, nor was he involved with the racially-divisive question of conscription for overseas service. This question, which had split the country so badly in 1917, was again rearing its ugly head. The essentially conservative nature of Bracken's Government also had an appeal to many. Bracken was a westerner, unsullied by any contact with eastern "interests." The Conservative Party was in search of a leader. Bennett had retired to England just before the outbreak of war and had there received the reward which he had always desired, a seat in the House of Lords. His successor, R. J. Manion, had failed signally in the election of 1940, suffering defeat even in his own riding. In November, 1941, Arthur Meighen resigned from the Senate to resume the Conservative leadership but was defeated in South York in an attempt to enter the House of Commons. In casting about for a successor, Meighen's eye fell on Bracken.

Bracken filled every requirement but one – he was not a Conservative. This, however, was no obstacle either to Meighen or to Bracken. Bracken had never been a partisan; he had slipped easily from UF of M to Progressive to Liberal-Progressive to Coalition. It was no great feat to make a further step to the right. On December 11, 1942, Bracken accepted the leadership of the Progressive Conservative Party, so named at his insistence. As Progressive Conservative leader, he strove to create a favorable image for his party, but failed even in Manitoba. In the federal election of June 11, 1945, the Progressive Conservatives took sixty-seven seats; the Liberals, however, held 125 and retained the government. In Manitoba, Bracken was returned in Brandon and Col. J. A. Ross was re-elected in Souris; but ten Liberals and five CCF also captured seats. Bracken resigned his leadership to George Drew in 1948, and, after suffering personal defeat in Brandon, retired to his stock farm near Ottawa.

Bracken had resigned as premier of Manitoba on January 8, 1943, his mantle passing to Stuart S. Garson, Liberal-Progressive MLA from Fairford since 1927 and provincial treasurer since 1936. As premier, Garson continued the same careful stewardship as had Bracken. Like his predecessor, he was firmly wedded to the idea of implementing the Rowell-Sirois report. Under Garson, the transition from a wartime to a peacetime economy was accomplished with little disturbance and with far less unemployment than had been thought likely. The wartime tax-sharing agreements with Ottawa were to run out at the end of 1946, and there was little prospect for any general agreement on Rowell-Sirois. Mr. Garson secured for Manitoba a five-year agreement with Ottawa whereby the province kept out of the income, corporation, and inheritance tax fields in return for an annual payment of some $13,000,000, an amount which would rise with population and national income. The province now stood a fair chance of securing a measure of economic stability. The last power sites on the Winnipeg River were put under development. With this power, D. L. Campbell, as minister in charge, was able to make great strides in the rural electrification of Manitoba. On October 15, 1945, Stuart Garson led the coalition to its second test at the polls. There were fewer acclamations, but the Government took forty-three seats. The CCF, which had left the coalition in 1943, won ten seats, while Independents took two.

In 1948, Stuart Garson moved to the national level as minister of justice, succeeding Louis St. Laurent, who became prime minister on the retirement of Mackenzie King. In Manitoba, the Liberal-Progressive caucus had almost an embarrassment of ability and experience from which to choose its leader. The rural preponderance again prevailed over the claims of Winnipeg, and Douglas L. Campbell became premier. Doug Campbell was highly qualified and in the Progressive tradition. Manitoba-born, a farmer and fuel dealer, he had represented Lakeside in the legislature since 1922 and had been minister of agriculture since 1936. He was the first native of the province since John Norquay to hold its highest elective office. It is perhaps an indication of the province's growing maturity that all three of his successors have been native Manitobans. Amiable, quick-witted, and with all the caution attributed to his Scots ancestors, Campbell had made a sound reputation in a most important department of government and had also been the driving force behind rural electrification. As in the case of the transfer from Bracken to Garson, few ripples appeared on the political scene though one or two veterans of the cabinet soon departed for the bench or for senior appointments in the federal service.

The end of the war had not been followed by a depression, as had been World War I. But neither had it been followed by any great forward movement. There was the expected contraction of war-boomed industries, though without serious unemployment. War-imposed restrictions were quickly eased and taxation was somewhat reduced. The manufacturing and processing industries at Winnipeg converted to peacetime operations and maintained high levels of production and employment. There were great gaps to be filled in the field of farm machinery and an immense backlog of individual needs to be met. For more than fifteen years, Manitobans had been denied many things by depression and war. The need for metals brought increased production at Flin Flon, as well as the opening of further sources of copper and zinc. As with metals, there was a high demand for grain and other agricultural production, and this continued for some years. Selkirk Wheat, as developed in the Rust Research Laboratory at the University of Manitoba, proved a boon to all western farmers – a result of its high protein, high yield, and especially its rust-resistant qualities. Farm labor became short, but machinery was now available as a replacement and the horse retired from his labors to become the concern of sportsmen. The financial position of the Government moved from sound to healthy, though it remained very cautious. Much needed to be done in order to overcome the enforced neglect of the years of depression and of war. Some start was made on the development of modern highways, and that with considerable federal help. Little was done in education, and in other fields where the need was equally great. The Government suffered from a depression-induced paralysis. There was an incapacity to strike out and to spend where spending had become mandatory.

The caution of the Government was not resented by the rural electorate. As a producer of wealth, agriculture had yielded first place to processing and manufacturing. But political power still rested solidly on the farms. The legislature was redistributed and Winnipeg became a multiple and multi-membered constituency. Still, of the fifty-seven seats in the new house, less than twenty were demonstrably urban. D. L. Campbell took his case to the people on November 10, 1949. The coalition remained, but it was showing signs of strain. Social Credit had disappeared from the cabinet through attrition. Errick Willis, the Conservative leader since 1936, and James O. McLenaghan, his chief lieutenant, were members of the Government. They appeared content to let things be, but some of the Conservatives were moving to a resumption of the political wars. In 1949, however, the Government was strongly upheld. It could count on forty-five of the fifty-seven members of the House. Three anti-coalition Conservatives and one anti-coalition Liberal were elected. Albert Prefontaine, Liberal MLA for Carillon, was restless at the Government's inaction on schools. Joe Renouf of Swan River and Jack McDowell of Iberville were old-school Conservatives who felt betrayed by the continuation of the coalition after the war. So did the newly-elected Dufferin Roblin of Winnipeg, dedicated as he was to the restoration of both the Conservative Party and the name of Roblin in Manitoba's political life. The powerful force of nature on the rampage was soon to come to Roblin's aid in beginning the work of demolishing the creaking structure of the Progressive administration.

The winter of 1949-50 reproduced the same conditions that had existed in 1825-26. There was much snow, a late and rapid spring thaw, and more precipitation. Again in May, as in 1826, the Red River rose throughout its length. At Winnipeg, it could no longer receive the equally-engorged waters of the Assiniboine and the Seine. In addition, the heavy ice of the southern basin of Lake Winnipeg denied easy entry to the torrent. During May, the floods came almost as high as in 1826, and this time there were close to half a million people and a metropolis in their path. There had not been adequate preparation. Indeed, there had seemed no need for any. There had been years of high water in the not too recent past – the last of any note in 1916 – and flooding of the lowlands along the Red, the Assiniboine, and the Seine was regarded as a matter of occasional inconvenience. The Government hesitated to proclaim an emergency, though its information from both sides of the border indicated unprecedented levels. There was no panic, but there was indecision and public disagreement about the extent of the potential trouble by the ministers most closely concerned.

While the authorities bickered, the waters rose. From Emerson to Netley, the Red was one great slow-moving lake of tawny, refuse-laden water, narrowing with increasing menace where it crawled through Winnipeg. Emerson, St. Jean, Morris, and Ste. Agathe were engulfed in spite of the best efforts of their people and of the armed forces to block the relentless flow. Winnipeg and St. Boniface, together with their suburbs, stood besieged as the rivers poured through between hastily-built and constantly-manned dykes. Some dykes gave way and, among other areas, Elm Park, Scotia Street, and much of East Kildonan were overrun. Most dykes held, largely as the result of constant and well-organized attention by civil and military authorities working under general military direction. There was no thought of proclaiming martial law, nor was the city evacuated – though that extremity was prepared for. Most schools closed. Many bridges were impassable, due to the flooding of their approaches, though none were carried away. Literally thousands, chiefly women and children, left for near or distant safety. Still, the life of the city continued without any general dislocation. Essential services continued without interruption. As the ominously-dark waters slipped silently by, lapping testingly at the containing sand-bagged ramparts, the air was filled with the thump and roar of a multitude of pumps. Pumps in the thousands worked perpetually to keep the water from rising disastrously behind the dykes. The flood reached well over thirty feet above mean winter ice level before it stopped rising, paused, and then began to recede with agonizing slowness. As in 1826, there was a minimal loss of life – only one person was drowned.

The flood of 1950 differed greatly from that of 1826 in the amount of damage and the cost of restoration. Much was owed to the work of the Red Cross and other relief agencies. The armed forces played a major party in relief work, as well as in the successful fight to maintain the principal dykes. There was a heartening camaraderie among all Winnipeggers and the exhilaration of a shared danger. The rest of Manitoba, together with the people of Canada and the United States, were generous with their help. Large sums were contributed for relief and rehabilitation. However, it was some years before the effects of the flood were completely cleared away and all damage claims had been settled. Many of the dykes were built as permanent fixtures – the university in Fort Garry, Elm Park, Glenwood Crescent, and Scotia Street being examples along the Red. Others were built at points west along the Assiniboine. Many new and large pumping stations were built to help control any future flood. Much thought was also given by municipal and provincial authorities as to how the danger could in future be obviated, or at least reduced to a minimum. A diversion channel around Winnipeg came to be considered as the best solution, particularly if accompanied by a diversion of the Assiniboine into Lake Manitoba at Portage la Prairie, thus preventing the two rivers from cresting simultaneously at Winnipeg. The cost, however, was enough to boggle the minds of men who were still preoccupied with "penny wisdom."

After its successful struggle with the angry waters of the Red, the Government resumed its steady, old, nonpartisan course, little changed as it approached its thirtieth year of power. The flood, however, had done damage to the Government and this was universally apparent. The amiable and high-principled Errick Willis had clashed openly with the premier as to the extent of the flood emergency, and in August, 1950, he resigned from the cabinet. His Conservative colleague, William C. Miller, chose to remain. With the exception of Miller, the Conservatives joined the CCF in opposition. The legislature, long unaccustomed to the interplay of the forms and forces or responsible government, saw new life. Campbell and his colleagues, still certain that a nonpartisan approach was the right one, were by no means dismayed. They continued on their slow and careful course and were upheld again in the increasingly unrepresentative constituencies in the election of June 8 1953, the now Liberal-Progressive Government returned thirty-two members plus three Independent L-P's on whose support they could generally count. The Conservatives elected twelve and the CCF five. A somewhat revived if unrepentant Social Credit elected two and the Labor Progressive Party (Communist) elected one. Stephen Juba, a liquor law reformer of the wet persuasion, was returned in Winnipeg.

With this election, the old Progressive regime entered on its last phase of power. The ministers were firmly wedded to their administrative tasks, and though they played musical chairs with cabinet seats from time to time, they seemed to view themselves as holding office as of right. The atmosphere of the Government was generally sterile of ideas. The corps of dedicated civil servants of high rank who had sustained the Government in the dark days of depression and war was depleted by death and retirement. In their places were men who, to a considerable degree, reflected the rigidity and "don't rock the boat" attitude of the ministers they served. In all matters, the Government acted with a high level of efficiency within the limits of its vision. The members of the Government were not entirely out of touch with reality, though their attitude is best described in the words which Adlai Stevenson applied at the time to the Republican Party in the United States: "They had to be dragged, kicking and screaming, into the twentieth century." Though not unaware that changes had taken place, the Liberal-Progressives could not themselves undertake to introduce major changes or even know what changes might be necessary. They worked under the prairie's "this year and next year" philosophy – next year might be a bad one, so be prepared for disaster. They had lived through the greatest disaster which Manitoba had ever suffered, and the memory dogged their steps.

There were new departures made under the pressure of public opinion. In 1954, the general clamor for a liberalization of the liquor laws led in the House by Winnipeg's Steve Juba, brought Campbell to form a Royal Commission on Liquor Laws under the chairmanship of John Bracken. The commission sat throughout the province and heard submissions, few of which reflected the militant prohibition of forty years before. They investigated the liquor legislation of Ontario, Quebec, and of several of the American states. Bracken's report recommended a system which included the sale of liquor with meals, cocktail bars, the wider licensing of social clubs, mixed beverage rooms, and extended hours of sale in liquor stores, with the elimination of purchase limits and of the permit system. The new regulations concerning public drinking were to be subject to local option and soon much of the province reflected an easier attitude toward liquor. Many areas whose residents were personally dry opted for the new regulations in order to attract tourist traffic. To no one's regret, the bleak all-male beer parlor began to fade into the realm of forgotten horrors. Doug Campbell led the way here, once he had seen which way the people wanted to go.

By 1955, roughly one half the people of Manitoba lived in the greater Winnipeg area. And yet Winnipeg controlled only about one quarter of the seats in the legislature. The mining districts of the north clamored for more adequate representation. Campbell moved to remedy the situation. Hitherto, the legislature had been the arbiter of its own destiny, alloting seats and drawing constituency boundaries through a representative committee of the House on which the government held the majority. All this was changed by the Redistribution Act of 1955, which abolished the single transferable ballot and established fifty-seven single-member constituencies. Boundaries were to be drawn by an independent commission consisting of the chief justice of Manitoba, the president of the University of Manitoba, and the chief electoral officer. The commission was to work under a formula which gave some favorable consideration to geographical representation, but not to the extent that had prevailed previously. For example, the rural riding of Lakeside had 4,000 names on the voters' list, while suburban Springfield had 40,000. The first redistribution made under this act was implemented in 1957, setting up twenty-six rural and twenty-one urban constituencies. Slowly, but inevitably, the balance of political power was swinging to the areas where most of the wealth was produced. In 1955, the Manitoba Power Commission took over the development, production, and distribution of electric power – with the exception of Winnipeg Hydro, which was jealously guarded by its citizens. Rural electrification was practically complete and extensive surveys were undertaken to assess the northern potential for future needs. A start was made on a highway program, but it was dwarfed by similar programs in Ontario, North Dakota, and Minnesota. The Campbell Government was moving into action, but it was more a matter of being pushed.

The inadequacy of the province was probably seen most clearly in its educational facilities. Schools were traditionally a charge on local property taxes and had been left to local devices since the 1920's. The result was an extremely low standard of public schools, except in the greater Winnipeg area – and even here some schools left much to be desired. Most rural children could expect, at best, a reasonable elementary education, but they had little chance of obtaining good secondary schooling, such as would fit them to enter university or one of the skilled trades. An increasingly technical society and the ever-present threat of an atomic holocaust made a hitherto listless people wake to a concern that their children be equipped to handle a civilization which appeared in danger of getting out of hand entirely. There were some demands that the University of Manitoba and the trades lower their standards, but even the Department of Education realized that there was no substitute for knowledge. The matter was largely taken out of the hands of the Department of Education and the whole question was entrusted to the searching investigation of a Royal Commission on Education under the chairmanship of R. O. MacFarlane. Dr. MacFarlane, brought from Carleton University at Ottawa, was well equipped for his task by virtue of long service in Manitoba as a professor of history at the university and as deputy minister of education. The MacFarlane Commission commenced work in 1957 and was still at work when the Progressive regime finally came to an end.

The 1950's saw the greatest exploitation of the province's mineral resources. The copper- and zinc-refining complex at Flin Flon expanded as it was fed with the ore of ten new mines. Since 1954, it had been receiving copper ore from Lynn Lake by rail. Power for the mining operation was generated by two plants on the Laurier River. The major mining development was that of the great nickel ore body at Moak and Mystery lakes. Here, by agreement with the International Nickel Company, the town of Thompson was built *de novo* in the rock, muskeg, and slash pine of north-central Manitoba. After a first start at town-building through the use of tractor trains, a line of railway was built to connect with the Hudson Bay Railway at Sipiwesk in 1957. With the development of hydroelectric power at nearby Kelsey Rapids on the Nelson, Thompson became the world's first fully-integrated nickel mining and processing plant. Most exciting in prospect, but disappointing in result, was the development of oil wells in the southwest corner of the province. This region, an extension of the Williston Basin of North Dakota and Montana, was test-drilled in 1951 and 1952. In 1953, wells were put into production in the Virden-Roselea and Virden-Scallion fields. There were high hopes of another oil Golconda, such as that of Texas or the rich Alberta fields at Leduc. Manitoba's oil production, however, reached a peak of only 4,750,000 barrels in 1962, a mere trickle of the total Canadian production.

In 1957, Canada awoke to find John Diefenbaker as prime minister and the Conservatives in power after a lapse of twenty-two years. Of the fourteen seats that were now Manitoba's portion, eight had gone Conservative and five CCF. The farmers had deserted the Liberal Party and its provincial allies stood to suffer as well. In March, 1958, Diefenbaker went to the people to gain a majority and did so beyond his wildest dreams. The Progressive Conservatives took 208 of the 265 seats. All of Manitoba's seats went into that total. Even the CCF Nirvana, Winnipeg North Center, rejected its own Stanley Knowles. No Liberal gained election in the four western provinces. In this dismal atmosphere, a Manitoba election was called for June 16, 1958. Campbell and his associates were confident of victory, and precedent was certainly in their favor.

The Progressive Conservative phenomenon was not merely federal, nor was Diefenbaker its only knight in shining armor. In June, 1954, the brilliant and forceful Duff Roblin, a politician who had proven his worth both in the House and on the hustings, deposed the amiable and complacent Errick Willis and assumed the Conservative leadership. From the moment of his election at the bottom of the poll in Winnipeg in 1949, Roblin had been the party sparkplug. He worked long and hard to master the intricacies of government. He was assiduous in doing his homework and put new life into a moribund party. He recruited scores of like-minded, forward-looking people who might otherwise have scorned to be called Conservatives. Under Roblin, the Progressive Conservatives became the liberal party in Manitoba and remained so for as long as he led them. When the votes were counted in June, 1958, the Liberal Progressives had been reduced to nineteen seats, the CCF went to eleven, and the Progressive Conservatives held twenty-six. After an unseemly delay, Campbell announced the resignation of his Government and on June 30, 1958, Duff Roblin became premier of Manitoba. An era had ended with few regrets and a new era hopefully dawned.

15

Years of Hope Reborn

THE DECADE OF THE ADMINISTRATION of Duff Roblin is too recent to be viewed in proper perspective, though it is already evident that it was one of great and far-reaching changes for Manitoba. Most of these changes were initiated by Roblin's Government, while others were begun in the last years of the Progressives and were carried forward under the Progressive Conservatives. Manitoba had been too-long reluctant to tackle new problems or even to solve its old ones. In that respect, the old regime had reflected the will of the effective majority. When redistribution made the effective majority more representative of the people, their preference for change was realized. However, the increased taxation which these changes necessitated apparently made the electorate pause and reconsider. Then, on the eve of the centennial year of the province of Manitoba, and with a further redistribution in effect, the people were given the opportunity to pass judgment on the heirs of Duff Roblin. They then showed a decided preference for a change, endorsing an administration which all the self-appointed pundits prophesied would cost them more dearly in cash and even in freedom. The fundamental reasons for this action will be clear to the recorder of Manitoba's bicentenary. In the meantime, the principal events of the period can be set down in outline, though any assessment must be viewed in the light of its proximity to events.

Duff Roblin selected a cabinet which reflected his own eagerness to break new ground, but it was one which also reflected the political facts of life. Errick Willis was a direct link with the political past, but on the basis of his ability alone, he deserved a place and found it. Others were about as similar to the ministers of the former government as is Tweedledum to Tweedledee, and were about as effective. There was, however, a full leavening of newcomers – Progressive Conservatives in whom the progressive exceeded the conservative – Sterling Lyon as attorney-general, George Hutton as minister of agriculture, George Johnson as minister of health and public welfare, and a number of others. Together, they brought a new light into the dark corridors of the great mausoleum on Broadway.

In a short legislative session in the fall of 1958, Roblin indicated that he would tackle such matters as education and highways through the immediate provision of more money from the province. This money would come in the form of direct and matching grants, and the national government would be approached for all possible assistance. The Red River Flood Committee had recommended the construction of a floodway from St. Norbert on the south of Winnipeg to Lockport on the north to carry surplus waters around the city. This would be built and Ottawa would help with the cost. Over the winter, Roblin and his ministers prepared a program of expansion in almost every field of government. There was a sense of purpose and a feeling of confidence. Such a program, however, would cost a great deal, and this prospect was far from pleasing to those who manned the citadels of finance along Main Street and Portage Avenue. Their unrest found plaintive voice in the *Free Press* which, more than before, merited the epithet of "the old lady of Carlton Street." Its readers were warned that Duff would seek an excuse to go to the people and would take advantage of their credulity to secure a clear majority. Whether guided by the *Free Press* or not Roblin got his election and his majority.

On March 31, 1959, he was defeated in the House on a procedural motion, though its mover, D. L. Campbell, had stated that he did not regard the matter as being one of nonconfidence. The CCF joined the Liberals, and the Government was defeated on a straight party vote, thirty to twenty-six. Roblin secured a dissolution from Lieutenant-Governor J. S. McDiarmid and went joyfully to the fray. The issue was clear. In order to get Manitoba in step with the twentieth century, it would take much spending, and only the provincial government could do it. Debt was not to be incurred for its own sake, but the province had the natural resources as well as the skills and the people required to develop those resources. The Liberals stuck to the line that caution was necessary. They dropped the Progressive from their title, but implications of the thirty-six years of Progressive rule remained and old habits are not soon forgotten. The CCF had much of their thunder stolen by Roblin and could only chime in with "me too," and the warning that you never can trust a Tory no matter how appealing he may be. Voting took place on May 14, 1959, and the worst fears of the *Free Press* were realized. Thirty-six Progressive Conservatives were returned against eleven Liberals and ten CCF. Roblin now had his mandate, and he proceeded to execute it.

Over the next nine years, the province was transformed – if not out of all recognition, at least to the extent that everyone was made aware of the change. Previously, only a few roads could be described as being "first class": the Trans-Canada Highway, running across the province through Winnipeg and Brandon; Number 75 to the United States; and Number 10 running north from the Peace Garden, through Riding Mountain, Swan River, The Pas, and Flin Flon. Now a veritable network of good roads covered the province, opening much of its scenic beauty to the tourist and greatly easing communication for Manitobans. A perimeter road was built around Winnipeg, thus making it easier for traffic to by-pass the city and somewhat relieving the travel problems of its citizens. The Red River Floodway was undertaken and completed, an effort which required the movement of more earth than had been shifted for the building of the St. Lawrence Seaway. The cost was decried as ruinous and the project described as approximating the building of the pyramids of Egypt in terms of usefulness. Its worth, however, was clearly proven in the spring of 1969 when a potentially dangerous flood threat passed without the flooding of one metropolitan Winnipeg basement. For this alone, half the people of Manitoba owe Duff Roblin and George Hutton an eternal debt. A similar diversion of the Assiniboine into Lake Manitoba at Portage la Prairie ran afoul of local sensibilities, with the result that Portage la Prairie returned to the Liberal persuasion.

The Government of Manitoba also launched a frontal attack on the problems of greater Winnipeg. Here, a clutch of lesser governments – some affluent, others destitute – clung to the skirts of the City of Winnipeg, at once its joy and its despair. The city proper resented the services which it perforce provided its suburbs on an unpaid or underpaid basis. For their part, the satellite municipalities complained of their inability to raise a revenue to match that of the city, while at the same time they attracted Winnipeggers with the lure of lower taxes. They complained at the inadequacy and high cost of public transit, but they were unwilling to help underwrite the perpetual transit deficit. Tuxedo boasted the finest homes and had among the lowest tax rates.

Brooklands abounded in broken sidewalks and had a medieval sewage system; it was always without funds and its schools lagged far behind those of the city proper. The local councils were jealous of their brief and small authority, and the Council of the City of Winnipeg tended to lord it over their lesser cousins – much to the latters' vociferous resentment.

In 1960, Roblin cut the Gordian Knot. All efforts at voluntary co-operation had failed, though many attempts had been made over the years. The Legislature used its undoubted power and legislated into existence the Metropolitan Corporation of Greater Winnipeg, thus establishing a middle level of government between that of the province and those of the nine full and three partial municipalities of greater Winnipeg. Metro encompassed the whole of the area from the junction of the Red and the Assiniboine, north to St. Andrews, south to St. Norbert, west to Assiniboia, and east to Transcona. It was practically a re-creation of the District of Assiniboia of the days of the fur trade. Not surprisingly, much fur flew. Winnipeg's mayor, Steve Juba, was mortally offended at this blow to the primacy of Winnipeg, which he and his council had hoped to expand to engulf the suburbs. The suburbs themselves bewailed both their loss of authority and the introduction of another taxing authority. With little grace, they all submitted to the inevitable, secure in the knowledge that they now had a scapegoat for all of the failings of man and nature in Metro. The citizens may groan at the taxes, but they now enjoy many benefits in the form of roads, bridges, parks, and other amenities. Metro provides a uniform property assessment and an over-all building and zoning code. There is at last some hope that the rivers may be cleaned up and that their banks will be used for purposes other than industrial slums and highrise apartments. In due course, it is hoped to unite police and fire services, as well as other public necessities. The struggle, however, is far from over.

Again in 1960, the Roblin administration began a massive campaign to rehabilitate education in the province. The University of Manitoba and its affiliated colleges were able to embark on a much-needed building campaign and to recruit staff. This dawn had been heralded in the latter days of the Progressive regime, with a healthy assist from the federal authority. Of more immediate concern, however, was the public school system. The MacFarlane Royal Commission tabled its report in 1960 and its recommendations did much to gladden the hearts of every teacher. The report called for a general raising of standards, particularly in the secondary schools, and for a wider use of central examinations by the Department of Education. It also asked for higher educational standards for entry into Teachers' College and higher academic standing for the Faculty of Education.

The MacFarlane report has served to raise the educational standards of teachers, but the proposed system of central examinations has been put aside in the interests of local autonomy – though possibly also in the interests of administrative convenience and economy. As to educational administration, the report recommended that Manitoba's proliferation of local school boards be replaced by consolidated districts such as that pioneered at Dauphin-Ochre River. Such divisional boards would be able to supply the necessary facilities for a full secondary education, hitherto seldom seen outside greater Winnipeg. One or two high schools in the average rural division would give every child an equal opportunity. The Roblin Government accepted this, and school divisions for secondary education were set up by referendum. The Government encouraged public acceptance by making larger grants contingent upon a favorable vote for the divisional concept. Grants from the province for teachers' salaries were made according to a scale which takes into account both qualifications and experience. As to primary schools, the nettle was not grasped; they were left to the local boards on the grounds of the greater virtue of local democracy. The suspicion remains, however, that any wholesale removal of local authority would so wound local pride as to prove electorally dangerous to any MLA who supported it.

Dr. MacFarlane and his colleagues urged much higher scales of provincial grants for school buildings, equipment, and teachers' salaries – the implication being that all education costs are a proper charge on the province. Most shattering, however, was the commission's reccomendation that the province provide full financial assistance to separate schools provided that such schools follow the curriculum and maintain the standards of the public schools. In addition, it was proposed that encouragement be given to the use of French as a language of instruction in elementary schools and as a subject of study in all schools from the earliest grades. The very breadth of the concept was staggering. The Catholic community reacted with surprised and pleased disbelief. The inflexible Protestants, who proved more numerous than had been believed, were dismayed and even outraged. The shade of Thomas Scott was invoked and Louis Riel was again consigned to the deepest reaches of the Orange inferno.

The separate school recommendation was a surprise in terms of its scope, but not in terms of its underlying principle. At least two of the commissioners believed that it was high time the province corrected an old injustice. It is difficult to avoid the thought, however, that the commission's wide-open approach to the question might have been made simply to demonstrate the practical impossibility of its ever becoming a working system. The recommendation applied not only to Catholic schools, but to any denomination which might care to operate its own schools. Visions loomed of an educational theocracy. The *Free Press* dusted off and reprinted its editorial thoughts of 1890. Whether by intention or not, the concept was simply too bold for execution. A limited scale of shared services was introduced, as was a wider use of French in the elementary schools, especially as a subject for study. Yet even this was resented by many, and the resentment precluded further concessions.

In the meantime, the needs of industry were not neglected. The province established an Industrial Development Board to encourage new enterprises and to assist established ones. The ventures in question were ones which could not attract private capital at economic rates and were indicative of the confidence of the Government in the future of the province. When the risks for which the fund was established became evident in one or two cases, there was unjustifiably harsh criticism from both left- and right-wing elements. The left accused the Government of underwriting the expensive mistakes of capitalism at the cost of the taxpayer, while the right viewed the Government's endeavor as a wasteful effort to maintain areas of employment which were uneconomic and therefore a cause of higher taxation. A large-scale power development with a connecting highway was put under way at the Grand Rapids of the Saskatchewan River. Thompson grew to the status of a small city, with its own microcosm of social problems. New mining properties were exploited, and in the area of The Pas an immense complex for the use of forest products was backed with the assistance of Swiss interests. Still, the industrial progress of Manitoba was painfully slow; and emigration, though slowed, did not cease. A total population of one million, believed to be within reach at the time of the expansion of 1896-1911, was not reached even in the years of the second Roblin.

The Government's electoral record remained excellent. On December 14, 1962, the Progressive Conservatives elected 35; the Liberals, 13; the New Democratic Party, 8; and Social Credit, 1. On August 3, 1961, the CCF had changed its name and refurbished its image. Henceforth, it was to be the New Democratic Party and its philosophy was labelled "social democratic" – which apparently meant less socialism and more democracy. Its personnel, however, remained largely the same in the Manitoba Legislature. Russell Paulley was its House leader, and its appeal in 1962 was still largely confined to those who had supported the CCF. In the same period, there was a change in the Liberal leadership. D. L. Campbell resigned as party chief to a general convention of the party, though he retained his seat in the House and his active interest in politics. The convention chose Gildas Molgat as House leader. Gil Molgat was the first French-speaking party leader in Manitoba since the establishment of regular party organizations.

The inadequacy of municipal government organization and the inequity of the burden of school taxation were other long-standing problems for which the Roblin Government undertook to find solutions. A royal commission was appointed under the chairmanship of Roland Michener, former Ontario provincial secretary and speaker of the House of Commons, later to become governor-general of Canada. The Michener report was received in 1963. It recommended fewer and larger local government districts, each of which should be entrusted with the educational functions which had hitherto been handled by local school boards. This reorganization of local government would, it was hoped, increase the efficiency and thus lower the costs of municipal administration. The commission recognized that even with the new and higher scale of provincial grants, the costs of education in many areas were too great a burden on local property. It therefore recommended that all costs of education be assumed by the province in the interests of higher uniform standards. It would also permit the municipalities to devote their resources to other purposes. As with that of Dr. MacFarlane, the Michener report offered a remedy which was beyond the political capacity of the province to swallow. The old habits, forms, and boundaries of local government were firmly set. There was massive opposition to so radical a change – and understandably so. To be relieved totally of school costs would be a mixed blessing, since with it would come a loss of local autonomy and interference on the part of the bureaucrats of the Department of Education The capital was beginning to loom in many rural eyes as a bullying rather than a benign and affectionate parent.

The many and necessary changes which had so far been made by the Roblin administration had been accomplished with no increase in general taxation. The Government used the carefully-hoarded reserves which had been accumulated under Garson and Campbell; and the credit of the province was borrowed on with care. The need for funds, especially by local governments, was still great and the continued tendency to pile taxes on land could not be justified. Consideration was given to a general provincial sales tax, a move which had hitherto been avoided. Freedom from provincial sales tax was an achievement which Manitoba shared only with Alberta. Duff Roblin avoided the tax at this time by resorting to a series of taxes on a wide variety of goods and services. These taxes did not have the full impact of a sales tax, but they were equally irritating – perhaps even more irritating by virtue of their very selectivity. The old reliable fund raisers, liquor and tobacco, were tapped once more, and amid the welter of minor impositions was a five-percent tax on fuel. Taxing fuel in a climate which requires artificial heat for at least eight out of twelve months revealed a lack of imagination such as had not been seen since the Progressive administration left office. But despite the public's reaction to diverse taxation, the obvious improvement in government services generally was much appreciated. Education, from nursery schools to postdoctoral studies, flourished as never before. The roads were a pleasure to drive on, and their extension and improvement went on apace. Hospitals were built and health services multiplied. The people of Manitoba were being well served.

The only fly in the ointment was money – or rather, the lack of money. All of the recent improvements were expensive and, as in the case of all government expenses, there is only one source of revenue – namely, the individual taxpayer. It served little purpose to point out that much of the current cost was due to past neglect or incapacity to pay. Nor did it help to point out that widespread improvements made the province a more attractive place in which to live. Human frailty intervened to give the Government the image of a spendthrift, on the one hand, and of a penny-pincher on the other. At the same time, the Government of Canada altered the nature of its income-tax collection procedure. In so doing, the federal government made it abundantly clear that the portion of income tax returned to the various provinces was less in some provinces than it was in others. Lester Pearson, the new Liberal prime minister, had enough trouble without bearing more than his share of the blame for the high level of taxation in Manitoba. The economic situation was relatively bright and tax money was being well spent. There was, however, no outwardly visible economic expansion taking place. The province seemed to be on a sort of plateau. Immigration remained slight, though it might be added that immigration in Canada in general was not great. Emigration continued, especially among the young and the highly skilled.

The inevitable recipient of blame was the provincial government. On June 23, 1966, there was a provincial election. Roblin appealed for support on the basis of his undoubted achievements. Both the Liberals and the NDP countered by pointing to the cost of these achievements and to their doubtful validity. The result sustained the Government, but it also indicated growing reservations. The Progressive Conservatives dropped from thirty-five to thirty-one and lost one of these when Gordon Beard, MLA from Churchill, assumed the status of an Independent because of his dissatisfaction with governmental inaction in the north. The Liberals gained one to hold fourteen, while the NDP advanced from eight to eleven. The results were deplored or approved, depending on the point of view being expressed, but there was no sign of serious political discontent.

Indeed, it was a period of general good will, marred only by a few niggling criticisms. Canada celebrated her centenary in 1967 and none were better Canadians than the people of Manitoba. Projects of all kinds greeted the new Canadian century. Outhouses were burned to mark the completion of a new sewage system. Concert halls and museums were erected. The Pan-American Games were held at Winnipeg with great fanfare and success, providing valued additions to the city's sports facilities. The increasing concern with the viability of the "two nations" concept in Canada was exemplified in Manitoba by the amending of the School Act so as to permit the use of French as a language of instruction for up to one half of each school day. The increasing sophistication of higher education was recognized by the granting of full autonomy to United College at Winnipeg and to Brandon College. After July 1, 1967, they became the University of Winnipeg and Brandon University respectively, with full degree-granting powers.

The other side of the coin was seen in the implementation on June 1, 1967, of a five-percent sales tax. This measure had been avoided as long as possible, both because of its essential inequity and because of its political dangers. The sales tax as instituted had many exemptions. It was not added to the existing tobacco levies and it went almost unremarked by the already tax-groggy customers of the Liquor Control Commission. Food was exempt, as were meals of moderate price, children's clothing, mortgage payments, and rent. Books were also exempted, though not without a struggle from the Progressives. Generally speaking, if you could eat it or read it, you paid no tax on it. As long delayed as it had been, and as necessary as it was, the provincial sales tax was poorly received. Everyone had to pay, and though the Government had long warned of the inevitability of the tax, it was accused of bad faith.

The achievements of Duff Roblin had not gone unnoticed in the rest of the country. He was generally regarded as an outstanding candidate for the national Progressive Conservative leadership. In Winnipeg in 1963, he had even been hailed as a possible heir by John Diefenbaker himself. It was a blessing the Tory chieftain soon repented of, but Roblin's image loomed as Diefenbaker's faded. A national leadership convention of the Progressive Conservative Party was called for September, 1967. After considerable hesitation, Duff Roblin announced his candidacy for the mantle of Sir John A. Macdonald. On announcing for his party's national leadership, Roblin also announced that whether he won or lost, he would vacate the premiership of Manitoba. The Progressive Conservatives chose Robert Stanfield of Nova Scotia. In conformity with his promise, Roblin resigned his provincial leadership in November, 1967. The candidates for successor were George Johnson of Gimli, Sterling Lyon of Fort Garry, Stewart McLean of Dauphin, and Walter Weir of Minnedosa – all members of the Roblin cabinet. The final contest was between Sterling Lyon and Walter Weir, with Weir carrying off the laurels. The choice was due to Weir's solid rural support and the resurgence of small "c" conservatism – a reaction among those who felt that Roblin had gone too far, too fast. The same thought swung some Winnipeg votes to Weir. That city's "establishment" was very restless under what they considered to be the reckless course being pursued by the Government, and they feared more of the same from Lyon. Perhaps it was merely a return to the traditional rural-based leadership, and Lyon, in spite of the efforts of his friends, bore a city lable. In any event, on November 25, 1967, Walter Weir became premier of Manitoba and his erstwhile opponents remained as his cabinet colleagues at least for the time being.

Duff Roblin remained a prominent figure in his party and a potential member of any future Progressive Conservative government of Canada. In the spring of 1968, Lester Pearson resigned as prime minister and Liberal leader and was succeeded by Pierre Trudeau, the enthusiastic choice of a national Liberal convention. Trudeau led his party and Government into a general election that was held in late June, 1968. Duff Roblin was nominated to contest South Center Winnipeg in the PC interest, but he was soundly defeated by E. B. Osler, the Liberal candidate. Conservative candidates elsewhere in

Manitoba fared reasonably well. In spite of a Canadian total of 155 Liberals elected to 72 Progressive Conservatives, Manitoba returned five PC's, five Liberals, and three NDP members. The extent of Roblin's defeat indicated deep public resentment at the sales tax and the other unpopular exactions of his Government. The spectacular advance which he had led for Manitoba had since been forgotten. It was a classic case of public ingratitude.

The Weir administration undertook to flutter no dovecotes. It soon became apparent that caution was once again the order of the day. At a conference of provincial premiers at Toronto early in 1968, Manitoba firmly maintained its position of active co-operation with Ottawa in the equitable distribution of taxing power and governmental responsibility. Though only comparatively a "have not" province, the re-confederation of Canada along the lines proposed by the Rowell-Sirois Commission was still the goal of Manitoba. There were four by-elections early in 1969, of which the Government won three. The prospects for the Weir Government appeared pleasing. Its legislation in the session of 1969 indicated no change in the "go slow" policy being followed by Walter Weir.

During the spring of 1969, the Government determined to proceed with the development of a high-level dam at Southern Indian Lake. The purpose of the dam was to produce a head of water which could be diverted into the Nelson in order to get maximum output from the Kettle Rapids power plants, which were already under construction. The Southern Indian Lake dam would greatly increase the area of the lake and inundate a large tract of land, thus dispossessing the relatively prosperous Indian and Métis settlement of Southern Indian Lake. Provision was to be made, of course, for the compensation and resettlement of the more than six hundred persons concerned. Unexpectedly, the residents of Southern Indian Lake opposed the whole idea. They had considered other cases of resettlement which had been far from fortunate for those who had been resettled. Questions were raised as to the propriety of the means used by the Government in the conduct of hearings on the proposed removal of Southern Indian Lake village. There were protests from environment experts and water resource specialists, including suggestions that the diversion of the Churchill River might have unfortunate repercussions for the port of Churchill. The Government temporized, hesitated, and changed its mind on the conduct of public hearings. Different stories were given by different governmental sources. It was claimed that Southern Indian Lake was the only power source available. This was a distinct shock to the people of Manitoba, since they had been led to believe over a period of some sixty years that the province was inexhaustibly rich in hydroelectric resources. Why else had such a determined campaign been waged to secure this vast and uninviting hinterland? There was deep public concern. Whatever the case for the inundation of the settlement of Southern Indian Lake, it was obvious that the Government was being less than frank. To clear the air, or in anticipation of further difficulties, Walter Weir decided to seek a public mandate. An election was called for June 24, 1969.

Weir's timing seemed perfect. The Government had been sustained in three of four by-elections. The Liberals had just changed leaders. Gildas Molgat resigned and was succeeded by Robert Bend, a former minister in the Campbell Government and superintendent of schools in Transcona-Springfield. Bobby Bend was enthusiastically received by the *Free Press* as a sound man in the tradition of Bracken, Garson, and Campbell. Similarly, the NDP had called a leadership convention to replace its ailing leader, Russell Paulley. The convention took place after the election writs had been issued. The NDP chose Edward Schreyer, MP for Selkirk and former MLA for Brokenhead. Schreyer was in the best Manitoba rural tradition. He was a native of Beauséjour and had a farm background. He had taught high school and had been a university lecturer in political science. He was in his late thirties, a forceful speaker, and an attractive public personality. The Redistribution Commission had again altered constituency boundaries in the direction of representation by population, thus increasing both urban and far-northern representation. There were many factors at work, and the final result surprised everyone – especially the NDP which had cried long and loud over the unnecessary calling of an election. The NDP emerged with 28 seats; the PC's were reduced to 21; the Liberals to 6; and the *Free Press* to despair. For some days, there was indecision on the part of Mr. Weir and his advisors. But the Government had been repudiated beyond any doubt and so it resigned. On July 15, 1969, Ed Schreyer became premier of Manitoba.

Manitoba entered upon its second century with a new government. Its people had been brought belatedly into the mainstream of the twentieth century by Duff Roblin. An attempt had been made to arrest, or even to reverse, this advance. The people decided that they preferred Schreyer as Roblin's successor. The province now in his care is one with many problems. The whole of Canada is full of unrest. The age-old problem of linguistic duality is at a critical phase. The West's century-old resentment of the domination of the East is agitating the prairies from the edge of the Canadian Shield to the foothills of the Rockies. The lessons of the past indicate that the current crises, both racial and sectional, will pass. The give and take between the races and the regions is as much a source of strength as it is a source of weakness. It is sufficient to say that whatever future Canada may have, Manitoba will be a part of it.

The province has reached a population of one million, but there are now no loud boasts that it will be two million by the end of the century. Growth will be as growth has been; there is not likely to be a great surge forward, but rather a series of advances and retreats. The province is still the crossroads which it has been since man first set foot on its rolling plains or gazed at its rock-girt lakes and white-watered rivers. It is the great center of exchange between the East and the West, but it remains firmly a part of the West. The North is beginning to disgorge the riches of its rocks, rivers, and forests, but this is still only a beginning. Manitoba has passed far beyond its position as an island colony in the midst of a continental wilderness. Its links are as firm with the world as modern technology can make them. The raiment of civilization becomes the province. It houses athletic events as grandly as does any of its peers. It serves the fine arts, and its scholars in many fields have made the name of Manitoba honored throughout the world.

But there is still much to be done. Manitoba's polygot origins still tend to hinder the full and fruitful co-operation of her people. The province still has a debt to its Indians, Métis, and halfbreeds which it has hardly begun to pay. There is much reform to be effected in the thinking of official and financial circles, which still look back to a "golden age" that never really existed outside of their own narrow imaginations. Manitoba's prospects are not boundless, nor are her horizons unlimited. They are visible, but they are bright – especially to the north. The control by Manitoba of its eastern and western hinterland is limited – and the courage must be found to go to the north. The recorded history of Manitoba began there, and its unfolding has brought the province, not to fulfilment, but to expectation for the future.

Index